Preface
Origins and Perspectives

"Too often, disciplines are sealed off, in sterile
pedantry from significant influences."
> Victor Turner, *Dramas, Fields, and Metaphors*

"Cada loco con su tema"
> Dicho mejicano

This book, like Mesoamerican cosmogonies, has several beginnings. Some of the beginnings that I can assign to it reflect still earlier influences and contributions. In a significant way, this book began on a cold, windy November afternoon in 1972 when I first met Pedro Armillas on a Chicago street near the University of Illinois, where he was teaching anthropology. My graduate studies in the history of religions at the University of Chicago had led me into the field of Mesoamerican history and religion. In major books and articles, I discovered the name and perspective of Pedro Armillas, always at strategic points. The manner in which Armillas asked questions and developed conceptions about the complexities of Mesoamerican settlements and subsistence was outstanding. Whether the topic was historical reconstruction, the role of elites in the Classic Period, the meaning of certain deities, or the impact of the changes of frontiers on human migrations, Pedro Armillas had, in the words later written by Eric Wolf, "led the way." And so, as a graduate student eager to learn the way, I sought him out.

On that afternoon of our first meeting, I had invited Armillas to lecture on the influences of pre-Hispanic history on contemporary Mexican culture at the Chicano community center, Centro de La Causa. For three hours, Professor Armillas, using the Plaza de las Tres Culturas as his symbolic structure, educated, entertained, and charmed the gathering with information and insights about the character of Mexican culture. Everyone in the audience, from the intellectuals to the social workers and the street gang members, understood and appreciated something about his remarkable perspective.

xi

It was "perspective" that I sought in Armillas' work, a perspective that would enhance my own attempts to understand the complex processes that characterized the history of Mesoamerican religions. During the next several years, I sought out Pedro Armillas's point of view on the role of ceremonial centers in the integrations of city-states, the meaning of Toltec ideology in Aztec history, and the patterns of Mesoamerican frontiers. Questioning and listening to him uncovered his depth perceptions about the vital relations between material conditions, social settings, and religious ideas. Pedro's perspective informed parts of my subsequent book, *Quetzalcoatl and the Irony of Empire: Myths and Prophecies in the Aztec Tradition*. In a way, the subtitle of this book, "Center and Periphery in the Aztec World," was conceived in those many discussions with Pedro in different Chicago locations. It was Pedro Armillas who sponsored my research in archaeological zones in Mexico (he called it "pedestrian archaeology . . . so you can experience the fantasmas still lurking in the ceremonial centers") by introducing me to Eduardo Matos Moctezuma, then Sub-Director de Monumentos Prehispánicos at the National Institute of Anthropology and History in Mexico City and one of the coauthors of this volume.

My meeting with Eduardo in 1976 began a ten-year working relationship that involved the growth of our different approaches, all of which was intensified with the discovery of the Coyolxauhqui stone in 1978 and the establishment of Proyecto Templo Mayor. Eduardo's earlier publication, *Muerte a filo de obsidiana*, represented a substantial integration of several perspectives including archaeology, art history, and the history of religions. It was significant to me that Eduardo included in his work on the cult of the dead in pre-Hispanic Mexico the insights of Mircea Eliade, the master historian of religions who had taught me at the University of Chicago.

In 1979 Eduardo Matos was given the Herculean position of coordinating the excavation of the Templo Mayor, the quintessentially sacred enclave of the Aztec Empire. In many discussions with Eduardo concerning the exciting evidence being uncovered at the Templo Mayor, it became clear that no single interpretive framework was sufficient with which to even begin a substantial interpretation of the symbolic, political, ecological, and artistic significance of the Aztec center of the world. I was particularly impressed with the archaeological *and* artistic dimensions of Eduardo's descriptive approach. We both saw a need not just for perspective, but for perspectives in the plural to come into communication with each other on a new understanding of Aztec religion and society. In October 1978 I invited Professor Matos to the University of Colorado, where he gave the first lecture, outside of Mexico, to a standing-room-only crowd on "New Discoveries at the Great Temple in Mexico City." Like Armillas, Eduardo's vision emerged from an attraction to the concrete material dimensions of Mesoamerican society and manifested itself in vivid, descriptive presentations of political and symbolic patterns embedded in the Templo Mayor. The University of Colorado, principally through the Religious Studies Department, displayed an in-

GREAT TEMPLE OF TENOCHTITLAN

The Great Temple of Tenochtitlan
Center and Periphery in the Aztec World

JOHANNA BRODA
DAVÍD CARRASCO
EDUARDO MATOS MOCTEZUMA

UNIVERSITY OF CALIFORNIA PRESS
Berkeley   Los Angeles   London

We wish to thank the following for permission to reproduce the photographs listed below:
Instituto Nacional de Antropologia e Historia, 1, 4, 5, 6, 7, 8, 9, 10, 11, 14, 15, 16, 17, 18, 19, 20, 23, 24, 25, 26, 27, 28, 30, 31, 32, 33, 34, 35, 36, 37, 38, 39, 40, 42, 43, 44, 45, 48, 49, 50, 52, 54, 55a, 55b, 55c, 55d, 56, 57
Lawrence G. Desmond, 2
Kenneth Garrett, 3, 12, 13, 21, 22, 29, 47, 51
National Gallery of Art, 46, 53
Jose Cuellar, 41
We are also grateful to Lawrence G. Desmond for his assitance with the photographs.

University of California Press
Berkeley and Los Angeles, California
University of California Press, Ltd.
London, England
Copyright © 1987 by The Regents of the University of California

Library of Congress Cataloging-in-Publication Data

Broda, Johanna.
    The Great Temple of Tenochtitlán.

    Bibliography: p.
    Contents: The Templo Mayor of Tenochtitlán / Eduardo Matos Moctezuma—Templo Mayor as ritual space / Johanna Broda—Myth, cosmic terror, and the Templo Mayor / Davíd Carrasco.
    1. Templo Mayor (Mexico City, Mexico) 2. Aztecs— Religion and mythology. 3. Indians of Mexico—Religion and mythology. I. Carrasco, David. II. Matos, Moctezuma, Eduardo. III. Title.
    F1219.1.M5B76 1988   972'.53   87–5938
    ISBN 0–520–05602–7 (alk. paper)

Printed in the United States of America

1 2 3 4 5 6 7 8 9

*In Memory of
Mircea Eliade
and
Pedro Armillas*

Contents

Abbreviations Used in the Citations and Bibliography

CISINAH	Centro de Investigaciones Superiores del Instituto Nacional de Antropología e Historia
FC	Florentine Codex—Bernardino de Sahagún
GA	Gesammelte Abhandlungen—Eduard Seler
HG	Historia General—Bernardino de Sahagún
INAH	Instituto Nacional de Antropología e Historia
INI	Instituto Nacional Indígenista
SEP-INAH	Secretaria de Educación Pública-Instituto Nacional de Antropología e Historia
SEP-INI	Secretaría de Educación Pública-Instituto Nacional Indígenista
UNAM	Universidad Nacional Autónoma de México

terest in developing a working relationship with Mexican scholars in attempting to understand Aztec religion. Eduardo's archaeological expertise and sensitivity to symbolic order were matched by his generosity in opening a series of discussions with North American scholars at the University of Colorado and elsewhere on the significance of Templo Mayor. A series of conferences at the University of Colorado in Boulder, codirected by Professor Matos and myself, has resulted in the establishment of the Mesoamerican Archive and Research Project, which has provided some of the intellectual orientation and financial support for the generation of this volume. As we explain in the Introduction, we agreed along with Johanna Broda, upon the common theme of sacred space to order our inquiries. Eduardo's descriptive approach illuminates the archaeological and architectural dimensions of sacred space at Templo Mayor. As Eduardo's present contribution shows, his command of information about the material remains at Templo Mayor is combined with his understanding of symbolic order in a distinct and illuminating way.

This book also has a beginning in the outstanding work of Friedrich Katz, whose *The Ancient American Civilizations* still contains one of the best general descriptions of the structure and evolution of the Aztec Empire. It was Professor Katz who guided my own graduate research on historical reconstruction of Aztec and Inca polities and encouraged me to read the work of Johanna Broda on ritual, ideology, and cosmovision. While doing research in Mexico, I had the opportunity to become personally acquainted with Dr. Broda's scholarly perspective, and it nurtured my earlier formulations of the patterns of center and periphery in the Aztec empire. I came to realize that Johanna's special knowledge of the ethnohistorical sources, exemplified by her seminal study "Tlacaxipehualiztli; a Reconstruction of an Aztec Calendar Festival from 16th Century Sources," coupled with her creative studies on the social anthropology of tribute, ritual, astronomy, and ideology, constituted one of the most solid perspectives for the study of Aztec urbanism. This special combination was manifest in a series of visits to the University of Colorado, where she lectured and collaborated on a number of the major issues that became part of the Mesoamerican Archive's research agenda. As her contribution in the present book demonstrates, Broda has made new discoveries about the ritual space at Templo Mayor as well as pointed us in a new direction for research. The power of Johanna's contribution emerges from her ability to synthesize pieces of information from dispersed documents and organize these pieces into an illuminating design and then relate the design to the social context of Aztec life.

As the excavation in Mexico City continued to reveal ritual objects and structures related to Aztec myth, ceremony, tribute, political hierarchy, astronomy, warfare, agriculture, a vision of this book formed in my mind, and I suggested to Eduardo and Johanna that a collaborative effort was needed to begin the construction of new and larger perspectives by which to study and understand the Aztec world. For all our differences in method and theoretical orientation, we shared some common interests, including the understanding of Mesoamerican religions; we were also attacking a common problem—how to use the Templo Mayor as a window to see into the social and symbolic complexities of the last pre-Columbian empire of Mesoamerica. It became evident that the perspectives we shared were enhanced by the different views we each held and vice versa. I was encouraged toward our collaboration by Clifford Geertz's and Paul de Man's comments on the interdisciplinary study of meaningful forms: "Specific commonalities of intellectual interest make scholarly interchange possible and useful; and the creation of such interchange demands, and indeed consists in, the discovery and exploration of such commonalities."

And so, with the help of Jack Miles, who was then an editor at the University of California Press, we entered into this project. We hoped that a new beginning was at hand in Aztec studies and that three heads, with their many influences and perspectives, were better than one.

David Carrasco

Mexico City and Boulder, Colorado

Introduction

In the early morning hours of 21 February 1978, electrical workers laying down lines behind the Cathedral of Mexico City (Metropolitan Cathedral) uncovered the edges of a huge round stone with unusual carvings on it. When archaeologists from the Instituto Nacional de Antropología e Historia (INAH) (National Institute of Anthropology and History) visited the site and made a preliminary excavation, they realized that a major piece of Aztec sculpture had been found. Their excitement was enhanced by the fact that this stone, depicting the ritually dismembered body of the goddess Coyolxauhqui, was the most significant Aztec monument to be discovered since 1790, when the now famous Aztec Calendar Stone was unearthed several blocks from the site. It appeared that the discovery signified more than simply another addition to the heavy, awesome collection of monuments in the National Museum. This discovery hinted of a new era in both public awareness and scholarly research regarding Aztec religion and society. Further excavation of the immediate area uncovered six rich ritual offertory caches containing statues of gods, human skulls decorated with obsidian eyes, ancient masks, and sea shells. It had long been known that this was the site of the Templo Mayor (Great Temple) of Tenochtitlan, but previous excavations had barely touched the corner and fringes of the ceremonial precinct. The astonishing richness and significance of this discovery rekindled interest in the Templo Mayor and the ancient capital, and within a month a major excavation of the shrine, *Proyecto Templo Mayor*, was ordered by the president of Mexico, Miguel López Portillo. Since February 1978 Eduardo Matos Moctezuma has served as general coordinator of the project, and the excavation was successfully concluded (under his direction) in November 1982.[1]

For five years—from 1978 to 1982—truly fabulous discoveries startled public and scholars alike as some 7,000 ritual objects were excavated within the thirteen phases of enlargement of the Great Temple. Most of these treasures were obtained from offertory caches where effigies of deities, ritual masks, sacrificial knives, jade beads, human sacrifices, and minor sculptures were deposited together with an enormous amount of real animal species. These stunning offerings have a complex symbolic meaning that can be analyzed from many different points of view, approaches, or disciplines. The present volume contains three such interpretative efforts of approximation to the many aspects of the Great Temple.

An important characteristic of the excavation is the interdisciplinary collaboration which has made it possible. At the National Institute of Anthropology and History, scientists from many disciplines have been involved in the digging, restoration, mapping, photography, and interpretation of the treasures at Templo Mayor. Biologists are identifying the geographic origin and the species of animals found in the offerings. Chemists are analyzing the soils and stones, while geologists are studying the types of rocks and minerals scattered throughout the site. Physical anthropologists have studied the human remains. A team of restorers has examined the wood, bone, and stone objects, while a team of ethnohistorians has carefully scanned the sixteenth-century sources for references to the history and ritual of the Templo Mayor. Archaeologists who have supervised the entire project are now dedicated to classifying the characteristics of sculptures and architectural structures. Thus far one volume of these interdisciplinary studies and excavation reports has been published; a second one is in press. A volume containing maps of the constructive periods of the temple has also appeared. Another volume constituting a collection of earlier studies on the Templo Mayor was edited earlier by Eduardo Matos Moctezuma; these publications have appeared in Mexico.[2]

While this work has been proceeding in Mexico, several conferences on the Templo Mayor and Aztec religion were held in the United States. The first meeting took place in November 1979 at the University of Colorado in Boulder when thirty scholars from ten institutions in Mexico and the United States participated in a week-long conference, organized by Davíd Carrasco of the Department of Religious Studies, entitled "Center and Periphery: The Templo Mayor and the Aztec Empire," to discuss the exemplary role of the Templo Mayor in the organization and expansion of Aztec urbanism.[3] The discussions focused on the temple and economic tribute, human sacrifice and ideology, spatial symbolism in Teotihuacan and Tenochtitlan, magical flight, and Mesoamerican cosmology. The categories of "center" and "periphery," which have recently animated discourse in the history of religions and urban geography, were a recurring theme in the deliberations. Since 1979, scholars from the Departments of Religious Studies, History, Fine Arts, and Anthropology at the University of Colorado, Boulder, have utilized the information and interpretations of visiting Mexican scholars to assist in constructing an interpretative framework for future studies of Aztec religion and society. In 1983 the Mesoamerican Archive and

Research Project was founded at the University of Colorado at Boulder. This project places the recent Templo Mayor excavation within the wider context of Mesoamerican studies and the comparative study of world religions.[4]

At the October 1983 annual Pre-Columbian Studies meeting at Dumbarton Oaks, Washington, D.C., dedicated to the Templo Mayor,[5] the latest excavation results were presented and several new lines of investigation developed.

The present study, by three of the scholars who participated in these meetings, is guided by our interests in the vital interrelationships that existed between city and empire, religion and society, and cosmovision and nature in ancient Mesoamerica. The treasures from the Templo Mayor establish a new empirical basis for inquiring into several major problems of Mesoamerican history. Never before have scholars of pre-Columbian Mexico had the opportunity to combine such rich primary sources—painted, written, *and* archaeological—related to one major ceremonial center, as a means of addressing such difficult questions as (1) the nature of Aztec tribute, (2) the structure of the Aztec empire, (3) the complexity of Aztec artistic styles, (4) the significance of incremental human sacrifice, (5) the character of Aztec religion, and (6) the relation between cosmology and the observation of nature.[6]

The present volume presents three views of the nature and significance of the Templo Mayor as the quintessential sacred space within the Aztec empire. This collaborative work, by an archaeologist, an ethnohistorian, and a historian of religion, seeks to illuminate several major religious, political, and economic strategies utilized by the Aztecs to effectively organize the center and peripheries of their empire.

The excavation has brought to light firsthand material to learn about a multitude of aspects of Aztec society. The exemplary character of the Templo Mayor demands an interdisciplinary reflection and interpretation. Among the theoretical concepts that have been of basic concern to the authors, the one of center and periphery operates as a unifying concept of the three chapters in this volume.[7] The understanding of the dynamics of center and periphery in comparative perspective has been one of the research agendas of Davíd Carrasco and the seminars conducted by the Mesoamerican Archive.

The categories "center" and "periphery" are utilized in this work on three planes of reference: (1) geographic-ecological, (2) sociopolitical, and (3) symbolic. In the first case, it is clear that the ecological potentials of the Valley of Mexico provided a foundation for the consolidation of the Aztec state in and immediately around the lakes. The Aztec consciousness of their power to integrate the wider geographic order of Mesoamerica is reflected in the patterns of the offerings uncovered at the Templo Mayor. As Matos demonstrates in text and lists in this volume, a huge number of ritual objects came from peripheral communities of the empire *and* the oceans marking the edges of the Aztec world. In the case of the social order of the Aztec empire, historical analysis reveals that Tenochtitlan was in constant tension and conflict with city-states within and on its borders and that the interaction influenced the character of

Aztec life. Broda's earlier essays demonstrated a parallel between conflicts with peripheral communities, patterns of conquest, and the increase in human sacrifice. Perhaps the clearest example of interaction between center and periphery is in the symbolization of space and society by Aztec elites. For instance, within the metaphorical space called *Cemanahuac* (land surrounded by water), a pattern of quadripartition with four quarters surrounding a quintessential center, permeated myriad aspects of ritual, myth, and symbolic art. As Carrasco shows, the antagonisms between center and periphery are symbolized in the myth of Huitzilopochtli's birth.

Another concept that served to unite and organize our work was that of "sacred space." This category is taken from the discipline of history of religions, where it is associated, above all, with the work of Mircea Eliade.[8] In the present volume it is integrated by the three authors into the specific approach used by each and is explored regarding its relation to architecture, social order, and the symbolic structure of the ceremonial complex. It is our judgment that the category of sacred space, utilized in an interdisciplinary discussion, will lead to a deeper understanding of the site and a refinement of the concept itself in the light of Aztec evidence. Our use of this concept stems, in part, from the recent advances in understanding the role of the ceremonial capital in comparative studies of traditional societies. The monumental contribution of Paul Wheatley to these studies has led the way.[9] This author writes, "it is the city which has been, and to a large extent still is, the style centre in the traditional world, disseminating social, political technical, religious and aesthetic values, and functioning as an organizing principle conditioning the manner and quality of life in the countryside."[10]

In the study of Mesoamerican cultures considerable new knowledge has been accumulated in recent decades which has demonstrated the major role of cities in the organization of Toltec, Maya, and Aztec society.[11] Pre-Hispanic society on the eve of the Spanish Conquest was a world dominated by the form known as the traditional city, specifically the great capital of Tenochtitlan. The Aztecs themselves were aware of the complex power and authority that they possessed. Consider their own statement about their capital:

> Proud of itself
> Is the city of Mexico-Tenochtitlan
> Here no one fears to die in war
> This is our glory
> This is Your Command
> Oh Giver of Life
> Have this mind, oh princes
> Who would conquer Tenochtitlan?
> Who could shake the foundation of heaven?[12]

Díaz del Castillo describes the Spanish account of their arrival at the capital:

During the morning we arrived at a broad causeway and continued our march towards Iztapalapa and when we saw so many cities and villages built

4

in the water and other great towns on dryland and that straight and level causeway going towards Mexico, we were amazed and said that it was like the enchantments they tell of in the legend of Amadis, on account of the great towers and cues and buildings rising from the water, and all built of masonry. And some of the soldiers even asked whether the things that we saw were not a dream. Gazing on such wonderful sights we did not know what to say.[13]

The dynamic midpoint of authority, ritual, and architecture of the capital was the great ceremonial center, which was organized around the Great Temple. As Eduardo Matos Moctezuma has stated, the excavation proves that the Templo Mayor was the economic, political, and symbolic center of the entire empire. The objects uncovered at the excavation show that the intertwining of tribute, political ideology, and ritual took place at the Templo Mayor in a purposeful, dramatic fashion. It appears that the Templo Mayor and the city of Tenochtitlan were akin to what Clifford Geertz calls "a microcosm of supernatural order—'an image of . . . the universe on a smaller scale'—and the material embodiment of political order."[14]

As our study will show, the Templo Mayor is paradigmatic in at least three major ways. First, for millions of people in the Aztec world, it was the *axis mundi* of the empire, the main center in the political, economic, and religious sense. It was the great meeting point of heaven, earth, and the underworld from which emanated supernatural authority for priests and rulers to organize the world. It was the center for pilgrims, warriors, rulers, and enemies of the Aztec world. It was the place where tribute and monument were deposited and erected on a grandiose scale. Second, it was an *imago mundi*, an image, a living screenfold, in its own time and space, of the elite conceptions of authority, power, aggression, and orientation in the world. It served as the backdrop and stage for the theatrical presentation of myth, military policy, and economic order. Third, the Templo Mayor was a center in the manner referred to by Edward Shils as a "structure of activities," a series of actions that gave motion and authority to the Aztec capital.[15] This structure of activities, articulated most vividly in the elaborate calendrical cycle celebrated in the temples, was based on large-scale human sacrifice and the redistribution of great quantities of tribute in luxury goods that were concentrated in the capital from the faraway tropical regions of the empire.[16] In this context the three chapters in this book present new data on the practice of human sacrifice in the Aztec capital and add substantial points of view to the recent discussion of this topic among academic circles in the United States.[17]

This book combines the viewpoints of anthropology, archaeology, and the history of religions to present a preliminary effort of understanding this complex structure of the Templo Mayor and the world it reflected and organized. Our general purpose is twofold: (1) to examine and interpret the history, symbolism, and ideology of the temple itself and (2) to utilize the Templo Mayor as a lens to see the social reality behind it and penetrate deeper into the socioeconomic, political, and symbolic structure that characterized the Aztec empire.

Another concept that provides a common background to the contributions of the present volume is the "functional polyvalency" of pre-Hispanic institutions. As Pedro Carrasco[18] has shown, in an archaic civilization such as Mesoamerica, we do not find a separation between economic, political, and religious institutions comparable to that existing in modern industrial society. Rather, we find that political institutions share simultaneous socioeconomic and religious functions, while ritual expresses the existence of social stratification and is the vehicle for the dramatization of mythic traditions and the propagation of the political ideology. In this sense, the Templo Mayor demonstrates in an exemplary way how social, political, and religious aspects of Aztec society were intertwined in the architectural complex and the offerings of the site.

Although the three authors of this volume share the latter concepts in their broad outline, the general theoretical position into which they are integrated varies considerably. Matos and Broda are concerned with elucidation of the role of ideology in ancient Mesoamerican society, analyzing its expression in the material conditions of existence. From a different perspective, Carrasco also sees mythic traditions integrating material and social structures. Although Broda's and Matos's approaches are also far from being uniform, they coincide basically in viewing ideology as a system of symbolic representation of the relations within society and between society and the natural environment. Ideology serves the function of legitimizing and justifying the existing order of society. In this sense, Broda and Matos are concerned about distinguishing between "objective social reality" and the "explanation" given of that reality, the "phenomenon" and "essence," according to the terminology used by Matos. According to this approach, cosmological systems are viewed to form part of the ideological apparatus of a society. The term *cosmovision*, which is frequently used in this volume, is borrowed from the common Spanish and German usage and denotes the structured view in which the ancient Mesoamericans combined their notions of cosmology relating to time and space in a systematic whole.[19]

Carrasco bases his study of myth and the Templo Mayor in what he sees to be religious subject matter, namely, the symbolic and ceremonial life of the Aztecs. His method is morphological and historical, meaning an empirical procedure ordered by the forms he is studying. The forms that dominate the physiognomy and related songs and stories of the Templo Mayor are human sacrifice, royal temple rededications, combats, extravagant processions, and offerings. In other words, the Templo Mayor was the center of a constant dramatization of Aztec obsessions of conquest, expansion of authority to the periphery, and hierarchical dominance. In Carrasco's view, however, the thundering rituals of Tenochtitlan were not simply devices for reconsolidation of the society and state: they "were not means to political ends, they were the ends themselves, they were what the state was for."[20] In an altered formulation, rituals were not *only* vehicles for political power; rather, political power was a vehicle carrying the mythic force of rituals.

As our study will show, each one of us utilizes a different set of tools to explore

the organizing principles of Aztec Mexico. This results in both convergence of interpretation and different ways of understanding the Aztec world. The simultaneous
divergence of theoretical positions and coincidence of lines of interest can be well
documented in the preceding example of the "urban tradition." There exists a coincidence in how we view the Templo Mayor—microcosm of the Aztec world—as the
culmination of 1,500 years of urban historical tradition. This coincidence emerges
from the scholarship of Pedro Armillas, Friedrich Katz, Angel Palerm, William
Sanders, Eric Wolf, and others who have uncovered the complex historical processes
that led to the formation of the Aztec world.[21] Broda synthesizes aspects of the background when she points out[22] that when studying Aztec social and political institutions, it is necessary to realize that the formation of the state and of class society in
Mesoamerica dates back to the end of the pre-Classic period and the beginning of the
Classic period (approximately the end of the first millennium B.C. and the first centuries A.D.) This circumstance determined historically the creation of a complex set
of sociopolitical institutions and a cultural tradition that was manifest in iconography, architecture, and the development of astronomy, calendrics, mathematics, and
technology. During the Classic period, a community of cultural traits was established
over the geographic area that today is called *Mesoamerica* (including modern Mexico south of the Panuco-Lerma drainage, Guatemala, Salvador, Belize, and western
Honduras to an approximate boundary formed by the Ulua River and Lake Yojoa).[23]
Numerous changes occurred over the following centuries until the formation of the
Aztec state; nevertheless, a continuous cultural tradition was maintained. In the central
Mexican highlands the great metropolis of Tenochtitlan was followed after its down-
fall by other important states ruled from urban centers such as Tula, Xochicalco, and
Cholula.[24] In the Valley of Mexico, city-states such as Culhuacan, Azcapotzalco, and
Tetzcoco held political power before the rise of domination of the Aztecs. In no other
area of the ancient Americas has there existed such a long uninterrupted tradition of
political dominance as in the Valley of Mexico, today absorbed into modern Mexico City, whose population of 17 million inhabitants steadily continues to expand.

The Templo Mayor is not merely one more archaeological site to be excavated;
it consists of a combination of unique features: (1) it provides evidence of the very
last period of Mesoamerican cultural history before the Spanish conquest, thus
representing the most mature achievement of this civilization in terms of architecture
and symbolism; (2) it was the main temple of the empire, the symbolic as well as
material center of the most powerful state in Mesoamerica on the eve of the Spanish
Conquest; and (3) no other site of comparable complexity dating from the fourteenth
to the sixteenth centuries had been excavated and no other one has survived in such
a complete way. Despite the destruction following the Spanish Conquest, the ground
structures of the Great Temple were preserved for more than 450 years below the
Zócalo—the main square of Mexico City—right next to the Catholic Cathedral and
the Palace of Government that the Spaniards erected in the sixteenth century. When

the Spaniards leveled the Aztec temple to the ground in 1521 in order to build in its place the Christian Cathedral as a demonstration of their own access to power, they did not realize that below the last visible double pyramid, the earlier structures remained hidden. This fact has spared the bases of previous constructions from their annihilation, and has made it possible that today—460 years after the Spanish Conquest—they have come to light through the excavation of the Templo Mayor, as a living testimony of the history of Aztec rule as well as of its downfall.

In the first chapter of the book, Eduardo Matos Moctezuma presents a descriptive, informative panorama of the history and content of the excavation. Utilizing the eyes of an archaeologist and anthropologist who has worked intimately with every phase of the excavation, Matos presents the historical background and description of the excavation as well as an interpretation of the major symbolic objects found at the Templo Mayor. In his chapter, Matos speaks of the archaeological findings made in the area of the Great Temple prior to the initiation of the project under his direction. He begins his survey to the year 1790, when some of the most important Aztec monoliths such as the Calendar Stone and the colossal statue of *Coatlicue* (mother goddess) were discovered. Matos then provides the relevant information on the main results obtained during the five years of excavation, regarding the architectural findings as well as the offering caches. It should be noted that the list of objects found in the offerings is the only published (to date) survey of this kind. His presentation enables us to appreciate the diversity of objects and the complexity of their symbolic relationship within a general view of the site.

According to Matos, the Templo Mayor, with its twin temples to Tlaloc and Huitzilopochtli, represented the horizontal and vertical center of the cosmos. From this center emerged the different planes of the universe: the thirteen heavens and the nine underworlds, which were also coordinated with the four cosmic directions. He argues that the temple itself constituted this symbolism, with the general platform representing the plane of the earth, the different bodies of the pyramid indicating the levels of ascension, and the two temples at the top constituting the *Omeyocan* (place of duality). In this way, the Templo Mayor is seen as synthesis of Aztec cosmovision.

In the second chapter in this volume Johanna Broda analyzes the "Templo Mayor as Ritual Space" from the point of view of Mesoamerican ethnohistory and anthropology. Her presentation combines the interpretation of sixteenth-century chronicles and codices with a careful examination of ritual objects that have been revealed during the excavation. Further, the material is complemented by modern ethnographic data. Broda's point of departure were her previous studies on Aztec ritual and society in which she dealt with the role played by the warrior nobility in the spectacular calendrical ceremonies that were staged periodically at the Great Temple.[25] These studies showed that the ritual space of the Templo Mayor was used for the intimidation of conquered peoples and conveyed to both spectators and participants the ideology of the Aztec state. The investigation presented in this book has led Broda far away from the initially formulated enquiry into the social and political functions of cult at the Templo Mayor, however. The detailed analysis of the offerings that were buried at the temple during the process of its construction compels Broda to conclude that we are dealing here with an aspect of Aztec religion that is quite different from that manifest in the great public rituals of state cult. While the latter were clearly connected to the legitimation of political power and the role played by different social groups in Aztec society, the former seem to derive from ancient traditions of cosmological thought that were related to political ideology only in a more indirect way.

In this way Broda detects, through her analysis of the offerings, fundamental aspects of Aztec cosmovision centered around a basic symbolism of water and the earth (as well as mountains, caves, and the sea) which are present at the Great Temple but are also manifestations of a cult system with ancient roots in previous cultures. This study points to perspectives of time depth of Mesoamerican cosmology as well as to an ancient pan-Mesoamerican distribution of certain mythic and ritual concepts.

Following the interpretations of Matos and Broda, Davíd Carrasco utilizes a comparative perspective to discuss the Templo Mayor as a "mythic space" that replicated several crucial episodes in Aztec cosmology and cosmogony. Utilizing as a point of departure his previous studies of the symbolic character of Mesoamerican cities and the nature of cosmo magical thought utilized by priestly elites to organize complex state societies,[26] Carrasco discusses the ways in which the myth of Huitzilopochtli's birth and the myth of the Fifth Sun influenced not only the location, shape, and authority of the Great Temple but also provided a ferocious model for massive human sacrifices of warriors. Carrasco's work attempts to combine a historical interest in Aztec religion with a sensitivity to symbolic forms. In his view, the Templo Mayor as an axis mundi can be understood historically through an application of the categories of "center" and "periphery" to the ritual objects found at the excavation and the historical chronicles that describe the antagonistic relationships that existed between Tenochtitlan and the tributary communities in the empire. Throughout the project, Carrasco's work has been nurtured by the discoveries of both Broda and Matos. In the third chapter of the book, we will see how the enlargements of the temple, the expansion of the empire, and the increment in human sacrifices were reflections of symbolic and political tensions between the central area of the Aztec state and the peripheral areas of the Mesoamerican world. The complexity of these forces and their reflection in the anarchical growth of the Templo Mayor throughout the fifteenth and sixteenth centuries permit us to gain new insights into the mythic structures and the psychology of this remarkable state.[27]

To assist the authors in attempts at reflection and interpretion, the book includes photographs of architectural features and ritual objects that represent the history, symbolism, and ideology of the Templo Mayor. We have tried to base our selection of these illustrations on the content and meaning that they convey in accordance with the interpretation present in each chapter. Our objective is to use the photographic material not only as an aesthetic attraction for the reader but also to convey an approach and a certain interpretive line.

In our view, the multidisciplinary approach developed in this book may suggest new perspectives for the understanding of the origins, and significance, of the symbolic and material power of the great Aztec shrine. Our occasional failure to reach common denominators and similar conclusions may not necessarily reflect an incoherence but may, in fact, enrich a broader vision of the subject. This book represents only an initial attempt at interpretation. With the advance in the analysis of concrete aspects of the excavation and the development of new aspects of theory, to be carried out in the near future, it will become possible to deepen our understanding of the varied phenomena of the Templo Mayor. Further research, academic exchange between specialists, and a comparison with studies on other ancient civilizations are required in the future.

Acknolwedgments

We would like to express our acknowledgments to the National Institute of Anthropology and History, Mexico, for having provided all the facilities for access to the excavation in the past years, as well as many of the photographs in the present volume. Johanna Broda acknowledges her gratitude to the Instituto de Investigaciones Históricas of the National University of Mexico as the institution that has sponsored her investigation and to its director, Robert Moreno de los Arcos, for his steady support. Finally, we would like to express our warm appreciation to the University of Colorado at Boulder, particularly the Department of Religious Studies and the Mesoamerican Archive and Research Project, for having initiated support to carry on these interdisciplinary studies on Templo Mayor, the product of which is the present book.

Eduardo Matos would like to acknowledge the contributions of John Copeland, Department of Spanish, for his generous assistance in the translation of his article. Also, thanks to José Cuellar of Stanford University for his oral translation of Professor Matos's 75th Anniversary Lecture on Templo Mayor at the American Academy of Religion in Chicago. Appreciation is also extended to John Hoag, Department of Fine Arts at the University of Colorado, for his warm hospitality during numerous visits to Colorado and to Anthony Lozano and Ralph Kite for their translations of lectures in Boulder.

Professor Carrasco acknowledges the generous financial support of the University of Colorado, especially the office of President Arnold Weber, who clearly saw the significance of the excavation in Mexico City and assisted in establishing an academic center, the Mesoamerican Archive and Research Project, in which interdisciplinary collaboration can take place. Appreciation goes to Charles H. Long and Paul Wheatley for their wisdom and guidance. Research support was also given by the National

Research Council and the Council on Research and Creative Writing at the University of Colorado and Doris and Frank Havice, who supported one of the initial research trips to Mexico during the planning stages of this book. Thanks also to William B. Taylor for advice on how to organize the framework of the book, Larry Desmond for tireless hours of collecting and developing some of the photographs, Gene Aparisio for assisting in the final choice and ordering of the photographs, Gladys Bloedow for typing parts of the manuscript while manifesting the patience of a saint, and Phil Arnold, Rebecca Herr, Bryan Dennis, Tracey Hovda and Lois Middleton for working on the vital details of the project. Also, we are grateful to the Department of Religious Studies, specifically Frederick Denny and Rodney Taylor, for support in mind and heart during the development of the book. Finally, much gratitude to my parents David and Marjorie Carrasco for their love and support of my work. Red roses for Jane Marie.

Notes

1. For a discussion of the material character of the Templo Mayor excavation at an earlier stage, see Matos, Moctezuma Eduardo, "Los Hallazgos de la Arqueología," in *El Templo Mayor*, Miguel León-Portilla and Eduardo Matos Moctezuma (Mexico: Bancomer, S.A., 1981a), pp. 103–284; Eduardo Matos Moctezuma, *Una Visita al Templo Mayor de Tenochtitlan* (Mexico: Instituto Nacional de Antropología, 1981b); Eduardo Matos Moctezuma, "El Templo Mayor: Economía e Ideología," in *El Templo Mayor: Excavaciones y Estudios*, Eduardo Matos Moctezuma, ed. (Mexico: Instituto Nacional de Antropología, 1982a).

2. See Matos, Moctezuma Eduardo, ed., *Trabajos Arqueológicos en el Centro de la Ciudad de México (Antología)* (Mexico: SEP-INAH, 1979); Eduardo Matos Moctezuma, *El Templo Mayor: Excavaciones y Estudios* (Mexico: Instituto Nacional de Antropología, 1982b); Eduardo Matos Moctezuma, *El Templo Mayor: Planos, Cortes y Perspectivas*, Dibujos Victor Rangel, ed. (Mexico: Instituto Nacional de Antropología, 1982c).

3. Participants included Jose Arguellas, Pedro Armillas, Johanna Broda, Davíd Carrasco, Edward Calnek, Jose Cuellar, Wilfred Gingerich, Richard Hecht, Doris Heyden, John Hoag, Alfredo López-Austin, Eduardo Matos Moctezuma, Henry B. Nicholson, Esther Pasztory, Payson Sheets, Paul Shankman, William B. Taylor, and Paul Wheatley. Also participating from the Department of Religious Studies were Frederick Denny, Ira Chernus, Robert Lester and Rodney Taylor.

4. The project is directed by Davíd Carrasco, and the following scholars from the University of Colorado at Boulder collaborate on it: John Hoag, Department of Fine Arts; Paul Shankman, Payson Sheets, and Russell McGoodwin, Department of Anthropology; and Larry Desmond, Mesoamerican Archive and Research Project as well as members of the Religious Studies Department.

5. Speakers included Elizabeth H. Boone, Frances F. Berdan, Johanna Broda, Carlos J. Gónzalez, Doris Heyden, George Kubler, Miguel León-Portilla, Alfredo López-Austin, Cecelia Klein, Eduardo Matos Moctezuma, Augusto F. Molina M., Henry B. Nicholson, Esther Pasztory, Juan A. Roman B., and Richard F. Townsend. Their contributions are published in Elizabeth H. Boone, ed., *The Aztec Templo Mayor* (Washington, D.C.: Dumbarton Oaks, 1987).

6. For a general survey of scholarship on these issues, see Anthony F. Aveni, *Skywatchers of Ancient Mexico* (Austin: University of Texas Press, 1980); Burr Brundage, *A Rain of Darts*

(Austin: University of Texas Press, 1972); Davíd Carrasco, *Quetzalcoatl and the Irony of Empire: Myths and Prophecies in the Aztec Tradition* (Chicago: University of Chicago Press, 1983); Pedro Carrasco, "Social Organization of Ancient Mexico," in *Handbook of Middle American Indians*, vol. 10, R. Wauchope, G. Ekholm, and I. Bernal, eds. (Austin: University of Texas Press, 1971); Alfonso Caso, *The Aztecs: People of the Sun* (Norman: University of Oklahoma Press, 1958); Nigel Davies, *Los Mexicas: Primeros Pasos Hacia el Imperio* (Mexico: Instituto de Investigaciones Históricas UNAM, 1973); Friedrich Katz, *The Ancient American Civilizations* (New York: Praeger, 1972); Migúel León-Portilla, *Aztec Thought and Culture* (Norman: University of Oklahoma Press, 1963); Migúel León-Portilla, *Pre-Columbian Literature of Mexico* (Norman: University of Oklahoma Press, 1969); Henry B. Nicholson, and Eloise Quiñones Keber, *Art of Aztec Mexico: Treasures of Tenochtitlán,* catalog of an exhibition at the National Gallery of Art (Washington, D.C., 1983); Esther Pasztory, *Aztec Art* (New York: H. N. Abrams, 1983); and Eric Wolf, *Sons of the Shaking Earth* (Chicago: University of Chicago Press, 1959). For a selection from the vast field of specialized publications on specific aspects of pre-Hispanic central Mexican society, see Pedro Armillas, "Tecnología, Formaciones Socio-Económicas y Religión en Mesoamérica," in *Selected Papers of the 29th International Congress of Americanists*, Sol Tax, ed. (Chicago: University of Chicago Press, 1951); Frances Berdan, *Trade, Tribute and Market in the Aztec Empire*, Ph.D. dissertation, Department of Anthropology (Austin: University of Texas, 1975); Johanna Broda, "Estratificación Social y Ritual Mexica: Un Ensayo de Antropología Social de los Mexica," *Indiana* (Berlin) 5 (1979*b*): 45–82; Johanna Broda, "Astronomy, Cosmovision and Ideology of Prehispanic Mesoamerica," in *Ethnoastronomy and Archaeoastronomy in the American Tropics*, vol. 385, pp. 81–110, Anthony F. Aveni and Gary Urton, eds., *Annals of the New York Academy of Sciences* (New York: The New York Academy of Sciences, 1982*a*); Edward Calnek, "The Internal Structure of Tenochtitlan," in *The Valley of Mexico*, Eric Wolf, ed. (Albuquerque: University of New Mexico Press, 1976); Davíd Carrasco, "Templo Mayor: The Aztec Vision of Place," *Religion* (London) 11 (1981): 275–297; Pedro Carrasco, *Las Bases Sociales del Politeismo Mexicano: Los Dioses Tutelares*, Actes du XLII Congrés International des Americanistes (Paris, 1976); Pedro Carrasco, Johanna Broda, et al., *Estratificación Social en la Mesoamérica Prehispánica* (Mexico: SEP-INAH, 1976); Pedro Carrasco and Johanna Broda, eds., *Economía Política e Ideología in el México Prehispánico* (Mexico: Nueva Imagen—CIS-INAH, 1978); Charles Gibson, "Structure of the Aztec Empire," in *Handbook of Middle American Indians*, vol. 10, part I (Austin: University of Texas Press, 1971), pp. 376–394; Doris Heyden, "Caves, Gods and Myths: World-View and Planning in Tenochtitlan," in *Mesoamerican Sites and World Views*, Elizabeth Benson, ed. (Washington, D.C.: Dumbarton Oaks, 1981), pp. 1–40; Paul Kirchhoff, "Mesoamerica: Its Geographic Limits, Ethnic Composition, and Cultural Characteristics," in *The Heritage of Conquest*, Sol Tax, ed. (New York: Random House, 1968); Alfredo López-Austin, *Cuerpo Humano e Ideología: Las Concepciones de los Antiguos Nahuas*, Instituto de Investigaciones Antropológicas (Mexico: UNAM, 1980); Robert McC. Adams, *The Evolution of Urban Society* (Chicago: University of Chicago Press, 1967); Henry B. Nicholson, "Religion in Pre-Hispanic Central Mexico," in *Handbook of Middle American Indians, Guide to Ethnohistorical Sources*, 15 vols. (Austin: University of Texas Press, 1971), vol. 10, pp. 395–445; William T. Sanders and Barbara J. Price, *Mesoamerica: The Evolution of a Civilization* (New York: Random House, 1968); and Eric Wolf, *The Valley of Mexico* (Albuquerque: University of New Mexico Press, 1976).

7. For a general introduction to categories of center and periphery, see Mircea Eliade, *The Myth of the Eternal Return* (New York: Pantheon Books, 1965) and the remarkable comparative enterprise of Paul Wheatley, *The Pivot of the Four Corners* (Chicago: Aldine, 1971),

as well as Jonathan Z. Smith, "The Wobbling Pivot," in *Map is Not Territory* (Leiden: E. J. Brill, 1978). Also see several applications of these categories in D. Carrasco, "Templo Mayor: The Aztec Vision of Place," and Heyden, "Caves, Gods and Myths."

8. Mircea Eliade, *Patterns in Comparative Religions* (New York, Meridian Books, 1967).

9. For a broad summary of various uses of the category of sacred space and the exemplary center, see Paul Wheatley, *The Pivot of the Four Corners*, especially chapter 3, entitled "The Early Chinese City in Comparative Perspective."

10. Quote from Paul Wheatley, "City as Symbol," inaugural lecture presented at University College, London, 1967.

11. See D. Carrasco, *Quetzalcoatl*, especially pp. 205–220.

12. Miguel León-Portilla, *Pre-Columbian Literature of Mexico* (Norman: University of Oklahoma Press, 1969), p. 87.

13. Bernal Díaz del Castillo, *The Discovery and Conquest of Mexico* (New York: Farrar, Straus & Giroux, 1956), p. 191.

14. See "The Myth of the Exemplary Center," pp. 11–19, in Clifford Geertz, *Negara: The Theatre State in Nineteenth Century Bali* (Princeton: Princeton University Press, 1980).

15. Edward Shils, *Selected Essays* (Chicago: Center for Social Organization Studies, 1970). See especially his article entitled "Center and Periphery."

16. See P. Carrasco and J. Broda, eds. *Economía Política e Ideología*, and Broda, "Estratificacíon Social y Ritual Mexica."

17. See Michael Harner, "The Ecological Basis for Aztec Sacrifice," *American Ethnologist* 4 (1977), and Marvin Harris, *Cannibals and Kings: The Origins of Culture* (New York: Random House, 1977). The ecological basis for Aztec sacrifice defended by Harner and Harris was severely criticized by Marshal Sahlins, "Culture as Protein and Profit," *New York Review of Books*, November 23, 1978; Barbara J. Price, "Demystification, Enriddlement, and Aztec Cannibalism: A Materialist Rejoiner to Harner," *American Ethnologist* 5 (1978) and Bernard R. Ortíz de Montellano, "Aztec Cannibalism: An Ecological Necessity?" *Science* 200 (1978): 611–617.

18. See Pedro Carrasco, "The Peoples of Central Mexico and Their Historical Traditions," in *Handbook of Middle American Indians, Guide to Ethnohistorical Sources*, 15 vols. (Austin: University of Texas Press, 1971), vol. 11, pp. 459–474; P. Carrasco, *Las Bases Sociales del Politeismo Mexicano* and P. Carrasco, "La Economía del México Prehispánico," in *Economía Política e Ideología en el México Prehispánico*, Pedro Carrasco and Johanna Broda, eds. (Mexico: Nueva Imagen—CIS-INAH, 1978), pp. 13–74.

19. Johanna Broda, "Astronomy, Cosmovision and Ideology of Prehispanic Mesoamerica": 81.

20. C. Geertz, *Negara*.

21. See Armillas, "Tecnología, Formaciones Socioeconómicas," Sanders and Price, *Mesoamerica: The Evolution of a Civilization*, Wolf, *Sons of the Shaking Earth*, and Wolf, *The Valley of Mexico*.

22. See Johanna Broda, "Ideology of the Aztec State and Human Sacrifice," paper presented at the symposium on "Center and Periphery: The Templo Mayor and the Aztec Empire," University of Colorado at Boulder, November 5–9, 1979. To be published in *Societies in Transition: Essays in Honor of Pedro Carrasco*. Edited by Roger Joseph, Frances F. Berdan, and Hugo G. Nutini (in press).

23. See Kirchhoff, "Mesoamerica: Its Geographic Limits," p. 7; and Sanders and Price, *Mesoamerica: The Evolution of a Civilization*, pp. 6–7.

24. See D. Carrasco, *Quetzalcoatl.*

25. See Johanna Broda, "Relaciones políticas ritualizadas: el ritual como expresión de Una ideología," in *Economía Política e Ideología en el México Prehispánico*, Pedro Carrasco and Johanna Broda, eds. (Mexico: Nueva Imagen—CIS-INAH, 1978), pp. 219–255, and bibliography quoted in the chapter by Broda in the present volume.

26. See D. Carrasco, *Quetzalcoatl*, especially chapters 2 and 3.

27. For an important model of continuity and change seen in relation to cultural ecology and religious ritual, see Roy Rappaport, *Ecology, Meaning and Religion* (Richmond, Calif.: North Atlantic Books, 1979), p. 148, and J. Smith's challenging study of Judaism in the chapter entitled "Earth and Gods," pp. 104–129, in *Map is Not Territory*.

The Templo Mayor of Tenochtitlan
History and Interpretation

EDUARDO MATOS MOCTEZUMA

General Coordinator
Proyecto Templo Mayor

LA CAPTURA DEL TIEMPO

Un dia me asomé a la ventana del tiempo
Encontré rostros antiguos, ojos que me miraban
    con cristal de obsidiana
     y con ojos marinos
Ví el cuchillo que da muerte
Y el caracol que da vida
Miré el rostro de la vida y de la muerte

Pude detener el tiempo
    con mis manos
    con mis barbas . . .

El tiempo que buscaba por años
  y que me obligaba
  a permanecer
En el tiempo ido,
el tiempo capturado,
  en todos los tiempos

          Eduardo Matos Moctezuma

The excavations of Proyecto Templo Mayor in Mexico City have provided important archaeological data that, combined with ethnohistorical data, greatly broaden

15

our knowledge of the Templo Mayor of Mexico-Tenochtitlan, the sacred place that controlled the destiny of fifteenth- and sixteenth-century pre-Hispanic Mexico. Beginning in March 1978, the excavation was based on specific questions and strategies that were applied to the archaeological and historical data, in order to provide a new understanding of the Great Aztec Temple and its power to integrate the symbolic and political traditions of the Aztec world.

The essay presented in this chapter places my interpretation of the symbolism of the Templo Mayor within a historical survey of major cultural and archaeological developments in Mexico City prior to 1978. My discussion begins with a review of the discoveries of major Aztec monuments and the controversies surrounding their significance and orientation. The historical background is followed by a concise description of the plan of excavation and the archaeological discoveries made during the excavation. This includes a description of both major sculpture and ritual objects found in the offerings buried in the foundation of the Templo Mayor. In my view, the Templo Mayor symbolism represents a precise example of the Mexica view of the cosmos. As we shall see, the Tlaloc side and the Huitzilopochtli side of the temple are replicas of sacred hills which constitute the fundamental symbolic center of the vertical and horizontal cosmos of the Aztec universe. A discussion detailing the symbolic aspects of the sacred shrine and especially the integration of peripheral symbols into the temple concludes the essay. As an archaeologist committed to understanding the relationship of economic structures to ideological forms, I shall attempt to uncover and relate the material and symbolic character of the Great Aztec Temple in this chapter.

HISTORICAL ANTECEDENTS

Following the military conquest of the Mexicas by the armies of Hernán Cortés in 1521, there remained a more difficult enterprise, the imposition of a foreign ideology on the newly conquered peoples. What the force of arms could not accomplish was attempted by the warriors of Christ, the missionaries of Catholicism, who launched a massive effort to convert the Indians to the Christian faith. This effort involved various strategies to convert indigenous thought and society, including the staging of open-air theatrical masses to dramatize the Christian faith to the Indians. Two remarkable examples were the presentation in 1538 of the play the "Conquest of Rodas" in the city of Mexico and the presentation in 1539 of the "Conquest of Jerusalem" on the day of Corpus Christi in Tlaxcala. Great numbers of native peoples were baptized following these masses, leading to claims by Christian priests that Christianity was transforming the spiritual character of the New World. Another strategy was the use of pre-Columbian art forms to communicate biblical tales and sayings. For instance, the priest Jacob de Testera painted images of biblical scenes on *lienzos* (cloth banners) (a pre-Columbian art form), accompanied with Christian interpretations for the educated Indians. This priest also used native hieroglyphs to prepare letters of Christian doctrine to be read to the newly baptized.

It is not surprising, therefore, that during the sixteenth century a number of indigenous language dictionaries were produced and that there was widespread interest on the part of the Spaniards in understanding the customs of the conquered groups. This interest resulted in the creation of a large number of historical chronicles relating the history, politics, and religious traditions of the Indians which are highly valuable for our understanding of the complexity of pre-Columbian society. In many cases, these documents were produced by Spanish priests and laypeople in order to provide the missionaries with extensive knowledge of indigenous groups, to ensure the effective conversion of the natives to the ideology of the conquerors. An example of this strategy appears in the works of Bernardino de Sahagún, who wrote in the prologue of his *General History of the Things of New Spain*:

> The doctor cannot correctly apply medicine to the sick person without first knowing from what disposition and cause the sickness proceeds; therefore, a good physician should be knowledgeable in medicine and in sickness so as to apply correctly to each disease the corrective medicine; and the preachers and confessors, being doctors of the soul, should be experienced in the medicine and illnesses of the spirit in order to cure the spiritual ills; the preacher should know the vices of the republic in order to direct his teaching against them, and the confessor in order to know what to ask, and to understand what is relevant to the exercise of his offices, nor should the minister be careless in their conversion, believing that among this people there are no sins other than drunkenness, theft and lust, because there are many graver sins among them which are in dire need of remedy: the sins of idolatry, idolatrous rites and beliefs, omens, superstitions and idolatrous ceremonies have not yet totally disappeared.[1]

Sahagún further notes that his twelve-volume work, later known as *The Florentine Codex*, was produced to provide the mendicants with a fuller understanding of Indian life and to clarify their conceptions of nature and native idolatries.

The success of this evangelical venture and the Spanish achievement of economic and ideological control resulted, in a sense, in the second conquest of Mexico. For not only had the Aztec armies been defeated but also the Aztec temples had been dismantled. During the sixteenth century the masses of natives were converted into cheap labor and were exploited under a mode of production very different from the pre-Columbian system. The Aztec world appeared to be a dead civilization, while the society of New Spain came to vigorous life. The initial interest in the pre-Hispanic past gave way to a confidence that it was buried forever. The pre-Hispanic world did not receive attention again until the latter part of the eighteenth century. This revival of

17

interest had a number of different causes, but it appears that the various movements in the Americas for independence from Spain stimulated a serious look backward into pre-Columbian history.

Two examples illustrate the potency of this revival. The first was the stunning discovery in 1790 of two Aztec monoliths in the main plaza of Mexico City. The second was the controversial sermon of Fray Servando Teresa de Mier at the shrine of the Virgin of Guadalupe on 12 December 1794.

In 1790 the Spanish viceroy, Juan Vicente de Guemas-Pacheco y Padilla, ordered a resurfacing of the Zócalo of Mexico City. Work below the floor of the great plaza resulted in the discovery of the now famous Stone of the Sun and the huge frightening statue of the Aztec Mother Goddess Coatlicue as well as smaller objects of interest. These discoveries were described by Antonio de León y Gama in *Historical Description and Chronology of the Two Stones Which Were Discovered in the Principal Plaza of Mexico in 1790.*[2] Coatlicue (see pl. 31) was found on 13 August 1790 and the Sun Stone uncovered on 17 December of the same year. The discovery of these sculptures had a special impact in Mexico because it focused the beginning of a renewal of interest in indigenous society onto the cultural creativity expressed in Aztec art. For instance, León y Gama utilized these discoveries in order to defend Spain from the criticisms of its enemies. Writing of his purpose in publishing his work, the author states:

> I was also moved by the desire to present to the literary world part of the great knowledge possessed by the Indians of this America in the arts and sciences in the time of their paganism so that it may be known how falsely the enemies of our Spaniards have misrepresented the Indians as irrational or simpleminded in an effort to diminish their glorious deeds in the conquest of these kingdoms. By means of the narrative of this paper and the figures that are presented to the eye, the excellence of the work of the originals will be made manifest, for without knowing iron or steel, they sculptured with great perfection from hard stone the statues that represent their false idols; and they made other architectural works, using for their labors other more solid and hard stones instead of tempered chisels and steel picks.[3]

The second impressive example of a renewed interest in pre-Columbian life occurred on 12 December 1794, when Friar Servando Teresa de Mier delivered a sermon in honor of the Virgin of Guadalupe. The priest made direct criticisms of the authority of colonial officials. He insinuated in his sermon that the glory of the conversion of the Indians did not belong to the Spaniards but had been initiated over a millennium earlier when Saint Thomas appeared in the New World in the figure of Quetzalcoatl. Teresa de Mier presented a number of facts that served to support his interpretation that Saint Thomas was Quetzalcoatl, the revered holy man of the Toltecs. He also argued that the image of the Virgin of Guadalupe was painted not on the cloak of Juan Diego but on the Saint's cloak and that the popular religious cult at Tepeyac had been established long before the arrival of the *conquistadores* (conquerors). Friar Servando stated: "I added one thing and another in order to exalt, as I have said, the motherland and the image of the Virgin of Guadalupe." With this he immediately earned the hatred of the then archbishop of Mexico, don Alonso Nuñez de Haro y Peralta, who Friar Servando says was well known for his antipathy "toward Creoles and their glories."[4] The result was the persecution and trial of Friar Servando.

Friar Servando also lamented in his memoirs about the destruction of pre-Columbian relics by the Spanish bishops:

> It was a time when the bishops responded harshly to the native idols. The first bishop of Mexico surmised that all the symbolic manuscripts of the Indians were magical forms, demonic signs and witchcraft. He made it his religious duty to exterminate them and through his missionaries he collected all the libraries of the Aztecs.

Later he added, "El Señor Palofox almost destroyed all the Aztec statues which had stood in the street corners of Mexico and deprived us of much insight into ancient Mexico."[5]

Citing the censure of his sermon, which contained a peremptory order to seize the documents on which it was based, he says:

> When, finally, will there be an end to these truly scandalous acts which destroy our monuments, deprive us of the labors of our wise men, and retard knowledge of our antiquities in the name of religion? The king, to the contrary, only a short time ago issued, at the request of the Academy of History, a Royal Order not only to conserve all the monuments of American antiquity, but also inviting us to study them and write about them. This Royal Order was brought to our attention directly by the High Court of Mexico.[6]

In 1802, some years after these events, the brilliant German scholar Baron Alexander von Humboldt traveled from South America to Mexico City on the continuation of his research trip to the Americas. With a spirit of investigation and a sense of adventure he penetrated the vast American territories as no other explorer had done. He had a special interest in visiting archaeological sites and studying different pre-Hispanic monuments. His accounts of these travels and studies appear in his *Vistas de Las Cordilleras y Monumentos de Los Pueblos Indígenas de America*. The Mexican scholar León y Gama had already studied some of the monuments that Humboldt later examined. Especially interesting are León y Gama's comments about the great statue of Coatlicue, which had been moved from the place of its discovery to the University of Mexico on order of the viceroy who resided there.

> With pleasure I agree that the stone figure discovered in the excavations of the plaza of this place should be taken to the Royal and Pontifical University and placed in the most conspicuous spot in that building, taking care,

19

as has been suggested to me, to have it measured, weighed, drawn and engraved so that it may be published, along with the information that the Il-
lustrious Body may have or may ascertain about its origin.[7]

When Humboldt went to study the statue, he was informed that it had been buried
in an underground corridor at the university, so he petitioned the bishop of Monter-
rey to order its exhumation. It is important to understand the reason for the burial,
which was carried out so that the object would not be identified with the contemporary movement toward independence in Mexico. Pre-Columbian artifacts were being used as symbols of opposition to Spanish rule. Humboldt writes:

> The Viceroy Revillagigedo had the monument transported to the University
> of Mexico which he considered the most appropriate place for the conser-
> vation of one of the rare relics of ancient America. The professors, who at
> that time were Dominican priests, did not want to expose the idol to the
> youth of Mexico, so they had it buried again in one of the underground cor-
> ridors of the building, a half meter deep. I would not have been able to ex-
> amine it if the bishop of Monterrey, Feliciano Marin . . . had not visited
> Mexico in answer to my petition and made the rector of the University order
> it uncovered.[8]

Many years passed before real excavations took place in the center of Mexico
City. Various accidental discoveries, made during the construction of some buildings,
increased our knowledge of pre-Hispanic constructions and continued the growing
interest in the pre-Hispanic past. Such was the case of the discovery made in 1897 in
the southeast corner of the Zócalo of Mexico City on the corner of the entry to Mer-
caderes and Tlapaleros Streets. Another significant discovery took place on 5 December 1901 on the corner of the first streets of Relox and Cordobanes, where
construction under the direction of Porfirio Díaz, son of the Mexican president, was
being carried out. Today this is the site of the office of the Sub-Secretary of Culture.
In the patio they found part of a pre-Hispanic stairway that ran from west to east,
plus the head of a serpent with the date glyph 4 Reed and the great *cuauhxicalli* (sculptured recipients for human hearts) stone with the form of a jaguar, which is presently
at the entrance to the Mexica Hall of the National Museum of Anthropology. One
year earlier, in 1900, the archaeologist Leopoldo Batres, in his role as Inspector of
Monuments, examined a number of ritual objects found in the street of Las Escalerillas (now Guatemala Street; see Fig. 1) which can now be viewed in the National
Museum. Batres has left us detailed lists of the objects he located in his book *Archaeological Explorations in the Street of Escalerillas,*[9] where he demonstrates his interest
and dedication to understand the objects being discovered. His ideas about the location of the Great Temple were erroneous because he claimed that there was a structure beneath the cathedral oriented toward the south. In fact, the pre-Hispanic temple
generally had a principal orientation toward the west.

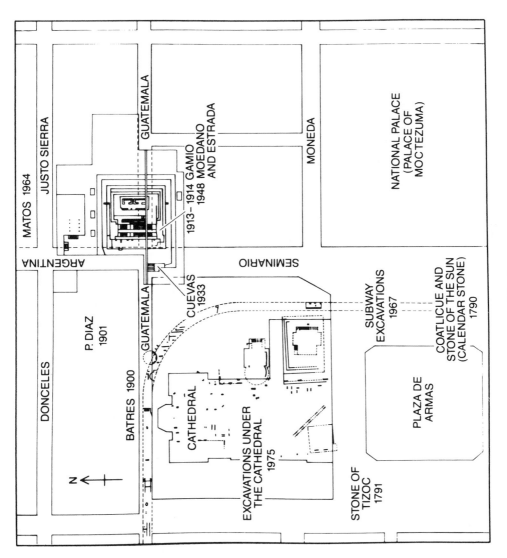

Fig. 1

Alfredo Chavero criticized the erroneous ideas about the location of the Great Temple in this manner:

> The Temple of Huitzilopochtli had to be located at the crossroads of the extension of the two major walkways. This is logical and it is hard to understand how we could mistake its precise location. At the same time, the center of the Teocalli ought to be somewhat to the west of the intersection of Escalerillas and Seminario Streets. In fact that is where it was located, even though Tezozomoc says it occupied the block where the houses of Alonso de Avila, Luis de Castilla and Antonio de la Mota are situated. No one doubts that the house of the unfortunate Avila was on the corner of Santa Teresa and the Relox. Here the front of the Teocalli corresponds to what is today the Plaza of the Seminario and its continuation to the entry of the home of the ex-archbishop, where the temple of Tezcatlipoca stood, following Duran's information.[10]

A. P. Maudsley located the Great Temple in the same place in a brief work entitled "A Note on the Position and Extent of the Great Temple."

Another significant find was the magnificent head of Coyolxauhqui carved in diorite which Antonio Peñafiel described this way: "The colossal head of diorite was found during the work on a foundation of a house on Santa Teresa Street, which was in the property of the convent of Concepcion. It was delivered by the abbess to the National Museum."[11]

Among the most important works carried out in this area of the city were the explorations of Manuel Gamio at the corner of Seminario and the second block of Santa Teresa.[12] During the demolition of a building on that corner, Gamio's excavation found the southwest corner of the Great Temple of Tenochtitlan. Gamio invited a number of specialists to participate in the study of the different objects and structures that he had excavated. For instance, the German archaeologist Hermann Beyer studied the benches, which were decorated with a procession of warriors, and Moises Herrera made a classification of the serpent sculpture discovered in the excavation.

In 1933, under the Office of Archaeology of the government, further archaeological digs were carried out on the corner of Guatemala and Seminario Streets, in the same block as the cathedral in front of the excavations of Gamio. These explorations were done under the supervision of the architect Emilio Cuevas,[13] who opened various trenches that covered the entire area where some buildings had been demolished. The most interesting element of these discoveries was the large, elaborate part of the stairway that was attached to the platform used to support one of the last constructions of the Great Temple.

In 1948 Hugo Moedano and Elma Estrada Balmori explored the platform decorated with serpent heads, as well as the great serpent head and the brazier that marked the middle of the building on its south facade.

In the following years, important objects from Tenochtitlan were uncovered under República de Cuba Street and in the place called *El Volador*. More recently, in 1964, a temple was excavated in Argentina Street, decorated with a magnificently painted mural that represented the god Tlaloc.[14] Another discovery was an offering excavated by Eduardo Contreras in 1966 which forms part of the Great Temple and was reported in the bulletin of the National Institute of Anthropology and History, 1966.

In 1966 the construction of the underground metro (subway) began, which resulted in the discovery of a large number of objects that have still not been organized into a general report, although some notes have been published in the bulletin of the National Institute of Anthropology and History, 1968.[15]

In 1974 excavations were done in the patio of Honor of the National Palace, uncovering what were probably the remains of the columns of the Palace of Cortés. Archaeologists also found a circular temple in the rear patio of the palace.

In 1975 the Department of Pre-Hispanic Monuments initiated the Cuenca de México project, with the goal of organizing the excavations in the Federal District and the border areas. This was done in response to the constant and uncontrolled growth of the city and the destruction of some archaeological remains. A project under the guidance of William T. Sanders was utilized by Eduardo Matos Moctezuma, who divided the urban zone into four sections, leaving each under the responsibility of specialists who would carry out work in such places as the Cerro de la Estrella, Azcapotzalco, Xochimilco, Ecatepec, Plan Tepito, and the Metropolitan Cathedral.

In 1977 the Museum de Tenochtitlan project was organized with the intention of excavating the area of the Great Temple and eventually building a museum for objects found in the ancient city. On 14 February 1978, I was named coordinator of this project and began to draw up the objectives in a new form. The fortunate discovery of the monolith of Coyolxauhqui on 21 February 1978 (pl. 1) necessitated the intervention of the Department of Archaeological Salvage and the procurement of funds to initiate the new project, which developed as a result of the Museum de Tenochtitlan project but had a form and structure of its own. This plan is the Great Temple project.

THE GREAT TEMPLE PROJECT

From what we have seen in the first part of this chapter, it is clear that all archaeological work done on the ceremonial center of Mexico-Tenochtitlan or in the border area of the city was salvage archaeology. This work was the response to accidental discoveries that demanded the intervention of specialists. The Great Temple project provided the first opportunity to develop a course of action and form a plan that we are striving to complete.

Another important dimension of the Great Temple project for social scientists is the opportunity to demystify our pre-Hispanic past. In general, the pre-Hispanic past has been the object of a distorted vision based on certain ideological principles

23

that depict the ancient world as one of grandeur, marvelous architecture, and superb astronomy, excellent in everything. For instance, the view that our museums transmit is narrow and ignores an integrated view of society. This results in a false vision of the past.

In the case of the Mexicas, this results in the "fashion" of Aztequismo, which is expressed on national levels of consciousness. This is detrimental to our understanding of other indigenous groups. For example, the monuments from the Mexicas occupy the central room in the National Museum of Anthropolgoy. This vision of the pre-Hispanic world ignores a more integrated view of the pre-Columbian societies which, if it existed, would present evidence of the many components of Mesoamerican social life and the complex interrelationships of groups and cultures. We do not really have a museum of anthropology, therefore; at best it is a museum of pre-Hispanic art.

In the case of the Great Temple project, we faced a unique opportunity to study a fundamental part of the Aztec state. We were interested in understanding the complex spheres that composed the total society of Aztec Mexico and the interaction between the capital and the peripheries of the empire. To clarify our approach, let me present a general outline of the project.

On 20 March 1978, one month after the discovery of the Coyolxauhqui stone, the first excavations of the Great Temple were begun. From the beginning, the project was divided into three phases, which can be summarized as follows.

First Phase: The collection of existing materials written about the Great Temple, both from ethnohistorical sources and from archaeological studies relating specifically to it. On the basis of this information, we established the *general principles*, both theoretical and practical, that would govern the process of the investigation. The relevant written materials were brought together in the volume *Archaeological Works on the Center of the City of Mexico*, an anthology that included the principal works of various researchers in the past as well as the plans for the project.

Second Phase: This phase covered matters related to the actual *excavation*; that is, to obtaining and mapping the archaeological data. A major concern was the use of adequate techniques that ensured control of data throughout the excavation. This included such techniques as cross-sectioning the area into sections 2 meters square and the placement of elevation markers in the area of excavation, with a central marker indicating 2,243 meters above sea level. Letters were used from east to west and numbers from south to north. The area to be excavated was divided into three sections, each one under the supervision of a professional archaeologist and his respective assistants. Support groups were established, such as a team of restorers with their field laboratory, as well as biologists, chemists, geologists, and other specialists from the Department of Prehistory. Also available were photographic laboratories, a sketching area, and an area for material control. The administration office coordinated all excavation activities (pl. 2).

Third Phase: This phase included the study and analysis of the materials obtained in the previous phase. Through the coordination of the interdisciplinary team of researchers we entered into the process of interpreting the masses of objects uncovered in the excavation.

PRESENTATION OF THE PROBLEM

Let us now consider what was obtained during each phase described above. The economic base of Tenochtitlán consisted of two interrelated aspects: agricultural production plus crafts and tribute paid by the many communities subject to the Aztecs. As our ethnohistorical and archaeological evidence demonstrates, significant parts of the production of a large number of tributary towns within the Aztec state were destined for Tenochtitlan. In this way, the peripheral units of the state were integrated by the "center" of the economic system. This system of tributary payments created fixed internal and external relations where production was concerned.

It is absolutely clear that the Great Temple of Tenochtitlan was the place, real or symbolic, where Mexica power was centered. It is significant that the shrines to the two great deities related to the economic structure of the Mexica state were located at the top of the temple: Tlaloc, god of rain, water, and agricultural production; and Huitzilopochtli, god of war, conquest, and tribute. Their presence at the Great Temple indicates a coherent relationship between structure and superstructure. The "structure," as I am using the term, refers to everything relating to the economic base of the group: productive forces, including habitat and natural resources, and humans as active components who use these forces and transform them with their tools in the process of production. Structure also includes the relationships that are created between those who exercise power and those who are subject to the controlling group, including the people conquered by the Mexica. The "superstructure" is made up of such aspects as art, philosophy, and religion (ideology), all of which is under the control of the governing class known in Aztec society as the *pillis*.

Concerning these vital relationships, we can propose two general postulates:

1. The archaeological context associated with the Great Temple such as offerings and sculpture has an ideological content that probably reflects the ideology of the dominant group and indicates how it uses two apparatuses of the state, the repressive and the ideological, to maintain its hegemony and assist in its reproduction. The first apparatus acts by

using force, and the second is expressed through religion, art, education, the family, and the political system. In both cases we see the ways in which the center of Mexica society dominated peripheral communities through ideological force.

2.   The different discoveries, including sculpture, murals, and offerings, probably reflect both internal and external Mexica control, through the presence of their own materials (Mexica) and other groups (tribute).

In order to understand what the Great Temple signified, we must refer to two categories that will help us in the process of our investigation: *phenomenon* and *essence*.

Our research begins with the study of a collection of phenomena related to the Great Temple, and these phenomena allow us to penetrate the essence that produced them. To analyze scientifically this motley collection of phenomena, we must use the two general categories that play an important role in the process of acquiring knowledge. The first refers to the outward appearance of objects and the processes of its objective reality, which moves and changes. *Essence*, the more stable of two categories, is the internal aspect of process that is contained within and manifested through a phenomenon. Scientific knowledge should be directed not only to the study of phenomena but to the study of internal processes, of the essence that produces these phenomena.

In figure 2 we have synthesized in flowchart form what we stated above, which can be explained as follows. The aspect of phenomenon (aspect A) is what we generally know as the presence of Tlaloc and Huitzilopochtli at the Great Temple, the symbols and elements proper to each deity, the rituals of the various festivals and their characteristics, and so on. This includes everything manifest and present before the priest and the participants, with all its religious complexity.

The essence (aspect B) is what is not directly present but that, nevertheless, acts as the basis of this process. For us, this is the ideological presence of the two deities at the Great Temple. First, there is Tlaloc, god of water and rain, a fundamental god for an agricultural people such as the Mexica, and we are well aware that part of the economic basis of Tenochtitlan consisted of agricultural production. Second, there is Huitzilopochtli, a tribal god, a solar god, a god of war, of the domination over other groups, a domination that required tribute from conquered areas. Tenochtitlan used this tribute to provide itself with a whole series of products necessary to its economy: loads of corn, beans, cacao, cloth, feathers, objects and raw materials such as skins, stones, and lime. In other words, the presence of these two gods, and not others, is a reflection of the economic and political base of Tenochtitlan.

Next we shall present a general summary of what was found in the second phase (excavation) of the project, such as the architecture and the offerings of the Great

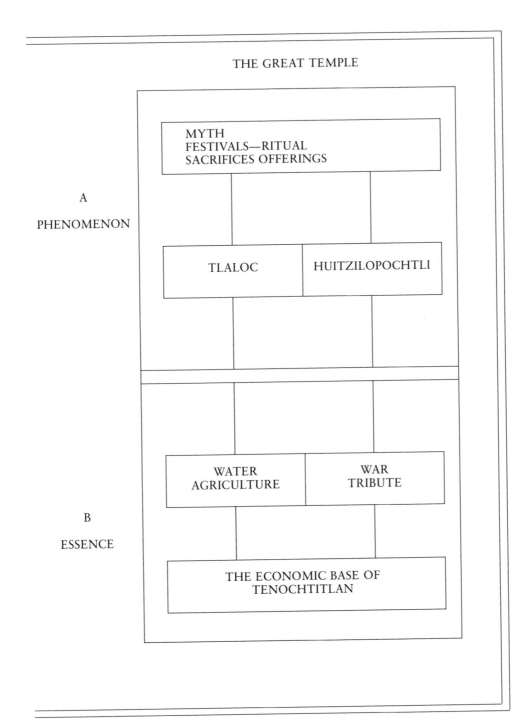

THE GREAT TEMPLE

A

PHENOMENON

MYTH
FESTIVALS—RITUAL
SACRIFICES OFFERINGS

TLALOC   HUITZILOPOCHTLI

WATER   WAR
AGRICULTURE   TRIBUTE

B

ESSENCE

THE ECONOMIC BASE OF
TENOCHTITLAN

Fig. 2

Temple. Later on we shall interpret the symbolic character of the Great Temple utilizing the archaeological data as well as data taken from historical sources. In this we shall have recourse to two branches of knowledge, archaeology and written history.

EXCAVATIONS

The following section is divided into three parts: (1) a brief look at indigenous accounts of the origin of the Templo Mayor, (2) a detailed survey of the stages of excavation, and (3) a description and list of objects found in the ritual offerings.

Origin Stories

The Mexica were the last Nahua group to penetrate the Valley of Mexico during the middle of the thirteenth century. Guided by their titular god, Huitzilopochtli, they left Aztlan, place of the white heron, and traveled until they arrived many years later at the promised island where they settled, prospered, and finally disappeared, annihilated several centuries later in the Spanish conquests. A beautiful Nahua text has survived that tells us of their original journey:

> "I shall act as your guide,
> I shall show you the road."
> At once the Aztecs began
> to move this way,
> they exist, they are painted,
> the places the Mexica passed by
> bear names in the Aztec tongue.
> And as the Mexica came,
> it was clear they moved aimlessly,
> they were the last who came.
> As they came,
> while they were following their road,
> they were not received anywhere.
> Everywhere they were reproached.
> No one knew their faces.
> Everywhere people said to them,
> "Who are you?
> Where have you come from?"
> So they could settle nowhere,
> they were always cast out,
> they were persecuted everywhere.
> They passed by Coatepec,
> they passed by Tollan,
> they passed by Ichpuchco,

> they passed by Ecatepec,
> then by Chiquihtepetitlan,
> then they came to Chapultepec
> where many people settled.
> The rule of Lord Azcapotzalco already existed,
> in Coatlinchan,
> in Culhuacan,
> but Mexico did not yet exist.
> There were still fields of rush and reed
> where Mexico is today.[16]

A number of historical chronicles relate how the Mexica arrived in the Valley of Mexico after many hardships and found the different city-states engaged in intense military struggles for control of the valley and its resources. The Mexica eventually submitted to the Tepaneca Lord of Azcapotzalco, who extracted tribute from them in exchange for the right to settle on the edges of their territory. This occurred in the year 2 House, or A.D. 1325.

It was here, in the middle of the lake, where the Mexica began to construct their first temple. One chronicle tells us:

> Seeing that everything
> was filled with mystery,
> they went on, to seek
> the omen of the eagle
> and wandering from place to place
> they saw the cactus and on it the eagle,
> with its wings spread out to the rays of the sun,
> enjoying its warmth and the cool of the morning,
> and in its claws it held an elegant bird
> with precious and resplendent feathers.
> When they saw it, they bowed down
> as if it were a holy thing.
> When the eagle saw them, it bowed to them,
> nodding its head in their direction.
> Seeing the eagle bow, and now that
> they had seen what they desired,
> they began to weep and give vent to their feelings,
> and to make displays and grimace and tremble,
> as a sign of their joy and happiness,
> and as an expression of their thanks, saying:
> "How have we deserved such a blessing?
> Who made us worthy of such grace
> and greatness and excellence?
> Now we have seen what we sought,
> and we have found our city and place.

Let us give thanks to the Lord of creation
and to our god Huitzilopochtli."
then, the next day, the priest
Cuauhtloquetzqui said to all of the tribe,
"My children, we should be grateful to our god
and thank him for the blessing he has given us.
Let us all go and build at the place of the cactus
a small temple where our god may rest."[17]

During the ensuing decades, the Mexica enlarged their temple, the Great Temple, numerous times by utilizing previous stages as the foundation for the larger structure. Our excavation shows that the temple was enlarged seven times on all four sides and on top, while the main facade received a number of partial enlargements. We will now present a description of the Great Temple, referring to both the archaeological data and reports from historical sources.

Architecture and Stages of Excavation

Until recently, our fundamental sources of information concerning the Great Temple were the chronicles written in the sixteenth century. Ignacio Marquina's famous model of the ceremonial center of Tenochtitlan was based on these written descriptions as well as the excavations of Manuel Gamio which uncovered a corner of the Great Temple in 1913–1914. Now that we have the excavated temple before us, we see that the historical descriptions were faithful to what the Spaniards saw and what they had learned from native sources. Also, the project has uncovered the very ancient stages of the Great Temple with which even the last generations of the Mexicas were not familiar.

In general, the temple was oriented with its principal facade toward the west. It was built on a large platform that supported a four-sided structure with two stairways leading upward to the two shrines of Huitzilopochtli and Tlaloc. Huitzilopochtli's shrine (on the south side) was the location of the titular god of the Aztecs, while Tlaloc (located on the north side) was the god of rain, water, and fertility.

The temple was enlarged many times for different reasons. On one hand, the city of Tenochtitlan suffered periodic floods, which required the base of the structure to be raised. The temple also had structural defects due to the sinking of the unstable earth beneath it. On the other hand, the historical sources reveal how some of the rulers ordered the construction of new temples on top of the existing ones, creating a pattern of the superimposition of new stages of the Great Temple. Today we know that the temple was enlarged on its four sides at least seven times, while there were six extra additions to the main facade. I shall give a general picture of each stage of the Great Temple by utilizing a system of Roman numerals that designate total enlargements of the four-sided structure. A Roman numeral accompanied by a letter refers to the additions on the main facade only (see the general plan in fig. 3 and pl. 4).

30

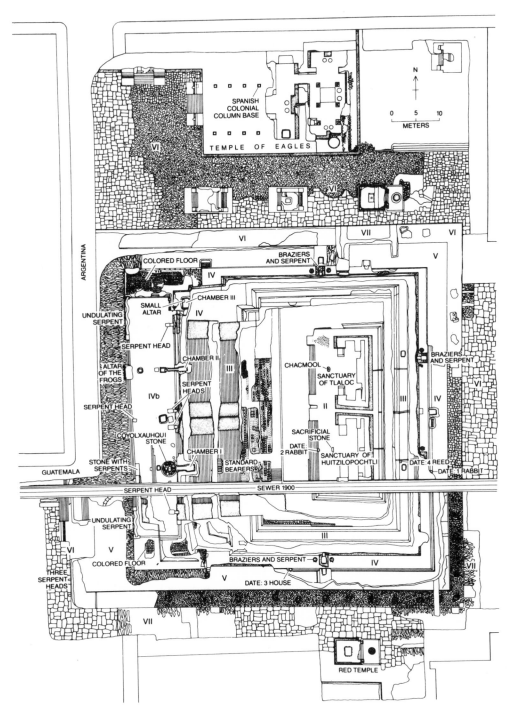

Fig. 3

Stage I: This refers to the first temple structure that historical sources indicated was a small hut constructed of perishable materials. No excavation of this structure is possible.

Stage II: This structure is extremely impressive because it still contains the upper section of the temple in nearly complete form. We see the remains of the two shrines constructed of stone with some of the stucco still covering the surfaces (a mixture of sand and lime). In front of the entry to the Huitzilopochtli shrine we found the notorious stone of sacrifice, a later version of which the Franciscan priest Motolinia describes: "They had a large stone, an arm's length long and a foot wide, and a good eight inches thick. Half of the stone was lodged in the earth, at the top, above the steps and before the altar of the idols."[18] On the last step leading up to the platform and on an axis with the sacrificial stone, we found the sculptured face of a person with the glyph 2 Rabbit carved above. This year sign is equivalent to the year 1390. In the interior of the shrine we discovered a bench that runs north and south. In the middle there is a small altar that apparently supported a statue of the deity Huitzilopochtli. On the Tlaloc side (the north side) we uncovered a marvelous *Chac Mool* sculpted in stone and covered with painted colors (see pl. 52). Chac Mools were divine messengers responsible for transporting the offering into the shrine. The pillars that mark the access to the inner shrine still show the murals that covered them. These paintings consist of black-and-white circles, possibly representing the eyes of Tlaloc, above a blue-and-red band. Below these bands are vertical black-and-white borders. In the interior of the structure we discovered the bench on which the image of Tlaloc probably sat. We consider this stage to be prior to 1428, the year in which the Mexica liberated themselves from Azcapotzalco and began their climb to dominance. It may correspond to the reign of the Aztec ruler Huitzilihuitl (see pl. 5). Following this stage, we found partial remains of superimpositions IIa, IIb, IIc, which show a deficient system of construction on the west facade of the temple.

Stage III: This stage reveals finely made, steep stairways bordered by vertically constructed foundations. Most significantly, we found eight impressive sculptures of life-size standard bearers reclining on the stairway leading to Huitzilopochtli's shrine. These figures were probably located at symbolic locations around the building before they were gathered together on this stairway when the next stage was constructed over them. This structure has the glyph 4 Reed carved into the rear platform wall of Huitzilopochtli's stairway. It is equivalent to the year 1431, which corresponds to the rule of Itzcoatl (see pls. 6 and 7).

Stage IV: This stage is one of the richest in the elements of the temple. Braziers and serpent heads adorn the large general platform on each of its four sides. The braziers on the side of Tlaloc (e.g., in the rear) show the face of this god, while braziers on the side of Huitzilopochtli have only a bow that symbolizes that deity. Beneath the braziers and serpents various offerings were found; the caches of these are still visible. Stage IVb is an addition to the main facade (on the west) that has yielded a great series of significant objects. It includes the great platform on which the Great Temple rests, a platform that contains stairways at both ends. Next to the stairways we found enormous serpents whose undulating bodies and great heads still carry some of the original pigment that covered them. The wide flight of steps to the platform is interrupted only by a small altar with two frogs resting on top of small pedestals. These sculptures are found in line with the middle of the stairway that leads to the upper part of Tlaloc's temple. On the side of Huitzilopochtli, in front of the stairway that leads to his shrine, we found a stone 2.5 meters long decorated with serpents which forms part of the fourth stairway of the platform.

The pedestal forming the base of the stairs that led to the upper part supports four serpent heads, two located at the extreme ends of the pedestal and two in the middle, which mark the union of both buildings. At the center of the Huitzilopochtli side of the platform we found the monumental stone sculpture of Coyolxauhqui, who is the dismembered sister of the war god. In Aztec myth, these two deities fought at the hill of Coatepec and together they constitute a major portion of the symbolism of the Great Temple. On this platform, we found various offerings, some around the Coyolxauhqui stone, others between the two serpent heads, and others in the middle of the stairway to Tlaloc. These offerings were found beneath the platform, while chambers 1 and 2 were found behind the stairways in the exact middle of each one of these buildings.

At the extreme north and south of this platform were found the remains of rooms with colored marble floors. Also, on the Tlaloc side was found a small stairway leading to a tiny altar within which were discovered two extremely impressive offerings. One contained more than forty-two skulls and bones of children, finely covered masks, and delicately painted funerary urns full of small seashells perhaps representing human hearts. Below this rich offering we found another offering called *chamber 3*. Both were dedicated to Tlaloc. Chronologically, we think that much of stage IV corresponds to the reign of Moctezuma I because we discovered a glyph 1 Rabbit on the Huitzilopochtli side of the platform which is equivalent to the year 1454. The additional elements of Coyolxauhqui and the serpents could well correspond to the reign of Ayaxacatl, for another glyph on the south side of the structure carries the symbol 3 House, which is the year 1469, coinciding with the ascent to the throne of that king (see pls. 8 and 9).

Stage V: We have found only the general platform of stage V, covered with stucco, as well as part of the floor of the great ceremonial enclosure formed by slabs that were joined by stucco.

Stage VI: This stage is the penultimate one to form part of the great platform. The principal facade reveals a wall with three serpent heads facing west, a decorated beam, and part of a stairway that was destroyed by the water conduit constructed here in 1900. The decorated beam was found by the archaeologist Emilio Cuevas in 1933. This stage of construction corresponds to the three small shrines found on the north side of the Great Temple and the foundation of the eagle precinct as well as an expansive patio of slabs on which are situated these smaller shrines. On the south side of the Great Temple we have another temple that we call *Red Temple*, and its architecture and paintings are similar to a corresponding temple on the north side.

I shall now describe each of these smaller structures located north of Tlaloc's temple.

Shrine A: This structure is situated on a small platform and contains two stairways leading to the upper part, one oriented to the west and the other to the east. The walls show no decorations.

Shrine B: This structure has a stairway facing west and is decorated on the other three sides with panels showing rows of carved skulls. There are about 240 skulls showing various coats of the stucco that covered them. We designate this structure as a *tzompantli* (skull rack) altar (see pl. 10).

Shrine C: The principal face of this temple is oriented east and is formed by a vestibule in whose center we found remains of a circular altar. On the sides are two walls decorated with circular stones painted red that symbolize *chalchihuitls*, or precious stones. At the back of the vestibule is a stairway. This building is totally decorated and preserved in the talus-panel style, which is the typical architectural order that prevailed in Teotihuacan from the second to the seventh centuries A.D. It shows that the Aztecs had a strong awareness of this more ancient culture.

Shrine D: This structure is a small shrine without decorations found on the extreme north side of the excavation. It faces west.

The Eagle Precinct: To the north of these three shrines we found a structure with its main facade oriented toward the west with beams decorated by eagle heads which still conserve remains of the original pigment. This facade is complemented by the south facade of a patio that we call the *eagle patio*. The floor supporting all these buildings shows various superimpositions, and it was found to be in magnificent condition. When we excavated beyond the facade, we discovered the complex which we have named the "Eagle Knight Precinct." It belongs to Epoch V but was rebuilt in Epoch VI (approximately A.D. 1500).

The precinct consists of a general hall that is approached by a staircase. The hall has a series of pillars that go from north to south and were used to support the roof that covered the structure. In the interior, along the walls of the rooms, there are benches formed by a series of stone slabs with a polychrome representation of a procession of warriors. A small frieze of serpents also adorns the benches. Above the benches located at the entrance or principal access to the precinct, two life-size clay sculptures were found, representing two eagle knights. It should be noted that this complex does not end here but continues to the north, beneath what is now Justo Sierra Street. The rooms apparently were covered by roofs.

Both the discovery of the eagle knight sculptures and the procession of warriors on the benches (resembling those of the Palacio Quemado in Tula, Hidalgo) lead us to believe that this complex was used for ceremonies of that military order so important in Mexica society (see pls. 11 and 53).

Rear Patio: Of the same epoch is the rear patio of the Great Temple which, like the one on the north side, consists of slabs of stone joined by stucco. This patio stops at the architectural limit on the east side of the great ceremonial precinct, which, according to Sagahún, contained seventy-eight ceremonial buildings. Architecture is composed of stretches of stairways alternating with beams, as can be seen in the ceremonial center of Tlatelolco, the twin city of Tenochtitlán.

Stage VII: This is the last stage of the Great Temple viewed by the Spaniards during their visit and battles in Tenochtitlan. All that remains is part of the stone floor of the ceremonial precinct and a trace of the place where the temple stood before it was eradicated. On the north side, however, one can see part of a platform that corresponds to the platform of the previous stage. When the Aztecs filled and covered the edifices previously mentioned (shrines A, B, and C and the eagle foundation) and built the floor of the last stage over them, they used the older platform, so that the Templo Mayor did not actually increase in size but utilized the platform that already existed.

An interesting discovery on the north side was the remains of a colonial house, possibly from the sixteenth century, which utilized the roof covering the eagle platform as its own floor. We can clearly see the colonial patio, which is formed by the bases of columns, stone pavements of corridors, and some walls, in which stones of pre-Hispanic constructions containing relief designs were utilized.

Other colonial remains can be found in different parts of the Great Temple. One is the circular fountain in the northeast corner of the excavation. Another object of particular interest is the faucet of a pool very close to the Red Temple on the south side. We see here the utilization of brick as construction material. Also, there is an arch embedded in the platform of stage V and in part of the stone floor of the last stage (VII) located near the southeast corner of the Great Temple.

We have conserved all these colonial elements because of their value in colonial studies. They are also a magnificent indicator of the depth of the foundations of colonial buildings and, in some cases, of their use of pre-Hispanic material for construction, as can be seen in the remains on the north side, already described.

Besides these elements of colonial architecture found at the Great Temple, we have uncovered colonial trash heaps and wells that contain ceramics in use at that time, including the notable presence of Chinese ceramics from the Ming and Ching Dynasties brought to Mexico from the East. These objects along with silks and other objects were part of the commerce of New Spain which found their way to the capital.[19]

Offerings

More than 100 offerings were discovered at the Great Temple, of which some were outside the context of the temple proper: that is, some were discovered as offerings in the smaller shrines nearby. The generalizations we will make here refer to those offerings directly associated with the Great Temple.

To begin with, we can say that all the offerings were found to be deposited in one of three different ways: (1) offerings placed in caches whose walls and floors were made of stone, with traces of stucco; (2) offerings placed inside movable chests or boxes of stone, with lids of the same material; or (3) offerings placed directly in the fill or nucleus of stone and earth that covered a construction period (see pls. 12–18).

As for location, we can state that generally they were placed along certain axes. On the main facade there were three main axes: the first and second, beneath the floor of the platform facing the middle of each of the two stairways; and the third, closer to the junction of the twin temples of Tlaloc and Huitzilopochtli. They were also located at the corners of the temple, as well as along the north-south axis. There are also three axes at the back part, at the middle of each building and at their junctions. Some offerings were placed around the base, equidistant from each other (see fig. 3). There exist some funeral urns that, although they are described as offerings in our nomenclature, actually have a function related to burial ritual.

In general, it can be stated that the placement of objects within the offering was not random but rather that their placement was premeditated; that is, the objects occupy a place according to a symbolism that we must decode. This means that the objects and their placement *have a language*. For example, there are materials that usually occupy the lower part of an offering, on the bottom, just as others always occupy the upper part. We have also observed that the materials are oriented in a certain way. Both the offerings on the west side (main facade) and in the back part of the temple are oriented toward the west, in the direction of the setting sun, while those found halfway down the temple on its north and south facades are oriented in those directions. Another interesting aspect is that the placement of objects within an offering also follows a specific plan. For instance, offerings 7 and 61, the first of which is located halfway down the south side of the structure and the other on the north side, had the same distribution of materials. On the bottom, *Strombus* mollusks oriented north to south; over these were placed crocodiles. On top were placed the seated gods whom we have designated *Xiuhtecuhtli*, since they represent old people. On the right side of these gods we have marine coral and on their left, a clay vessel with an effigy of the god Tlaloc. Could this distribution mean that the strombus represent the sea, the crocodiles an earthly level, and Xiuhtecuhtli and Tlaloc a heavenly level? The same pattern occurs with offerings 11 and 17; offering 11 is located on the main facade between the two serpent heads that mark the junction of the shrines of Tlaloc and Huitzilopochtli; offering 17 is located at the rear part of the junction of both edifices. Both are located in caches with stone walls, and their objects occupy similar positions in addition to being very similar in content.

The material obtained from the 100 or so offerings associated with the Great Temple is abundant and varied. More than 7,000 objects have been uncovered, including pieces that are clearly Mexica and others that definitely came from tributary areas. The great majority of the tribute objects originated from the present states of Guerrero, Puebla, and the Gulf Coast. It is important to note that not all "peripheral" communities were symbolically integrated into the Templo Mayor. For instance, not one single object came from either the Tarasca culture, which, as we know, was not under Mexica control, or the Maya culture.

Among the Mexica materials, the most numerous objects are the sculptures of seated old men, dressed only in the *maxtlatl* (loincloths) and wearing headdresses characterized by two protuberances. It is believed that they represent the ancient fire god Xiuhtecuhtli, although authors such as H. Nicholson suggest that they represent Tepeyollotl. We are inclined to accept the first explanation, since the sculptures depict an old man with missing teeth. The headdress may correspond to the two ritual sticks used to make fire. Also, we know that Xiuhtecuhtli was the father of the gods located on the macrocosmic level at the center of the universe and on the microcosmic level at the center of the family dwelling.

Other Mexica representations include numerous effigies of the god Tlaloc, carved out of *tezontle* (volcanic rock) and other kinds of stone. We also found coiled serpents, representations of rattlesnake heads made of obsidian, stone braziers with knotted bows, and, of course, the magnificent representations of conch shells, which constitute marvelous works of art.

There are other remarkable pieces from the tributary areas, such as a great quantity of Mezcala masks and figures of different sizes. There are also alabaster pieces from the Puebla region, including delicate deer heads, finely carved arrows, and seated deities. From the Gulf coast we have two magnificent funerary urns of orange ceramic, inside of which were found fragments of burned bones, necklaces, and other materials. The great variety of snails, shells, fish, swordfish swords, and corals come from the Gulf coast and the Pacific regions. The same wide distribution is true of the crocodiles and jaguars, which possibly come from Veracrúz, Tabasco, or Chiapas.

It is very significant that another group of objects belonged to societies that long preceded the Mexica. Outstanding examples include the magnificent Teotihuacan masks (see pls. 40 and 41) and the beautiful Olmec mask (pl. 39) that were excavated. The latter came from the region that lies within the borders of the states of Puebla, Oaxaca, and Guerrero, according to the petrographic analysis that has been made.

These objects are another example of the Mexica pattern of integrating peripheral materials within their central shrine.

All the material is under study, but a preliminary analysis reveals that the majority of the objects represent Tlaloc or symbols associated with him, such as the massive number of objects of marine origin. We also have objects associated with Huitzilopochtli such as the braziers with the knotted bows, skulls of the decapitated victims, and sacrificial knives (*tecpatls*) with eyes and teeth of shell. Huitzilopochtli's power is also manifest in the large number of objects from tributary areas, the products of military conquest. Significantly, not a single literal stone image of Huitzilopochtli has been found.

The foregoing description confirms our hypothesis that the Mexica were, of necessity, an agricultural and militaristic people whose substance depended on both agricultural production and tributary payments. Understandably, the major elements of water and war, life and death were symbolized in the Great Temple of Tenochtitlan. Moreover, the Templo Mayor represents the concentration of Mexica power and their control over the destiny of conquered and peripheral peoples, just as Huitzilopochtli conquered and took control of the *anecuyotl* (destiny) of his brothers. On a symbolic level this is important, for, as we shall discuss later, it shows how the Mexica continue the mission initiated by their tutelar god. They not only take control over the anecuyotl of the conquered peoples but also control their production of agricultural and other products such as warrior cloaks, war shields, and animal skins. We shall discuss this in further detail later.

So that the social, symbolic, and economic importance of these offerings may be appreciated, we shall transcribe two quotations given to us by Durán and by Bernal Díaz del Castillo. The first quotation states:

> When King Moctezuma saw the speed with which his temple was being built, he ordered all the lords of the land, so that his god would be more honored and revered, to take up a collection in all of the cities of a great quantity of precious stones: of green stones which they call chalchihuites and of glass and of bloodstones, emeralds, rubies and carnelians. In short, of every kind of fine stones and precious jewels and many valuable things, and that in each six foot layer as the structure grew, there should be thrown in among the mortar some of these stones which were precious, rich jewels.
>
> And in this way, collecting that tribute from each citizen, every city brought its jewels and stones to be placed in the walls, each in its turn and time, so that in every layer of the building they threw in such quantity of jewels and fine stones that it was astonishing, saying as they did so that since God had given that wealth it was fitting that it should be employed in His service, for it belonged to Him.[20]

This remarkable passage illustrates the Aztec pattern of renewing their axis mundi, the place of agricultural and military power, through the symbolic integration of jewels from "all the cities" in the empire. Again, the center of the world expresses its dominance over the peripheries.

The other quotation is interesting because it refers to the moment when the Great Temple was destroyed in order to build the first colonial structures:

Some very curious readers will ask how we came to know that into the foundations of that great *cu* [temple] they cast gold and silver and fine seeds and chalchihuis stones and sprinkled it with human blood from Indians they sacrificed, since it was constructed and made more than a thousand years ago [sic]. To this I answer that after we had won that great strong city and after catales had been divided up, we then proposed to build the church of our patron and guide St. James on that great *cu*, and a large portion of the site of the high *cu* of Huichilobos fell into the possession of the Holy Church and when they opened the foundations to make them stronger, they found a lot of gold, silver, chalchuhuis, pearls and seed pearls, and other stones. At the same time a resident of Mexico, who had received another portion of the same site, found the same thing, and the treasury officials of His Majesty sued him in behalf of His Majesty, to whom it lawfully belonged. There was litigation about it but I don't remember what happened, except that they took testimony from the leaders and chiefs of Mexico and Guatemuz (Cuautemoc) who was alive then, and they said that it was true that all the residents of Mexico of that time had thrown those jewels and all the rest into the foundations, and that that was the way it was recorded in their books and pictures about ancient things, and for that reason that wealth was left for the building of the Holy Church of St. James.[21]

Next we shall enumerate the different offerings that have been found, giving a general idea of their content and of the construction period to which they belong, following the preliminary classification that Carlos González and Bertina Olmedo have been developing. (See also table 1 for chronology of construction periods.)

Table 1
RULERS OF TENOCHTITLAN IN RELATION TO CONSTRUCTIVE PERIODS OF TEMPLO MAYOR AND CHRONOLOGY

Name	Periods of government	Constructive periods	Dates at the temple
Acamapichtli	1375–1395	Period II	
Huitzilihuitl	1396–1417		
Chimalpopoca	1417–1427		
Itzcoatl	1427–1440	Period III	(4 Reed, A.D. 1431)
Moctezuma I	1440–1469	Period IV	(1 Rabbit, A.D. 1454)
Axayacatl	1469–1481	Period IVb	(3 House, A.D. 1469)
Tizoc	1481–1486	Period V	
Ahuizotl	1486–1502	Period VI	
Moctezuma II	1502–1520	Period VII	

Drawing: Alberto Zuñiga R.

Period II (approximately A.D. 1390)

Offering 33.   (Cache). Interior, Shrine of Huitzilopochtli. Beads, bird (quail?), chimalli (shield?), copal, monofacial of jade (?), and fragments of charcoal.

Offering 34.   (Fill). Interior, Shrine of Huitzilopochtli. Obsidian funerary urn with cover of the same material; beads (many burned); obsidian earplugs; burned bones, miniature vessel of metal (?); copal; and stone knife. Inside there was a silver mask and a gold bell.

Offering 37.   (Fill). Interior, Shrine of Huitzilopochtli. Ceramic tripod vessel, cremated bones, obsidian knife, and gold and turquoise beads.

Offering 38.   (Cache). Sacrificial stone. Silex knives, bone fragments (?), bird, and jadite fragments.

Offering 39.   (Fill). Interior, Shrine of Huitzilopochtli (center). Beads, obsidian disks, earplugs, obsidian vessel, anthropomorphic vessel of alabaster with cremated bones and gold bell inside, black stone with carved human figure (?), jadite (?), and plaque with engraved human figure. Predominance of beads, obsidian disks, and earplugs.

Offering 40.   (Fill). Interior, Shrine of Tlaloc. Copal, charcoal, beads, bird, rubber (?), fragments of ceramic, and mineral (?).

Offering 42.   (Fill). Interior, Shrine of Tlaloc. Obsidian knife, potsherds, and obsidian chips.

Offering 44.   (Fill). Interior, Shrine of Huitzilopochtli (north platform). Monochrome ceramic vessel, zoomorphic vessel, and cremated bones.

Offering 45.   (Fill). Interior, Shrine of Tlaloc (center). Beads, sculpture of stone (?), fragments of obsidian nucleus, and copal. Predominance of beads.

There are nine offerings in this period; six are associated with the Shrine of Huitzilopochtli, and three are associated with the Shrine of Tlaloc. No marine items are present; this is significant, for it indicates that there still was no military expansion toward coastal areas and that our chronology may be correct in the sense that they were still under the control of Azcapotzalco.

Period III (approximately A.D. 1431)

Offering 8.   (Cache). East facade (south section). Potsherds, unidentified fish and animal, silex knives, raw rubber (?), snails, stone nail, wood, charcoal, and small ceramic head.

Offering 21.   (Cache). East facade (north section). Charcoal, potsherds, wood, bone, shells, ceramic Tlaloc vessel (polychrome and with a mask in relief), beads, copal, sawfish, bird, and silex knife.

Offering 25.   (Cache). East facade (north section). Ceramic vessel and ceramic bowl as a cover; beads inside.

40

Offering 26.   (Fill). East facade (north section). Orange ceramic vessel, ceramic bowl, charcoal and stone beads inside.

Offering 28.   (Fill). North facade (Shrine of Tlaloc). Orange ceramic vessel with trichrome ceramic pulque bowl and stone beads inside.

Offering 29.   (Box in fill). South facade. Box and lid of tezontle, ashes, bone fragments (?), bone awl, and bead inside.

Offering 32.   (Cache). East facade (north section).

Offering 35.   (Fill). North facade (east section). Tripod ceramic bowl, and ceramic vessel.

Offering 36.   (Fill). East facade (south section). Flint knife.

Offering 43.   (Fill). East facade (Shrine of Tlaloc). Bichrome vessel with handles and cover.

Offering 46.   (Fill). East facade (Shrine of Tlaloc). Silex knife.

Offering 47.   (Fill). East facade (Shrine of Tlaloc). Bichrome vessel with two handles and cover; copal fragments.

Offering 55.   (Cache). North facade. No material.

There are thirteen offerings in this period; in two of them, marine items are present and both are the only ones found to be directly associated with the structure of the base of Period III—the rest were found in the fill between Periods II and III; ten are in the east facade, two are in the north facade, and one is in the south facade. If we consider them in relationship to the north and south halves of the temple, there are ten in the north half and three in the south half. We consider that this stage of the construction was carried out immediately after the liberation from Azcapotzalco under the rule of Itzcoatl.

Period IV (approximately A.D. 1454)

Offering 56.   (Cache). North facade (central part). Polychrome Tlaloc vessel with a mask in relief, mother-of-pearl shells, beads, knife, copal (balls), remains of bird bones, wood, and snout of sawfish.

Period IVa (approximately A.D. 1454)

Offering   4.   (Cache). West facade (south—Coyolxauhqui section). Small Coyolxauhqui and shield (?).

Offering   5.   (Cache). West facade (south—Coyolxauhqui section).

Offering 30.   (Cache). West facade (central part). Stone beads, small lizard, small snail, copal, and rubber (?).

Offering 31.   (Cache). West facade (center). Polychrome ceramic Tlaloc vessel, Mezcala figurines inside, stone beads, shell, snails, coral, small bone fragments (?), and snout of sawfish.

Offering 85.   (Fill). Northwest corner. Mother-of-pearl shells, snails, strings of miniature beads, anthropomorphic figures, clay pots, pectoral figures, and alabaster objects.

Chamber I.   (Cache). West facade (north section). Sculpture of greenstone (Mayahuel?), objects of greenstone (Mezcala figures and axes, beads, engraved disks, head with headdress, serpent, pectorals, pendant, spindle, earplugs, and fragments), ceramic potsherds and lid, projectile points, small razors, knives, silex rattlesnake rattle, worked shell, turtle, coral, snails, wood, bone awl, large amount of copal, metal, and pyrites.

Chamber II. (Cache). West facade (north section). Gold (beads), Mezcala-style stone masks and figures, figures of copal, feline bone fragments, sculpture of Tlaloc of greenstone, penates, worked coral, copal, small snails, and ocean sand (lower levels). There are also a Chalchiuhtlicue and a worked shell.

Chamber III. (Cache). Northwest corner. Copal figures. Mezcala-style stone masks and figures, timbrels and tambours (teponaxtles) of stone (tezontle), serpent with turquoise mosaic, silex knife, stone snails in shape of a knife, beads, ceramic Tlaloc pot, polychrome pulque bowl, two polychrome anthropomorphic pots of Mixteca style with heads inside, clay flutes, worked shell, snails, coral, shells, sea urchin, a Xiuhtecuhtli, wood, textile, feline bone fragments with a knife, copper bells, bone awls, and unidentified bone fragments.

There are seven offerings in this period. Six contain marine items, and one does not; five are in the west facade, and two are in the northwest corner; two are in the south half, and five are in the north half of the temple. The presence of figurines from Mezcala and of marine elements is very important, since it indicates a military expansion toward Guerrero and the coasts. According to our chronology, they relate to the rule of Moctezuma I (1440 to 1469) (see pls. 33, 38, 42–45).

Period IVb (approximately A.D. 1469)

Offering   1.   (Cache). West facade (south section, Coyolxauhqui). Copper bells, disks, anthropomorphic seated sculpture of stone (Xiuhtecuhtli), stone Tlaloc vessels with lids, stone objects (knives, scepters of authority, Xiuhcoatl, serpent rattles and heads), mirrors, obsidian clubs and nose pendants, chicahuaztlis, small braziers and knives with deer heads of greenstone, projectile points, skulls and vertebrae, worked shell, disks with a mosaic of turquoise on hide, wood, bone atlatl and awls, bird, lizard, coyote with knife, turtle, fish, copal sculpture, copal, snails, coral, and sand.

Offering   2.   (Cache). West facade (south section, Coyolxauhqui). Skeletal remains of an infant, three gold bells, and beads of greenstone.

Offering 3. (Cache). West facade (south section, Coyolxauhqui). Gold (bells, beads, disks, small gold sheets or plates, figurine, earplug); copper and silver bells; worked shell; objects of obsidian and basaltic stone (scepters, disk, pendants, knives, turtle, mirrors, serpent rattle and head); bony remains of animals, turtles, human beings; shells; snails; coral; copal; bone awl; sheets of smelted silver; rods of copper (?); volcanic slag; and charcoal.

Offering 6. (Fill). West facade (south section, Coyolxauhqui). Snails, shells, beads, stone earplugs, turtle and bird, Tlaloc household god, alabaster Mictlantecuhtli receptacle, ceramic Tlaloc vessels, knives, atlatl, clubs, scepters, skulls and skull masks, copper bells, stone masks, copal, wood, turquoise disks, sawfish, and copal figures.

Offering 7. (Cache). South facade (center). Tlaloc vessel, fish and bird, beads, snails, shells, projectile points, small ceramic brazier and ceramic disks, Xiuhtecuhtli, bone awls, coral, copal, sand, sawfish, large snails, and crocodile.

Offering 9. (Fill). South facade (west section). Coral, shells, snails, copal, copal figures, bone awl, stone anthropomorphic sculptures (deities, including Tlaloc), stone items (atlatl, axe, beads), feline (next to the offering), potsherds, and sand. Much of this bears traces of having been burned.

Offering 10. (Fill). West facade (south section, Coyolxauhqui). Orange vessel with relief and cremated bones; pectoral of greenstone (serpent) (see pl. 46).

Offering 11. (Fill). West facade (center). Copper bells, bird, stone masks, obsidian points, small brazier, earplugs, mustache ornament, mortar pestle, skulls and vertebrae, sea urchin fragments, turquoise disks, ceramic anthropomorphic vessel, silex knives, sand, disfiguring cradle, anthropomorphic figures, skull masks, deer, scepter of authority and alabaster serpentine items, Xiuhtecuhtli, bone atlatl, strings of snails, sawfish, copal fragments, red pigment, and maguey points.

Offering 12. (Fill). East facade (south section). Small stone brazier, Tlaloc vessels of greenstone (?), anthropomorphic figure of greenstone, knife, and bells.

Offering 13. (Cache). West facade (center). Potsherds (possibly broken incense burners), bird, fish, copal, coral, knives, turquoise disks, stone items (beads, scraper, nose pendant, razor, points, clubs, buttons), bone atlatl and awls, copper bells, skulls and vertebrae, alabaster scepter of authority, obsidian serpent heads and rattles, worked shell, Tlaloc vessel, Xiuhtecuhtli, wood, metal, charcoal, feline claws, shells, snails, and wooden serpent.

Offering 14. (Fill). West facade (south section). Obsidian zoomorphic beads (small ducks), projectile points, bone awl, vessel with lid (funerary urn) and relief, burned fiber, and cremated bone.

Offering 15. (Fill). East facade (south section). Tlaloc brazier of tezontle, Tlaloc penates, small Xiuhtecuhtli, coral, sea urchin, snails, bone awls, fish, turtle, bird, animal claw, fish, copal, copal figures, stone items (razor, projectile points, knife), sawfish, disks and an eye of shell with an obsidian center, human jaws, skull masks, and potsherds.

Offering 17. (Cache). East facade (center). Worked and unworked wood, laminated metal (gold?), copper, stone fragments (deer, chicahuaztli, small brazier, atlatl, etc.), stone objects (beads, knife, buttons, scrapers, mortar pestle, obsidian points, earplugs), coral, sand, sea urchin, snails, shells, bone awls, bone atlatl, fish, turtles, stone sculptures (there are two stone Tlaloc pots with lids and two Xiuhtecuhtlis), turquoise mosaics, copper bells, copal, fine sand, textile, sawfish, skull masks with knives in the nasal openings, copper (?), earplugs, incised disks and shell eyes, skulls and vertebrae, potsherds as fill.

Offering 18. (Box in fill). West facade (center). Thirteen anthropomorphic sculptures of greenstone, copal, small snails, and shell (lower levels).

Offering 19. (Box in fill). West facade (center). Thirteen anthropomorphic sculptures of greenstone, beads and stone fragments, small snails, copal, and potsherds and obsidian as fill.

Offering 20. (Fill). East facade (center). Shells, snails, coral, sea urchin, copper bells, turquoise disks on wood, worked shell (nose pendant, atlatl, disks), objects of stone (beads, nose pendants, obsidian razor, knives, brazier, phytomorphic club, obsidian nose pendant, scepter, and club), feathers (?), charcoal, fine sand, skulls and skull mask (knife and hematite), Teotihuacán masks, penate, copper bells, wood, vessels of greenstone, Olmec mask, copal, copal figures, remains of human and turtle bones, sawfish, stone sculptures (Xiuhtecuhtli, Tlaloc, Mezcala), ceramic anthropomorphic vessel, stone masks (some Mezcala), Mictlantecuhtli cup of greenstone scepter of authority, serpentine of sliced snails, metal, and alabaster deer.

Offering 22. (Fill). Northeast corner. Ceramic deforming cradle, worked shell (drop pendants), copper bells, snails, shells, sea urchin, coral, skull mask, skull, ceramic anthropomorphic vessel, stone items (beads, small razor, obsidian nose pendant, earplug, fish, turtle), copal, sand, sawfish, alabaster items (chicahuaztli, deer, serpentine), and string of snails.

Offering 23. (Cache). West facade (north section). Xiuhtecuhtli, ceramic Tlaloc vessel, ceramic items (chicahuaztli, pot, anthropomorphic vessel, incense burners, vessel), bone awls, worked shell (pendant, disks, pectoral), stone objects (beads, knives, points), wood items (carved alligator), coral, shells, snails, skulls, turtle, fish, shark teeth, bird, feline, two lizards, lizard teeth, serpent, copper bells, string of snails, fish and lizard scales, fish skin and tail, sand, copal, sawfish, and potsherds as fill.

Offering 24.   (Fill). West facade (north section). Stone items (beads, knives, ear-plugs, obsidian nose pendant, pendant), bony remains (bird, feline, turtle, fish), worked shell (circles, plaques, disks), sawfish, Xiuhtecuhtli, ceramic Tlaloc vessel, skulls, skull mask, shells, snails, sea urchin, coral, alabaster (chicahuaztli, deer, serpentine), wood, and copper bells.

Offering 41.   (Box in cache). West facade (north section). Carved Tlaloc box with lid. Inside the box: two Xancus snails, two Mezcalan-style masks of greenstone, miniature canoes with atlatl, oar, harpoon and fish of shell, small brazier, Mezcalan zoomorphic serpent, bird (duck) and fish, figures, Tlaloc head of greenstone, anthropomorphic figures. Outside the box: snails and shells surrounding the box at its base.

Offering 48.   (Cache). Northwest corner. In the upper part there were eleven polychrome sculptures of the god Tlaloc (see pl. 47) and below a great quantity of infants' bones, with forty-two skulls among them. Two disks (pectorals?) of turquoise mosaic and beads of greenstone were included. It may be that this was a sacrifice in honor of the god Tlaloc, as indicated in historical sources.

Offering 53.   (Fill). Northwest corner. Stone beads, copal figures, silex knives, earplugs.

Offering 58.   (Fill). Northwest corner. Bird, wood, copal snails, copper bells, beads, skull mask, skull, mother-of-pearl shells, ceramic anthropomorphic vessel, turtles, wooden deer, alabaster (chicahuaztli, deer, serpentine), deforming cradle, obsidian mustache ornament, sawfish, and sea urchin.

Offering 60.   (Cache). Northeast corner. Skulls, Tlaloc vessel, Xiuhtecuhtli, marine shells, earplugs, obsidian mortars, serpents, bone awls, wood, coral, worked shell, copper bells, sawfish, fish, atlatl of wood and shell, and lizard.

Offering 61.   (Cache). North facade (center). Ceramic items (polychrome incense burner, Tlaloc vessel, two anthropomorphic vessels (Xochipilli?), brazier with remover, chicahuaztli, circle of water, small pot, sand, wood, copal, hay, stone items (knife, small obsidian razor, arrow points, beads), bone awls, Xiuhtecuhtli, worked shell items (pendants with drops, disk, circles), coral, snails, shells, lizard, fish, turtle, bird, snake, and fish scales.

Offering 62.   (Fill). South facade (east section). Coral, wood, copal, stone items (penates, large Tlaloc mask, Xiuhtecuhtli), snails, bird, human bone remains, skull masks, stone items (knife, beads, small obsidian razors), shell disk, potsherds of an incense burner, copal anthropomorphic sculpture, and copper bells.

Offering 63.   (Fill). North facade. Copal cylindrical form.

Offering 67. (Fill). North facade (west section). Copal.

Offering 69. (Fill). North facade (west section). Stone items [scepter of authority, flutes, miniature huehuetl (drum, bead)], snails, shells, ceramic items (potsherds, anthropomorphic figure), unidentified bone remains, penates, ash, copal, and copal figure.

Offering 75. (Fill). North facade (west section). Semicircular formation of copal.

Offering 76. (Fill). Northwest corner. Fragmented incense burner and obsidian knife.

Offering 82. (Fill). Southeast corner. Human skull, anthropomorphic masks, noseplugs, beads, miniature instruments, zoomorphic figurine, and stone hip ring.

Offering 83. (Fill). Southeast corner. Knives, copal, snails, wood, sculpture of Xiuhtecuhtli, anthropomorphic sculpture (basalt Tlaloc braziers, copal figure).

Of the thirty-two offerings of this period twenty-two contained marine items, while ten had no objects from the sea. Of the twenty-two that do contain marine items, ten are in the west facade, three are in the south facade, three are in the east facade, two are in the north facade, two are in the northeast corner, one is in the northwest corner, and one is in the southeast corner. A more concise analysis shows that there are eight in the south half of the temple and eight in the north half. There are six in the central east-west line, four in the west facade, and two in the east facade; there are two in the central north-south line, one in the north facade, and one in the south facade. Of the ten offerings without marine items, three are in the west facade, one in the east facade, three in the north facade, two in the northeast corner, and one in the southeast corner. There are five in the south half of the temple and five in the north half; none were found in the central lines of the temple. Of the ten offerings without marine items, nine are in fill and one (sacked) in a cache; of the twenty-two containing marine items, eight are in caches, eleven are in fill, two are in a box in fill, and one is in a box in a cache. We see the abundant presence of marine elements, which indicates control over coastal areas. According to our preliminary chronology, this would be during the rule of Axayacatl.

Period V (A.D. 1480 ?)

Offering 54. (Cache). Northwest corner. Beads of greenstone, potsherds, copal balls, impression of a leaf, bones, metal (?), bean seed (?), kernel of corn (?), oar, miniature atlatl and canoe, flutes, clay spiral disk, textiles, wood, sawfish, impression of a bird feather (?), and vegetable fiber.

Offering 77. (Cache, sacked). West facade (south section). Material found in the fill outside of the cache. Fragments of snail and shell were found.

Offering 80. (Fill). West facade (north section). Knife, bead, and shell fragments.

Offering 86.   (Fill). East facade (north section). Knives, shell disk, shell object, and beads.

Period VI (A.D. 1500 ?)

Offering 70.   (Cache). West facade (south section). Bird, unidentified bone remains (?), shells, snails, coral, sea urchin, copper bells, worked shell (disks, atlatl, graffiti, pendants), stone items (knives, arrow points, obsidian disks, beads), sand, copal figures, stone sculpture [Tlaloc, anthropomorphic figure (?)], bone awls, wood fragments.

Offering 79.   (Cache, sacked). West facade (south section). Shells and small snails were found, adhering to the floor of the cache.

Offering 87.   (Fill). West facade (central section). Four objects laminated with gold, stone anthropomorphic figures (Mezcala), snails, shell, copper bells, knife and knife fragments, copal, remains of organic and wood material, fragments of small bones, stone beads, Mezcalan remains with lime, and a vitreous substance.

Period VII (1500 and after)

Offering 49.   (Fill). East facade. Stone figures, copal figures, silex and flint knives, fish, snails, coral, and sand (lower levels).

Offering 51.   (Fill). East facade. Xiuhtecuhtlis, knives, copper bells, coral, and wood.

Offering 64.   (Fill). East facade. Knives, beads, arrow points, skull mask, turtle, feline claws, unidentified bone remains, shells, snails, bells, sawfish, copal, and unidentified material (corn dough?).

Offering 81.   (Cache). Southwest corner. Xiuhtecuhtli, bells, wood, bird (eagle), snails, and sea sand (lower levels).

Offering 84.   (Cache). North facade (southeast corner, altar of skulls). Snails, silex serpent, copal figures, flute with anthropomorphic face, obsidian serpents, coral, shells, bird, wood, and serpent bones. Although we cannot be certain, this stage may correspond to the rule of Moctezuma II.

SYMBOLISM OF THE TEMPLO MAYOR

We shall now discuss an extremely important subject. What does the complex structure we call the *Templo Mayor* signify? Why does it present certain characteristics? What rituals took place in it, and why? How do these rituals help us to understand the symbolic meaning of the temple? To attempt to answer these and several related questions, we shall begin with a discussion of the myth of the struggle between Huitzilopochtli and Coyolxauhqui on Coatepec, the Hill of the Serpent. This discussion will give special attention to the historical basis of the myth so that later we may see how the reenactment of this myth at the Templo Mayor is filled with historical symbolism representing social action at the center of the universe.

HISTORY AND MYTH

As the history of religions teaches us, on many occasions real historical events and people are converted into mythological structures. In a number of religious traditions, for example, an outstanding or charismatic individual is deified and is transformed into a paradigm, god, or hero. The same process of transformation from history into myth influences the creation of sacred places. These places are rendered sacred by the society that experienced a powerful event at a specific location. Once the place is rendered sacred or the individual deified, it becomes necessary to reproduce what took place during "mythic time"; therefore, the need emerges to reenact the mythic event through rituals. To understand Templo Mayor symbolism, we must explore the deeper significance of major Mexica rituals; as we shall see, behind the myth there lies a real, historical fact.

We can summarize the process of ritual formation as follows: (1) historical event is told in (2) myth, which is (3) reenacted in ritual. In other words, a person sanctifies the real event by "mythifying" it. From this process emerges the basis for ritual reenactment of myth that includes the reproduction of the places (now sacred) in which the myth occurred! We should state that the procedure of transforming history into myth is not always the same.

If we study carefully the myth of the struggle between Huitzilopochtli and his sister Coyolxauhqui, we can see how the process of mythic transformation influenced the symbolism of the Templo Mayor. Let us survey each step of this process.

The Historical Event

The chroniclers Alvarado Tezozómoc and Diego Durán tell us how in the process of the migration from Aztlan the Mexicas arrived at a place called *Coatepec* (hill of the serpent), where they settled. The Mexicas were part of a larger group, the Huiztnahua, who disobeyed their leader Huitzilopochtli. In retaliation, Huitzilopochtli attacked them and killed a woman warrior, Coyolxauhqui, decapitating her. In the ensuing battle, the Huitznahuas were defeated and their hearts were cut out.

Some scholars have argued that this is a mythic story, while others have correctly seen the historical event of a Mexica struggle at a hill called *Coatepec*. From reviewing the historical evidence, it seems certain that part of the Mexica group, made up of people from the barrio of Huitznahua, opposed the authority of the human leader Huitzilopochtli. The Huitznahua, led by a warrior woman, Coyolxauhqui, the woman with bells on her cheeks, were defeated in the confrontation. This rebellion signifies the historical attempt to usurp the power and control of the larger group led by Huitzilopochtli. It is a matter, then, of an internal power struggle that was remembered by subsequent generations as a turning point in their history.

As time passed, this event provided the basis for the myth of Huitzilopochtli's triumphant birth which was reported to the sixteenth-century priest Sahagún. Indian informants told Sahagún that Huitzilopochtli was born on the hill of Coatepec and immediately decapitated and sacrificed the attacking Huitznahua. In the historical version we find that he arrived there after a pilgrimage and then triumphed over the rebels. It is clear that historically and mythically what happened at Coatepec held great importance to the Mexica, who believed that the tutelar god and their own power were born there.

Let us now consider the myth of the birth and struggles of Huitzilopochtli, based on Sahagún's text and Miguel León-Portilla's translation.

Myth

On Coatepec, in the direction of Tula,
a woman had been living,
a woman dwelt there
by the name of Coatlicue.

She was the mother of the four hundred Southerners,
and of a sister of one of them
named Coyolxauhqui.

And this Coatlicue was doing penance there,
she would sweep, she was in charge of sweeping,
and so she did her penance,
on Coatepec, the Mountain of the Serpent.

And once
as Coatlicue was sweeping
some plumage fell on her,
like a ball of fine feathers.

Coatlicue picked it up at once,
she put it in her bosom.

When she had finished sweeping,
she looked for the feather which she had put in her bosom,
but she saw nothing there.

From that moment Coatlicue was pregnant.

When the four hundred Southerners saw
that their mother was pregnant,
they became very angry; they said:

"Who has done this to you?
Who has made you pregnant?
He has insulted us, he has dishonored us."

And their sister Coyolxauhqui
said to them:

"Brothers, she has dishonored us,
we must kill our mother,
the depraved woman who now is pregnant.
Who made what she carries in her bosom?"

When Coatlicue discovered this,
she was very frightened,
she was very saddened.
But her son, Huitzilopochtli, who was in her bosom,
comforted her, said to her:

"Don't be afraid.
I know what I must do."

Coatlicue, having heard
the words of her son,
took great comfort,
her heart was calmed,
she felt tranquil.

And meanwhile, the four hundred Southerners
gathered to take council,
and unanimously they agreed
to kill their mother
because she had disgraced them.

They were very angry,
they were very agitated,
as if their hearts were going to leave their bodies.

Coyolxauhqui greatly incited them,
inflamed her brothers' anger,
so they would kill their mother.

And the four hundred Southerners
were like captains,
they twisted and snarled their hair
as warriors fix their hair.

But one named Cuahuitlicac
was false in his words.

What the four hundred Southerners said
he went to tell it at once,
he went to reveal it to Huitzilopochtli.

And Huitzilopochtli answered:

"Be careful, be alert,
my uncle, I know well what I must do."

And when finally they had agreed,
when the four hundred Southerners were resolved
to kill, to destroy their mother,
then they began to move out,
Coyolxauhqui guided them.

They felt very strong, adorned,
decorated for war,
they distributed among themselves their vestments of paper,
their destiny, their nettles,
the painted stripes of paper hanging on them,
they tied little bells on the calves of their legs,
the little bells called oyohualli.

Their arrows had sharp points.

Then they began to move out,
they went in order, in a row,
in an orderly squadron,
Coyolxauhqui guided them.

But Cuahuitlicac at once went up to mountain
to speak from there to Huitzilopochtli,
he said to him:

"They're coming now."

Huitzilopochtli answered him:
"Look carefully at where they are."

Then Cuahuitlicac said:
"Now they're passing through Tzompantitlan."

And once more Huitzilopochtli said to him:
"Where are they now?"

Cuahuitlicac answered him:
"Now they are passing through Coaxalpan."

And again Huitzilopochtli asked Cuahuitlicac:
"Look carefully at where they are."

At once Cuahuitlicac answered him:
"Now they are coming up the side of the mountain."

And yet once more Huitzilopochtli said to him:
"Look carefully at where they are."

Then Cuahuitlicac said to him:
"Now they are on the mountain top, they are drawing near,
Coyolxauhqui is guiding them."

At that moment Huitzilopochtli was born,
he dressed himself in his finery,
his shield of eagle feathers,
his darts, his blue dart thrower,
the notable turquoise dart thrower.

He painted his face
with diagonal stripes,
with the color called "child's paint."

On his head he placed fine feathers,
he put on his earplugs.

And on one of his feet, the left one was very thin,
he wore a sandal covered with feathers,

and his two legs and his two arms
he had them painted blue.

And the one named Tochancalqui
took out the serpent made of candlewood,
whose name was Xiuhcoatl,
who obeyed Huitzilopochtli.

Then with it he wounded Coyolxauhqui,
he cut off her head,
which was left abandoned
on the slope of Coatepetl.

The body of Coyolxauhqui
rolled down the slope,
it fell apart in pieces,
her hands, her legs, her torso
fell in different places.

Then Huitzilopochtli raised up,
he pursued the four hundred Southerners,
he kept on pursuing them, he scattered them
from the top of Coatepetl,
the mountain of the serpent.

And when he had followed them
to the foot of the mountain,
he pursued them, he chased them like rabbits,
around the mountain.

Four times he chased them around.

In vain they tried to do something against him,
in vain they turned and faced him,
to the sound of their bells,
and they slapped their shields.

They could do nothing,
they could achieve nothing,
they could defend themselves with nothing.

Huitzilopochtli pursued them, he chased them,
he destroyed them, he annihilated them, he obliterated them.

And then he left them,
he kept on pursuing them.

But they begged him often, they said to him:
"Enough! Enough!"

But Huitzilopochtli was not satisfied with this,
with force he wrathfully attacked them,
pursued them.

Only a few could escape his presence,
could free themselves from his hands.

They went toward the south,
because they went toward the south
they are called Southerners,
those few who escaped
from the hands of Huitzilopochtli.

And when Huitzilopochtli had killed them,
when he had expressed his anger,
he took from them their finery, their adornments,
their destiny, put them on, appropriated them,
incorporated them into his destiny,
made of them his own insignia.

And this Huitzilopochtli, as people said,
was a portent,
because from a single feather
which fell into the womb of his mother, Coatlicue,
he was conceived.

No one ever appeared as his father.

The Mexicas venerated him,
made sacrifices to him,
honored and served him.

And Huitzilopochtli paid back
those who behaved that way.

And his cult was taken from there,
from Coatepec, the Mountain of the Serpent,
as it was practiced from times
most ancient.[22]

Reenactment and Symbolism

Before we begin our discussion of how the Templo Mayor is the reenactment of a living myth, let us return to the historical moment when the Mexicas founded Tenochtitlán and established their sacred space. In doing so, we shall see the relation between history and the sacred symbols embedded in the place chosen by their god Huitzilopochtli.

These symbols can be divided into two groups: those that the Mexicas took from the renowned cultural tradition of the Toltecs and those that they themselves added. Among the former are symbols of white rushes, junipers; fish, frogs, and snakes (also white); and springs of water gushing from the rocks. Some of these symbols are described in the *Historia Tolteca-Chichimeca*, which describes the famous Toltec pilgrimage to the city of Cholula. Upon their arrival, the Mexicas encountered these natural forms in abundance. The indigenous Mexica symbols related to the foundation of their city include an eagle perched on a nopal, devouring a serpent (according to Tezozómoc) or birds (according to Durán and Tezozómoc). In their narrative of pilgrimage and discovery the Mexicas are careful to separate both sets of symbols by having the Toltec symbols found on a specific day and their own symbols found on the following day.[23] Referring to the discovery of the first set of symbols, Fray Diego Durán tells us:

> The first thing they found was a juniper, all white and very beautiful, at the foot of which that spring flowed. The second thing they noticed was that all the willows which surrounded the spring were white, without a single green leaf; all the canes in that place were white as well as the reeds in the vicinity. There began to emerge from the water frogs that were all white and all white fish, and among them there were some beautiful white water snakes. The water originated between two large boulders.[24]

The next day they return to the same place and there they find a new symbolic order:

> and as they walked from one place to another they saw a prickly pear and on it was an eagle with its wings extended to the rays of the sun . . . and in its claws it had a beautiful bird with very precious and resplendent

55

feathers. The moment they saw it, they paid it homage, almost bowing to it, as to something divine.[25]

Within this terrain crowded with symbols, it is important to focus on the central image of eagle and serpent. In Mesoamerican religions, the eagle is a solar symbol associated with the power of the sun. It represents the god himself, Huitzilopochtli, patron of the capital. The act of devouring—whether of birds or a serpent—represents the action of conquering the enemy as occurred earlier in the historic events at Coatepec. Can this episode of discovery be a mythic version of that important event? Moreover, the triumph of the sun in the form of the eagle over the serpent (an earthly symbol but also a lunar one) appears to reaffirm the idea of the sun's defeat of the moon, or Coyolxauhqui, in the drama of Huitzilopochtli's birth. Further work on the symbolism of both these episodes is necessary.

The Mexica's first act upon settling in this place was to build a small shrine to Huitzilopochtli. They thus established their "center," the navel of the world, the sacred space from which would emerge the four fundamental divisions of the city. Within this supremely sacred space they attempted to reproduce architecturally the entire cosmic order, with the Templo Mayor serving as the axis mundi of this city and eventually their empire.

For the Mexicas, the universe consisted of two fundamental planes, one horizontal and one vertical. The former consisted of four quadrants associated with the four cardinal directions, each with its characteristic color, its own sign, and the god who ruled it. This was also the plane where Cemanahuac (the earth) was located, symbolized by a disk of earth completely surrounded by water. In the center from which the four directions radiated was located Tenochtitlan and the Great Temple. This sacred precinct was intersected by the vertical plane with nine levels below the earth and thirteen levels above. The souls of the dead traveled through the nine levels of the underworld in order to arrive at the deepest level—Mictlan. The thirteen upper levels led to the last and highest level called *Omeyocan*, in which resided the dual god, Ometecuhtli-Omecihuatl. The Mexicas symbolized this entire cosmology in the ceremonial and spatial order of the Great Temple and their city.

We can see other cosmological influences in the fact that the Temple of Ehecatl-Quetzalcoatl, god of the wind, is located opposite the Templo Mayor. Let us recall that in the myth of the emergence of the sun and the moon in Teotihuacan, it was Quetzalcoatl who looked toward the east and correctly identified the direction of the rising sun. In Tenochtitlan, his temple is located so that its main facade was oriented toward that cardinal point indicated by the center of the Templo Mayor. During the excavation we discovered another cosmic orientation in three shrines excavated to the north of Templo Mayor. We have named the center one a *tzompantli* (skull rack) altar, since it is decorated with more than 240 skulls. Its relationship to death is evident, and, contrary to our expectation that a shrine similar to this might appear on the south side, no equivalent temple was found. In Aztec cosmology Mictlampa (the place of the dead) is located by the north quadrant.

In my view, the Great Temple as a whole represents two sacred hills that as vertical symbols represent not only height but the entrance to the lower levels, the world of the dead. In one of his books, Sahagún points out that the Mexica believed that the first step in traveling to Mictlan consists of crossing two hills that clash with each other. It is possible that the Great Temple (the double temple-hill) was not only the horizontal center of the Mexica universe but also the place that gives vertical access to the world of the dead.

As a twin sacred hill the Temple has other symbolic aspects. Through the seven major stages of construction we find embedded in architecture the idea of duality: there exist two bases built on a common platform with the shrines of the god of water and the god of war on the upper level. Both bases and pyramidal sections represent hills or sacred mountains revered in Mexica tradition. We have ethnographic evidence of this architectural duality. Back in 1898 don Francisco del Paso y Troncoso, who had studied the *Codice Borbonicus*, told us that Sahagún referred to the temple of Huitzilopochtli as the *Koatepetl* and that Tlaloc was depicted on top of the hills. Referring to this god, the author says: "and that those hills . . . remind us of the cult which was now rendered not physically on the top of the hills, but rather on the platforms of the pyramids which, in order to preserve the steepness of the sides of the hills, were built with steep stairways."[26]

The hill on the south side, corresponding to Huitzilopochtli, is a specific hill: Coatepec. If we analyze the placement of the deities, we see that the god Huitzilopochtli is located on high, while his sister Coyolxauhqui lies conquered at the foot of the temple-hill, on the platform, decapitated and dismembered. These images were not placed randomly, but in the precise locations assigned to them by myth. On the huge platform supporting the Coyolxauhqui stone were found the huge serpent heads indicating the name of the hill-temple: Coatepec (hill of the serpent).

It is significant that in the third construction stage the material that forms the base of the temple contains projecting stone with no representations on them. This results in a realistic image of a hill. The stones simply are in their natural form and jut out from the walls. In the same construction stage eight anthropomorphic sculptures were found, some of natural size, which may very well represent the *centzon huitznahua*, the enemies of Huitzilopochtli who were vanquished in the myth of his birth. The sculptures were situated at the bottom of the stairways replicating their mythic defeat at the base of Serpent Mountain.

These correlations between myth, history, and architecture indicate that the Templo Mayor, on the south side, represents the real-mythical place of the birth and combat of Huitzilopochtli. Ethnographic evidence collected in the sixteenth century reveals that his myth was reenacted there, throughout the festival of Panquetzaliztli, culminating in the sacrifice of warriors conquered and captured by the Mexicas. Their hearts were taken out and their bodies thrown down the steep stairway. At the bottom the bodies were divided among those who captured them. That is, they would do to the conquered the same thing that Huitzilopochtli had done to his sister Coyolxauhqui: they would be killed and their bodies thrown down and dismembered. That is exactly the way Coyolxauhqui is depicted in the magnificent relief located at the foot of the temple-hill—dead and dismembered. It is appropriate to point out that this ritual of dismemberment is connected to the moon, which (unlike the sun, which descends into the world of the dead and emerges the following day) dies and is dismembered as in the lunar phases to be reborn again. This astronomical symbolism also allows us to reflect on the cosmic struggle between the sun and the moon, between light and nocturnal powers. The moon in various religions is associated with the feminine, while the sun is regarded as masculine. It is not surprising that in the historical record the leader Huitzilopochtli constantly had problems with Malinalxochitl and Coyolxauhqui during the pilgrimage. This could reflect a social change from the lunar to the solar calendars. Further research may tell us more about this aspect of symbolism.

For its part, the Tlaloc side of Templo Mayor also represents a hill.[27] We know from several chronicles that major rituals dedicated to the rain god took place on the tops of prominent hills and at sacred locations on the lake. In the *Codex Borbonicus*, Tlaloc is shown several times with his shrine on top of a hill. The distinctiveness of Tlaloc's hill from Huitzilopochtli's is suggested by the different kinds of serpents that adorn the platform that belongs to him at the Templo Mayor.

What is important to note here is that both hills are the living presence, made visible, of myths that were important to the Mexicas. On one side is depicted the myth of their ruler god, who was born to fight; on the other side is depicted the hill of sustenance, the place of Tlaloc, where the food that is used to sustain humans is obtained. In a broader sense, we are in the presence of a significant duality: the Great Temple is the place or symbol of life (Tlaloc) and death (Huitzilopochtli), in addition to serving as the entrance to the Omeyocan and the Mictlan, a symbolism that is implicit in the temple itself.

The architectural structure indicates these different levels to us: we believe that the *general platform* on which the temple rests represents the earthly level of the cosmos. This platform is characterized by having a single common stairway on which is located the altar of the frogs, an aquatic symbol. The braziers that surround the four sides of the temple are also on the platform, and on the main facade are the serpents that indicate the earth. The greatest number of offerings were found buried in this platform. Significantly, none of these characteristics is found on the four sides that form the pyramid. These stepped sides represent diverse heavens or levels of ascent until one arrives at the upper level (or heaven) where the two shrines in which the gods reside are located. It is there that the duality, the Omeyocan, is situated.

A broader view of Mesoamerican culture demonstrates that what is described here does not belong exclusively to the Mexica. Similar historical and cosmological patterns, with their own variations, characterized a number of religions that, although different in their time, had a socioeconomic development similar to that of Tenochtitlan.

Much remains to be investigated. We have attempted to suggest possibilities for research and general ideas that should be explored in more depth. Our intention has been to present a general view of what has been obtained from the Templo Mayor project during four and a half years of work at the site. It is clear that the Templo Mayor of Tenochtitlan symbolized a place of glory for the Mexicas and of misfortune for those who fell into their power.

(Translated by John G. Copeland, Associate Professor, Department of Spanish and Portuguese, University of Colorado.)

Notes

1. Fray Bernardino Sahagún, *Historia General de las Cosas de Nueva España*. 4 vols. Angel María Garibay, ed. (Editorial Porrúa, Mexico, 1956).
2. Antonio León y Gama, *Descripción Histórica y Cronológica de las dos Piedras . . .* (Mexico, Imprenta de don Felipe de Zúñiga, 1982).
3. Ibid.
4. Servando Teresa de Mier, *Memorias* (Madrid: Editorial América, n.d.).
5. Ibid.
6. Ibid.
7. León y Gama, *Descripción Histórica y Cronológica*.
8. Alejandro Humboldt, *Vistas de las Cordilleras y Monumentos de Pueblos Indígenas de América* (Madrid: Imprenta de Gaspar Editores, 1878).
9. Leopoldo Batres, "Exploraciones Arqueológicas en la Calle de las Escalerillas" (1902), in *Trabajos Arqueológicos en el Centro de la Ciudad de México*, Eduardo Matos Moctezuma, ed. (Mexico: SEP-INAH, 1979), pp. 61–90.
10. Alfredo Chavero, *Mexico a Través de los Siglos*, vol. I (Mexico, 1889).
11. Antonio Peñafiel, *Destrucción del Templo Mayor de México* (Mexico, 1910).
12. Manuel Gamio, "Los Vestigios Prehispánicos de la Calle de Santa Teresa (Hoy Guatemala)" *Boletín de Educación* (Mexico) 1 (1914): 3–8.
13. Emilio Cuevas, "Las Excavaciones del Templo Mayor de México," *Anales del Museo Nacional* (Mexico) V(1) (1934): 97–108.
14. Eduardo Matos Moctezuma, "El Adoratorio Decorado de las Calles de Argentina," *Anales del INAH* (Mexico) XVII (1965): 79–90.
15. See the Bulletins of the INAH for a series of articles published between 1966 and 1968.
16. Cited by Miguel León-Portilla in *Los Antiguos Mexicanos* (Mexico: Fondo de Cultura Económica 1972).
17. Fray Diego Durán, *Historia de las Indias de Nueva España y Islas de Tierra Firme* 2 vols. Angel María Garibay ed. (Mexico: Editorial Porrúa, 1967).
18. Fray Toribio (Motolina) Benavente, *Historia de los Indios de la Nueva España* (Mexico: Editorial Porrúa, 1979).
19. Eduardo Matos Moctezuma, *Una Visita al Templo Mayor de Tenochtitlán* (Mexico: INAH, 1981*b*).

20. Durán, *Historia de las Indias*.

21. Bernal Díaz del Castillo, *The Discovery and Conquest of Mexico*. (New York: Farrar, Straus & Giroux, 1956).

22. Eduardo Matos Moctezuma, "Symbolism of the Templo Mayor," paper presented in Templo Mayor Meeting in Dumbarton Oaks, Washington, D.C., 1983 (in press).

23. Durán, *Historia de las Indias*.

24. Ibid.

25. Francisco Del Paso y Troncoso, *Descripción, Historia y Exposición del Códice Borbónico* (Mexico: Editorial Siglo XXI, 1981).

26. Eduardo Matos Moctezuma, "El Templo Mayor, Economía e Ideología," *Boletín de Antropología Americana* (Mexico) (1980) and Rudolph Van Zantwijk, "The Great Temple of Tenochtitlan: Model of Aztec Cosmovision," in *Mesoamerican Sites and World Views*, Elizabeth P. Benson ed. (Dumbarton Oaks, Washington, D.C.: 1981). Pages 71–86. Recently there has been renewed interest in the Great Temple as the central site of the cosmological universe of the Mexicas. For example see Davíd Carrasco, "Templo Mayor: The Aztec Vision of Place," *Religion* (London) 11 (1981): 275–297.

Templo Mayor as Ritual Space

JOHANNA BRODA
National Autonomous University of Mexico

The Aztec empire destroyed by the Spaniards at the beginning of the sixteenth century was a highly complex society, product of centuries, millennia of cultural evolution in Mesoamerica and must be understood against the background of previous cultures in the area. To achieve this broader perspective and synthesis, the study of written documents should be complemented by archaeological studies and an interdisciplinary approach. There exists an extremely rich written documentation on Aztec society on the eve of the Spanish Conquest. The uniqueness of the excavation of Templo Mayor consists in the possibility of confronting the archaeological record with the abundant ethnohistorical information that refers to the same period and the very city of Tenochtitlan. It thus permits us to combine in an effective way the methodology of archaeology with that of anthropology and history.

My contribution to this volume interprets the archaeological findings from the point of view of Aztec society and religion in the fifteenth century and the beginning of the sixteenth century, the period during which the Aztec state experienced its rapid expansion and transformation into an empire that was to dominate large parts of the territory that today is known as ancient Mesoamerica. My interpretation in terms of anthropological concepts will be combined with the detailed ethnohistorical analysis of certain aspects of the excavation, concentrating primarily on the content of the more than eighty offering caches found at the site. Since we are dealing with a religious topic, this approach means that we will relate the Templo Mayor as a religious center to its socioeconomic and political functions. The analysis of the offerings further reveals important aspects of Aztec cosmology and ritual; these will also be explored in their social dimensions. Society is the soil on which the elaborate structure of cosmovision[1] and ritual was erected and to which the social and ideological[2] functions of religion were ultimately related.

I would like to point out that the confrontation with the material testimony of

61

the excavation as it was unearthed progressively between 1978 and 1982 and the attempt to reach an interpretative level encompassing a global vision of the symbolism of the site, led me quite far from the initial goal to focus only on the social functions of the religious symbolism at the Templo Mayor. The great public rituals that took place periodically at the Great Temple certainly had very important functions of the legitimation of Aztec power; at the same time, a close relation to agricultural cycles and climatological phenomena can be detected in the cult of Templo Mayor; I will refer to these points in the present chapter. Yet, the material remains of the huge temple structure and the remarkable quantities of offerings buried in it point, above all, to certain global concepts of pre-Hispanic cosmovision that have been revealed as a result of the present investigation. This analysis helps us to discern distinct aspects within the complex entities of cult activities and architectural structures. In fact, as I will try to show in this chapter, the construction of the twin pyramid, with all the offerings buried during this process, seems to constitute an aspect of Aztec religion rather *different* from the great public rituals of state cult that took place periodically at the Templo Mayor. While the latter were clearly connected to the legitimation of political power and the role played by different social groups in Aztec society, the former rather seem to derive from ancient traditions of cosmological thought that were related to political ideology, only in a more indirect way.

According to the methodology to be employed in this study, we must explain briefly our fundamental notions about Aztec social and political structure in order to combine its analysis with the one of cosmovision and ritual.

THE STATE CULT

Aztec Society and State Organization

Aztec society was complex and internally differentiated. It was based on a highly productive agricultural system that combined dryland farming with large-scale irrigation works. Economic exchange and trading relations integrated different sectors within that society and extended to remote regions of Mesoamerica. Long-distance trade dealt with luxury products—raw materials such as jade, turquoise, gold, quetzal feathers, and amber, as well as refined artisanry productions. Division of labor between towns and countryside had reached a certain degree of complexity, as well as the specialization into numerous crafts. The specializations served mainly to create a refined style of life in the towns and among the nobility which came to depend more and more on the luxury goods imported from remote parts of Mesoamerica. Long-distance trade supplied numerous types of goods, but even greater quantities arrived at Tenochtitlan through tribute. The ruling class, especially the royal court, came to rely increasingly on military expansion as a means of enhancing their power and maintaining the ostentations that political hierarchy and prestige required from them.

Central Mexican society on the eve of the Spanish Conquest was internally divided into social classes defined by their relation to the means of production (land, control of water resources, and human labor) and their access to political power. Basically there existed two antagonistic classes—the ruling class and the common people —but these, in turn, were subdivided into a number of hierarchically stratified groups. The ruling class, or nobility, held control over agricultural lands in the Valley of Mexico, received tribute, and exercised political power. It included warriors, functionaries, and priests. In Aztec society the warrior elite played the dominant role and controlled the state apparatus. The common people paid tribute to the nobles and were politically dependent on them. They included artisans, merchants, and peasants, as well as certain other urban occupational groups. Some of these groups, such as luxury artisans and merchants dealing with long-distance trade, occupied a more privileged position within society than the peasants; however, they also had to pay tribute and were not considered of noble origin. It should be borne in mind that the Aztec capital, on the eve of the Conquest, was a city of some 200,000 inhabitants. In the area of the southern lakes around Xochimilco and Chalco the agriculture of the chinampas was extremely important; however, the bulk of the population of Tenochtitlan had an urban composition.

As can be seen, the tribute system was an extremely important institution in Aztec society. It was the economic expression of the political relation of domination that existed within Aztec society as well as between the Aztec conquerors and the peoples they subjugated. Conquest and tribute were an expression of the violent expansion of society, therefore, and both contained important ideological elements.[3]

The Aztec warrior nobility, which assumed control of the state apparatus after the defeat of Azcapotzalco in 1427, in the course of the fifteenth century subjugated large parts of Mesoamerica and built up an empire that was to reach the Pacific and Atlantic shores, with Xicalanco on the southern Gulf coast and the Xoconochco at the Isthmus of Tehuantepec extending as far as highland Chiapas and Alta Verapaz in Guatemala. Following routes of expansion of earlier conquest states that had preceded them, the Aztecs were not only interested in controlling certain strategic regions but also sought to guarantee the access to the tropical lowlands as a means to acquire the luxury products on which they had come to depend so heavily. Warfare not only became a material necessity but was also incorporated into the ideological structure of cult and religion by means of mass human sacrifices of prisoners of war.

The sixteenth-century chronicles give ample evidence of this close interrelation between military expansion and cult. It is said that the sun—whose cult was the supreme religious task of the Aztec warrior nobility—required human blood and the slaying of victims. According to Aztec religious theory, blood had to be spilled to make the cosmos continue to exist. The sun, in order to send its light to earth, needed to be fed on human hearts and blood. The ruler's obligation was to provide this nourishment to the sun; for this purpose he led his armies into the war and exacted tribute in victims for sacrifice. These ideological concepts served to legitimate the dominant values of this expansionist warrior state and to motivate the subjects to act according to these values.

Military Expansion, Human Sacrifice, and Amplifications of Templo Mayor

The place where the grand ritual dramas of human sacrifices took place was the Templo Mayor of Tenochtitlan. It was not only the main temple of the capital but also represented symbolically its political integrity. It was the place where politics and ideology blended into one single structure. The chronicles of Diego Durán and Hernando Alvarado Tezozómoc, representing the Aztec historical tradition, describe in detail the military campaigns undertaken by successive Aztec rulers. At the return of their successful armies, several rulers ordered the structure of the Templo Mayor to be modified, enlarged, and made ever more impressive. The chronicles also tell how several new sacrificial stones were inaugurated by means of mass human sacrifices. As I have shown in previous studies, this documentary material can be analyzed in great detail with respect to the link that existed between the historical account and the successive enlargements of the Great Temple.[4]

Conspicuously enough, these references begin to appear only with the government of Motecuhzoma Ilhuicamina, the successor of Itzcoatl. Itzcoatl (1427 to 1440) was the conqueror of Azcapotzalco, the founder of the Triple Alliance between Tenochtitlan, Tetzcoco, and Tlacopan, and the *Tlatoani* (ruler; king) who destroyed the previous codices in order to "rewrite" Aztec history. The latter actually began to take on "imperial" shape under Itzcoatl's successor Motecuhzoma Ilhuicamina (1440 to 1469). This Tlatoani initiated the struggle for power with Chalco, the important city-state at the southern limits of the Valley of Mexico, a war that lasted for several years and ended finally with the defeat of Chalco. This conquest of the Triple Alliance opened the way to imperial expansion to the south beyond the barriers of the volcanoes. Motecuhzoma I successively made important conquests into areas surrounding the central highlands to the north, the southeast, and the southwest.[5] He also reorganized the state administration and decreed new sumptuary and criminal laws that exalted the power of the king and the nobility.[6] For the first time in Aztec history, the ascension to the throne of this Tlatoani was celebrated by extensive human sacrifices; this custom later became institutionalized in connection with the installment of his successors.

From Motecuhzoma's reign onward, particularly after the war with Chalco, the historical sources register a general increase in human sacrifices.[7] Motecuhzoma also established the *Guerra Florida,* a ritualized warfare directed against the local enemy states of Tlaxcala, Huexotzinco, Cholula, and Atlixco, situated to the southeast of the Valley of Mexico. It was designed as an exericse for young nobles to gain merits in war and to obtain victims for sacrifice.[8] Warfare and cult became even more closely intertwined through this new military institution, which was a peculiar creation of the Aztec period.

Motecuhzoma Ilhuicamina was also the Tlatoani who constructed a new temple for Huitzilopochtli. According to the chronicles, it was the first one of great dimensions that the Aztecs erected to their god. The inauguration of the temple and of several new sacrificial stones was celebrated by means of mass human sacrifices. To these festivities the Aztec ruler invited the lords of the allied and conquered city-states; curiously, however, the rulers of enemy territories were also invited to attend the ceremonies. It was an occasion for Motecuhzoma to show his generosity and magnanimity:

> [a fact that] . . . left the foreigners terrified, but it made very happy . . . all the lords and commoners of the town. From this time onwards, all the neighboring provinces and towns abstained from any further rebellions nor fighting with the Aztecs, since they saw how they excelled and in which way they dealt with their enemies.[9]

Successive *Tlatoque* (rulers) continued the task of enlarging the huge double pyramid and inaugurating these structures as well as several sacrificial stones at the Templo Mayor by means of mass human sacrifices of prisoners whom they brought back from successful military campaigns.[10] These festivities culminated in the amplification of the Templo Mayor undertaken by the eighth Tlatoani Ahuitzotl (1486 to 1502). We shall quote this case here as an illustrative example.

On the occasion of his ascension to the throne, this ruler undertook important works at Templo Mayor that were solemnly inaugurated in the year "8 caña" (1487).[11] For this purpose, Ahuitzotl ordered the *calpixque* (tribute collectors) to concentrate great quantities of tributes in the capital. The Tlatoani sent messengers to the conquered peoples asking them to hand in the captives whom they were obliged to give in tribute. Durán indicates detailed lists of places and provinces that the messengers visited for that purpose. Not only did the kings of Tetzcoco and Tlacopan, together with the lords from all the conquered groups in central Mexico, present themselves at Tenochtitlan but also the enemy lords from Tlaxcala, Huexotzinco, Cholula, Tecoac, Tliliuhquitepec, and Zacatlan, as well as those from faraway Michoacan, Metztitlan, and Yopitzinco were invited to attend the ceremonies. These detailed lists of Duran practically constitute a map of the Aztec empire and of the enemy territories during the reign of Ahuitzotl.

Tributes in luxury goods from all the conquered provinces were displayed before the guests. The enemy lords were duly impressed and terrified by such splendor and extravagance. At the same time, the Tlatoani had all the minor temples of Tenochtit-lan and its surroundings renovated, and he also invited the common people to attend the ceremonies. People from all over the Valley of Mexico poured into Tenochtitlan, crowding the streets and plazas of the city.

Durán mentions that the victims captured from enemy populations (whose detailed list he gives) amounted to some 80,400 men.[12] This figure obviously is not a real number but denotes the expression of an unlimited quantity according to the vigesimal system. The kings of the Triple Alliance personally initiated the sacrifices. According to Durán, these lasted for four days, at the end of which the temple and the entire city were covered by streams of blood and the atmosphere was impregnated by an acid and abominable stench.

After these sacrifices, the Tlatoani offered gifts to the allied nobles; at the same time he made particularly generous presents to the enemy lords. After the guests had departed, the Tlatoani distributed insignia to the Aztec warriors, the calpixque, and the priests, as well as the old and poor of the city. He further gathered all the artisans —Aztecs and foreigners alike—who had participated in the construction of the tem-ple and gave them goods as well.

Durán mentions several other occasions of new constructions at the temple precinct that were undertaken by the successor of Ahuitzotl, Motecuhzoma II (1502 to 1520). At their inauguration, captives taken in victorious military campaigns were sacrificed in spectacular ceremonies. The last event refers to the time shortly before the arrival of the Spaniards. Motecuhzoma wanted to inaugurate a new stone for the gladiatorial sacrifice (*temalacatl*); however, he could not put this plan into practice and interpreted his failure to do so as a foreboding of disaster.[13]

Durán and Tezozomoc, representing the Aztec historiographic tradition, both describe how military campaigns were deliberately initiated in order to make captives for the purpose of these sacrifices. The acquisition of sacrificial victims thus served as a pretext for conducting wars. This ideological justification might have motivated people to participate in these campaigns; however, the underlying reasons were of eco-nomic and political nature—of a dynamic state in expansion. At the same time, the cult of Templo Mayor became the symbol of political integrity of the Aztec empire, while the successive enlargements of the huge temple pyramid glorified the expansion of this state. The sacrifices of war prisoners in connection with these amplifications clearly had the effect of demonstrating the power of the conquerors. *It was political power transformed into supernatural power by means of the sacrifices.*

The cult of Templo Mayor expresses the ideology of a rapidly expanding con-quest state. In this sense I have undertaken the study of Aztec ritual in recent years, interpreting the cult as an aspect of the ideology of that society.[14] The ideology forms part of the superstructural relations and refers to the level of consciousness of the members of a given society. It is a system of symbolic representation, and its most im-portant social function is to legitimize existing conditions. It not only gives cohesion to social life but also permits in a wider sense the reproduction of the material conditions of existence.[15]

The concept of ideology permits us to analyze the interrelation that existed between society and cult, between the material conditions of existence and religious phenomena, and between politics and beliefs. We are thus compelled to apply a holistic approach in which the different aspects of pre-Hispanic society are studied as a unity and religious phenomena can be related to the social and political context.

Templo Mayor as a Symbol of Political Power

In this perspective it is valid to study the Templo Mayor as a symbol of political power among the Aztecs. This approach can be applied not only to the ethnohistorical sources but also to the archaeological remains. In fact, one outstanding feature of the excavation is the discovery of an entire series of superpositions of the temple structure that can be correlated to the history of Aztec imperial expansion. The archaeological evidence shows how, in a frantic building activity, the Great Pyramid acquired increasingly impressive dimensions; these modifications covered the older structures without destroying them (see pls. 2–7).

The excavation thus corroborates in general terms the data given by sixteenth century chroniclers such as Durán, Tezozómoc, and others who describe several important modifications of the temple pyramid and relate them to the reign of Aztec rulers and to military expansion. At the same time, however, the testimony of the archaeological findings goes far beyond the sporadic references of the written sources. It actually proves that during the reign of Aztec rulers from Acamapichtli (1375 to 1395) to Motecuhzoma II (1502 to 1520), the Great Pyramid was completely rebuilt seven times while its facade was remodeled six more times. In archaeological terms this fact proves that these modifications of the great double stairway leading up to the twin shrines on top of the pyramid mainly served the function of producing an increasingly spectacular frontal vision. An important general aspect of pre-Hispanic temple architecture was the dimension of giving an impressive visual perspective that, as an ideological phenomenon, was closely connected to Aztec political organization.

It is now possible to correlate these building phases tentatively with the government of successive rulers.[16] The first stage to be excavated, in which the twin shrines on top of the pyramid are fully preserved, actually corresponds to Period II. The latter received this denomination since there is at least one more building stage beneath it. Period II and the previous buildings cannot be dated accurately; at any rate, these structures are believed to correspond to the first rulers prior to Itzcoatl and before the conquest of Azcapotzalco.

The next important construction, Period III, the most solidly built thus far, corresponds to the reign of Itzcoatl and bears the date 4 Reed (A.D. 1431). The succeeding stage, Period IV (IVa, IVb), however, is archaeologically far more important than

Phase III. Its platform is adorned with braziers and serpent heads at its four sides, and numerous offering caches have come to light. A calendrical date, 1 Rabbit, may be correlated with A.D. 1454, corresponding to the reign of Motecuhzoma I (see Matos, this volume, table 1). The excavation proves the same circumstance that is confirmed by the historical sources: it is really under the ruler Motecuhzoma Ilhuicamina that the Templo Mayor takes on its grandiose dimensions, a fact corresponding to the thrust at military expansion undertaken by this ruler.

Period IVb only represents the construction of a new facade. The platform in front of this facade later proved to be the best preserved of all the building stages, however, as it contained an enormous variety of sculptural elements and offerings that have come to light: the enormous undulating bodies of two serpents, each measuring six meters in length, delimiting the north and south corners of the platform; the small altar of frogs situated at the central axis of the platform; the gigantic serpent heads at the base of the stairway; and finally, in front of Huitzilopochtli's stairway, the famous relief stone of Coyolxauhqui. On the same platform a series of important offering caches were located that have yielded a great variety of ritual elements. One of these caches, situated on the north side of the platform, contains some forty-two skulls and bones of children, buried together with Tlaloc vessels.

The date 3 House inscribed at the south side of the building, corresponding to Period IVb, suggests the year A.D. 1469 relative to the reign of Motecuhzoma's successor Axayacatl. The following three periods, V, VI and VII, are correlated by Eduardo Matos Moctezuma with the reigns of Tizoc, Ahuitzotl, and Motecuhzoma II, respectively (see Matos, this volume, table 1). The frontal platforms at the base of the twin stairway corresponding to these periods have been destroyed, however, and it is not possible to know their dimensions and the richness of their sculptures and offerings. Yet, the several small temples that were excavated on the north side of the Great Pyramid (the temple of the eagles, the tzompantli or skull rack, the Red Temple), as well as the recently discovered inner chambers with the magnificent relief frieze of Toltec warriors, which belong to Periods V and VI, give us an indication of the elaboration and wealth of this constructive stage. It is correlated with the reign of Ahuitzotl, whose spectacular inauguration ceremony is described in such an evocative way by Durán and Tezozómoc (see Matos, this volume, table 1). During Period VII, corresponding to the reign of Motecuhzoma II, the dimensions of the huge platform at the base of the pyramid were not enlarged further but remained of the same size. Unfortunately, this last stage was almost completely leveled to the ground during the Spanish Conquest and the succeeding colonial building activities.

Thus far we have analyzed the construction phases of the Templo Mayor in relation to the periods of government of the Aztec rulers and the expansion of the empire. We have commented on the ideological function of the creation of a progressively more impressive frontal vision as well as the ideological significance of mass human sacrifices of prisoners at the Great Temple. We have seen that the Templo Mayor was a symbol of political power and expressed the ideology of an expanding warrior state. At the same time it conveyed a vision of space; it was the territorial center of Tenochtitlan, capital of the Aztec empire. In the analysis of the offerings to be presented in the last section of this chapter, we will return to this symbolism of space within the territorial limits of Mesoamerica and see how it came to be expressed by means of certain objects and sculptures contained in the offering caches.

Now we will turn to the aspect of the Templo Mayor as the religious center of the Aztecs. The intimate connection which existed in Aztec culture between warfare, myth, ritual, and sacrifice found its most elaborate expression in the annual cult of calendar festivals.

Templo Mayor as a Religious Center

The Aztec state cult took place at the Templo Mayor and is described by a number of particularly detailed and informative sixteenth-century sources.[17] It is one of the aspects of society on the eve of the Spanish Conquest that is best known and permits one to make truly ethnographic reconstructions that can be interpreted in terms of anthropological theory.

This cult, based on the solar calendar, consisted of eighteen months and twenty days each, at the end of which one major festival dedicated to one or more gods was celebrated. In a parallel manner, innumerable minor ceremonies occurred continually. Several festivals also formed cycles, such as the cycle of the rain gods and related deities and the cycle of the maize deities; ceremonies to the dead, to the fire god, and to other gods. Finally, there were the large individual feasts dedicated to the Aztec patron god Huitzilopochtli or other important deities such as Tezcatlipoca, Mixcoatl, and Quetzalcoatl, in which mythical cycles of historical content were dramatically enacted. It is a difficult task to interpret the mythical content of these ceremonies in their manifold relations to nature and to society, since different cultural levels and historical dimensions interact in them in complex and not always logical ways.

Treatment of the extremely complicated structure of the annual cycle of festivals in greater detail is beyond the scope of this chapter. One major difficulty consists in the correlation of the great diversity of *form* of these ceremonies to their *function*.

These calendar festivals were celebrated with a tremendous display of people and decorative as well as symbolic elements. They were dramatic representations set against the background of the impressive temple architecture of Tenochtitlan. Many ceremonies took place at night, in the glaring light of torches and great fires, or at dawn before the sun rose. The richness of the array of the participants, with the lavish use of gold, splendid feathers, and beautifully woven materials, combined with the dramatic power of the ceremonies, must have had an overwhelming effect upon the spectator—an effect that cannot be grasped in modern secular terms. In this tense atmosphere the human sacrifices were performed. Myth was enacted and became reality in an overwhelming theatrical setting.

In these ceremonies the gods themselves were sacrificed; human sacrifice was based on a highly complicated mythical theory. There were different methods of sacrifice according to the association with specific deities; the most common one was the heart sacrifice. The hearts were torn out from the tensely stretched breasts of the victims and were offered to the sun. A *techcatl* (sacrificial stone) was found on the upper platform of Huitzilopochtli's shrine of Period II at the Templo Mayor, and several cuauhxicalli (sculptured recipients for human hearts) have also come to light in the archaeological context of the Templo Mayor. The victims representing the earth and maize goddesses were decapitated, as were some of the victims dedicated to the rain gods, and others were thrown into the whirlpool of the lagoon (Pantitlan) or were locked up into caves. Still other victims of Tlaloc were sacrificed by the ordinary heart sacrifice. The goddess of salt, Huixtocihuatl, sister of the rain gods, was sacrificed at the summit of Tlaloc's temple, and her throat was pressed down to the techcatl by means of the spiny snout of a swordfish. Sahagún describes this ceremony with dramatic power.[18] (A number of such snouts of swordfish have been found in the offering caches of the Templo Mayor.)

The idea of a contract between humans and the gods seems to have been fundamental for the notion of human sacrifice; in this contract, men offered their most precious stake in order to receive from the gods the renewal of natural cycles, the growth of vegetation and agriculture, and the maintenance of order in society. The concept of a contractual relationship between humans and the gods was inspired in the social reality of a complex and diversified society in which there existed numerous contractual relationships between different groups.

Cosmovision and the Observation of Nature

While Aztec cult had a manifold relation to society through the participation of social groups in the ceremonies as well as through its link to economic activities, it also had an important relation to the observation of nature. Actually, the point of departure for ritual was the observation of nature, and its basic motivation was control of the contradictory manifestations of natural phenomena. At the same time, in the complex calendrical structure of cult, precise observation, myth, and magic became intricately interwoven. A major topic of the study of ancient calendars and cult systems consists in analyzing this dialectical relationship between the development of the accurate observation of nature and its shading off into myth and religion.

The linkage to nature was manifest in Aztec cult in its relation to astronomy (the course of the sun and the moon, as well as certain stars and constellations; e.g., Venus, Pleiades), climatological phenomena (the rainy season and the dry season); and seasonal cycles and agriculture.[19]

The fundamental concern of Aztec ritual was with rain and fertility, as is to be expected in a culture whose sustenance was derived from agriculture. Another very important element was the extreme conditions of the natural environment of the central Mexican highlands. During the dry season there was a constant lack of water, while during the rainy season the waters could be dangerous by their excess. Thunderstorms and hail, and even frost, could threaten the young crops during the initial months of the rainy season. The obsession for controlling the rains within the religion thus had its direct material basis.

These natural phenomena, the rains, which stimulate plant growth and enable agriculture but that also present the threatening aspects of thunderstorms, frost, and inundations—came to be personified in the cult of Tlaloc. To the Aztec rain god Tlaloc corresponds the Maya god Chac, the Zapotec god Cocij, the Totonac god Tajin, and so on, whose cults are lost in the most distant Mesoamerican past. This group of gods belongs to the earliest deities worshiped since pre-Classic times, together with the ancient god of fire and of time (Huehueteotl—Xiuhtecuhtli). In Classic period Teotihuacan, Tlaloc seems to have been the main deity of the official state cult depicted on murals and sculptures.[20]

In most modern studies on Aztec religion, Tlaloc is characterized simply as "the god of water and rain," and among his attributes, the goggle-like eyes and the fauces with the fangs and the serpent motif are considered to be the most important ones. Esther Pasztory[21] and Cecelia Klein,[22] however, have recently shown that Tlaloc's iconography in codices, stone reliefs, sculptures, and archaeological monuments reveals a whole range of other aspects that are practically unknown in the descriptions of the god given by sixteenth-century chroniclers and have been neglected by modern scholars who rely too heavily on these written sources. Pasztory, on the basis of her study of the Tlaloc imagery of Classic period Teotihuacan, reached the conclusion that there are two iconographically distinct types of Tlaloc. One of these she calls "Tlaloc A," whose main features—which are always represented in a context of flowing water —are the direct antecedents to the Aztec rain god with his goggle-like eyes and his mouth and fangs. The second type, "Tlaloc B," appears in a terrestrial context in conjunction with jaguars and other nocturnal symbolic elements and is associated by Pasztory with the concept of the "night sun," that is, the sun on its nocturnal journey through the underworld.[23]

From Teotihuacan onward, this duality of Tlaloc can be traced up to Aztec times. Cecelia Klein combines the interpretation of iconographic material with the analysis of sixteenth-century and modern ethnographic evidence to reach the conclusion that those aspects identified by Pasztory as Tlaloc B link the Aztec Tlaloc with the earth, the underworld, the jaguar, caves, darkness, the night, the night sun and also with food, riches, and abundance, as well as pulque, drunkenness, and sexual license.[24] There are further relations to the moon, to Venus and the god Xolotl as the evening star, and to timekeeping and calendrical periods. Tlaloc's priesthood was the most important cult institution at the Templo Mayor, to which belonged the fire priests, *tlenamacaque*. As Klein points out, there exist certain interesting possibilities of exploring in greater detail the relationships between Aztec priesthood, the cult of Tlaloc, and social structure.[25]

Truly new insights into the complex character of the god Tlaloc can be gained from a systematic study of his iconography, but it is also very important to analyze his role in Aztec ritual. As with his iconography, his rites were intimately related to those of the deities of maize and fertility, the earth goddesses, and the night. The cult of the mountains results to be a fundamental aspect of the cult of Tlaloc, as we shall see below. His close association to the earth and the earth goddesses is another aspect that proves to be essential in understanding of the symbolism of Templo Mayor. All of Tlaloc's rites were performed during the hours of the night, and the human sacrifices took place at midnight or before dawn.[26] Different cycles of the cult of Tlaloc can be distinguished according to the rainy or the dry season—a fact that was also intimately linked to cosmovision.

Many of these ceremonies took place at the Templo Mayor, as is abundantly documented by the historical sources; their study can now be confronted with the results of the excavation. As I will show in the following section, the offerings of Templo Mayor, which in such an overwhelming way are centered around the cult of Tlaloc, can be understood in terms of the previously mentioned symbolic connotations of the god, as well as his ritual functions. At the same time, these material remains go far beyond the evidence of any single previously analyzed site, revealing certain aspects that really offer new insights into Aztec cosmovision. To explore further these new perspectives is a task that has barely been initiated.

Naturally, the symbolism of Templo Mayor is not dedicated exclusively to Tlaloc. Its essence is in the *twin pyramid* that supposes the cults of Tlaloc *and* of Huitzilopochtli as a blending of opposites. Certain identifications with nature were long recognized, and one has become skeptical of their simplicity: the opposition between the sun on the one hand and the moon and stars on the other hand, between day and night, between humidity and drought, between the sky and the earth, between agriculture and warfare, between life and death, and so on. After more than a century of studies of Mesoamerica, we now know that Huitzilopochtli is not exclusively a sun god and that Seler's interpretation of the myth of Huitzilopochtli's birth on the Coatepec cannot simply be represented as the fight between the rising sun and the moon and the stars, who are identified as his sister and brothers. The same myth has other symbolical aspects as well as historical ones. In the same way, the goddess Coatlicue is not solely the earth-progenitor of the sun, the moon, and the stars. Her

symbolism has various other philosophical connotations, particularly her close identification with Cihuacoatl-Teteoinnan. "Astral mythology," that is, the interpretation
of pre-Hispanic myths in terms of a direct linear correspondence to solar, lunar, and
stellar phenomena, which was fashionable at the beginning of this century, can no
longer be repeated in such a simplified way. *Yet*, many of the symbolic elements of
the above-mentioned oppositions of natural phenomena appear repeatedly in
the material remains, a fact that refers us to the underlying cosmovision and induces us
to reconsider the themes that were first discussed in the nineteenth and early twentieth
centuries by authors such as Chavero, Brinton, Seler, Nuttall, Lehmann, and Beyer.
The concept of dualism is extremely important at the Templo Mayor and is manifest
in numerous architectural and sculptural details. Recently M. Graulich has discussed
the significance of the huge serpent heads that flank the temple platform and that differ
between Tlaloc's and Huitzilopochtli's sides. The opposite symbolism that they reflect
seems to have ancient roots in the religion of the central Mexican highlands.[27]

The presence of Huitzilopochtli at the Templo Mayor was connected, above all,
with the enactment of "mythical drama," a circumstance that is fully confirmed by
the study of cult. The festivals dedicated to the Aztec patron deity during the annual
ritual cycle were precisely those related to mythical drama of the solar deity as well
as of the historical destiny of the Aztec ethnic group. The presence of Tlaloc was connected, however, to underlying fundamental concepts of cosmovision related to the
observation of nature and agricultural cycles. The sun (i.e., the sky) and the rains (i.e.,
water) are opposites and were related to the two Mesoamerican seasons—*tonalco*, the
"time of heat and the sun" (i.e., the dry season) and *xopan*, "when it is green" (i.e.,
the rainy season).[28] Elements of this opposite symbolism were intertwined in a complex way, as is evident in the architectural and sculptural elements and in the offerings of Templo Mayor.

In Aztec ritual the prototype of human sacrifices dedicated to Tlaloc and intended
to assure the rains necessary for agriculture were child sacrifices. In the cult of Templo Mayor these children were identified with concrete mountains of the Valley of
Mexico; they were converted into living representatives of the *tepictoton* (small sculptured figurines) or *tlaloque*, the host of small servants of the god Tlaloc who were supposed to assist him in producing the rains. The mountain sanctuaries where these
children were sacrificed during the months of *I Atlcahualo* through *IV Huey tozoztli*[29]
(corresponding to February through April) consisted of a quadrangle court encircled
by a wall; inside there existed an assemblage of small mountain idols, the so-called
tepictoton.[30]

Tlaloc's main sanctuary, high up on Mount Tlaloc, also comprised a quadrangle court encircled by a white-washed enclosure, which could be seen from a great distance. On one side of this patio there was a small temple; inside it there stood a statue
of the god Tlaloc surrounded by a multitude of small idols that represented all the

other mountains of the Valley of Mexico. These idols "all had their names, in accordance to the mountain that they represented; these names still persist today, and there is not a single mountain which does not have its name," wrote Diego Durán in the sixteenth century.[31] Most of these names are still used today. During the ceremonies of Huey tozoztli, the rulers of Tenochtitlan, Tetzcoco, and Tlacopan brought new adornments for the statue of Tlaloc and for all the small idols, and in a solemn ceremony they dressed the idols with these new garments.[32] The ruins of this sanctuary, at an altitude of 13,270 feet above sea level, can still be seen today. They have been superficially registered by archaeologists; unfortunately, however, no excavation of this important site was ever undertaken.[33]

Child sacrifices took place during the sequence of the driest months of the year, from February to May (I Atlcahualo to IV Huey tozoztli), although they might begin also two or three Indian months earlier (*Atemoztli, Izcalli*), and their main purpose was to ask for the coming of the rains. To these rites belonged certain processions with a kind of high paper banners decorated with liquid rubber, the *amatetehuitl* (paper strips) that were supposed "to produce the greenness, the growth and sprouting" of vegetation,[34] by effect of sympathetic magic.

In terms of the interpretation of Aztec cult, I am proposing here the hypothesis that the Aztecs made a basic division of the year into the dry and the rainy season, xopan and tonalco.[35] This division was based on the observation of the solar cycle in combination with climatic phenomena and agricultural cycles and was expressed in a complex manner in myth and ritual.[36] The initiation of the rainy season was celebrated by a big festival dedicated to Tlaloc; it took place during the month of *VI Etzalcualiztli*, corresponding to June. An impersonator of Tlaloc and his consort Chalchiuhtlicue were sacrificed; it was the great festival of the priesthood of Tlaloc who performed magic rites to attract the waters and guarantee the vigorous outcome of the rainy season.[37] Tlaloc thus presided over the ritual half of the year, corresponding to the rainy season, which began with Etzalcualiztli.

During the following two months, important ceremonies to the sun took place. These months corresponded to the summer solstice (June 21) and to the second zenith passage of the sun at Tenochtitlan (July 25). These months were dedicated to Xochipilli, a solar deity with important aspects of fertility and maize, as well as to the young maize goddess Chicomecoatl-Xilonen, and finally to Cihuacoatl-Chantico. The latter deity was an important aspect of the earth goddess Cihuacoatl, related to the underworld and to fire. According to Klein, Cihuacoatl-Chantico shared interesting iconographic traits with Tlaloc B.[38] She played an extremely important role at the Great Temple, as we shall see in the last chapter of this study. The presence of these deities leads one to conclude that the cult of the sun in the two months of the summer solstice and the second zenith passage was related to the cult of the dead and the underworld and also to the cult of maize and fertility. Important offerings to the dead took place during the months of *V Toxcatl*, *VIII Huey tecuilhuitl*, *IX Miccailhuitontli*, and *X Huey Miccailhuitl to Xocotlhuetzi*. During these months until the festival of *XII Teotleco*, "llegan los dioses" (end of September, beginning of October) the gods die or pass to the underworld (i.e., the rainy season presided over by the night sun). The importance of the cult of maize and fertility thus becomes obvious, since this was the time when the food plants germinated and grew.

This mythic representation of the solar cycle, in connection with climatological phenomena and agricultural cycles that I have interpreted purely on the basis of the Aztec cult, seems to have had old historical traditions. It is confirmed iconographically by archaeological material from central Mexico. In this sense, certain conclusions reached by Pasztory are highly suggestive. She proposes that

> In Postclassic Mesoamerican belief, the sun descended to the underworld where he married the earth goddess. The god of maize was born of this union. The god of maize, however, was not really an entirely separate deity, since he was the sun reborn in a new aspect. The sun god had two facets: during the dry season he was a deity of the sky and the day; during the rainy season he was a deity of the underworld and the night. As the night sun, the god was associated with water and fertility. He was believed to die in the underworld and to be reborn as the god of maize. He was, therefore, associated with symbols of death and sacrifice as well as with symbols of birth and fertility. As the night sun, the deity was associated with the jaguar; as the day, or sometimes descending sun, he was associated with a raptorial bird.[39]

This division of the yearly solar cycle into two parts, one corresponding to the "day sun" (i.e., the dry season) and the other part corresponding to the "night sun" (i.e., the rainy season)—in association with a whole complex of dualistic symbolic elements—not only seems to go back to Classic period Teotihuacan,[40] Xochicalco,[41] and Cacaxtla[42] but also may have been a fundamental concept of pre-Hispanic cosmovision that at least since Classic times came to encompass the whole area of Mesoamerica, from the central Mexican highlands to the Maya area.[43] These notions were expressed in ritual and in the iconography of sculptures and monuments.[44] They also seem to have been a fundamental concept underlying the dualism represented at the Templo Mayor. This hypothesis needs to be followed up in greater detail in future studies; however, it seems significant that the excavation of Templo Mayor has suggested to us that there are certain elements connecting these data on the cult of Tlaloc with this much wider context of pre-Hispanic cosmovision.

The all-pervasiveness of the symbolism of water in the excavation of Templo Mayor can thus be related to a complex intertwining of concepts, a kind of "philosophy of nature." As the god of the rainy season, of water and fertility in general, Tlaloc presided over the half of the year which was initiated by the festival of *VI Etzalcualiztli*. It was the rainy season, the "dark" time of the year associated with the moon, Venus, and the stars (including the Pleiades), as well as with the under-world; it was the time during which the plants grew and matured, culminating in the harvest and in the ceremonies of the gods of pulque, maguey, and fertility.[45]

While VI Etzalcualiztli initiated the half of the year presided over by the rain gods, *XV Panquetzaliztli* (nine indigenous months, or 180 days later) in an analogous way initiated the half of the year presided over by the sun as the deity of the sky and the day. This deity was Huitzilopochtli and the myth of his birth at Coatepec was enacted dramatically during the month of XV Panquetzaliztli. As we shall see below, Coatepec, "the serpent mountain," was in itself a symbol for the temple pyramid; and Panquetzaliztli was one of the most sumptuous festivals to take place once a year at Templo Mayor. The festivals of XVII Tititl, II Tlacaxipehualiztli, and V Toxcatl, which also belonged to this section of the ritual cycle, dealt with solar and sky sym-bolism interwoven with warfare and references to the destiny of the Aztec ethnic group. Certain monumental sculptures belonging to the context of Templo Mayor seem to have alluded to mythical events containing these references.

At the transition between the cycle of the rainy and dry seasons, coinciding with the time of the harvest of maize, we find two important festivals that were dedicated to a different aspect of the cult of Tlaloc which proves to be fundamental for our study of Templo Mayor: the cult of the mountains. During *XIII Tepeilhuitl*, correspond-ing to October, and *XVI Atemoztli*, corresponding to the latter part of December, mountain images were made of dough (tepictoton) and received the names of specific mountains of the Valley of Mexico. These mountains were also the patrons of cer-tain illnesses attributed to the tlaloque.[46] Some images were prepared in memory of those who had died in circumstances related to Tlaloc. Besides the names of moun-tains including the Popocatepetl and the Iztac Cihuatl, we find that some images were dedicated to Tlaloc, Chalchiuhtlicue, Matlalcueye, Ehecatl, Chicomecoatl, and Ci-huacoatl, in other words basically the same deities of the fertility cult that we have found to play an important role during the ceremonies of the rainy season. It is note-worthy that the god of wind Ehecatl-Quetzalcoatl also figures among these images. Finally, another important connection between XIII Tepeilhuitl and the pulque gods must be mentioned further. The time of harvest, which depending on altitudes and specific climatic conditions took place between October and December, was in this way intimately related to pulque and drunkenness. The varied aspects of this sym-bolism were expressed in the cult of the tepictoton, the small images of the mountain gods or tlaloque.[47]

It would lead us too far to search deeper into the complex subject of these fes-tivals. We have seen, however, the emergence of a coherent image in which the sym-bolism of rain, water, mountains, and agriculture was closely intertwined with, and yet opposed to, the solar symbolism. Huitzilopochtli as the "day sun" was born at Pan-quetzaliztli, whereas Tlaloc symbolized the "night sun" that presided over the rainy season and the mythical cycle of the germination and ripening of the maize plant. Solar events, climatological phenomena, and agricultural cycles formed the basis of that cosmovision, which was the driving force in creating that strange and fascinating product of human imagination, the Templo Mayor.

THE ARCHAEOLOGICAL SITE

Architectural and Sculptural Elements: The Reactualization of Myth

After having made such ample reference to the ceremonies of the state cult taking place at the Templo Mayor, we may now turn to the archaeological site itself and analyze aspects of the material remains in the light of our knowledge of the religious symbolism of the Great Temple.

The reactualization of myth is insinuated at the site by the presence of certain iconographic elements belonging to large sculptures that were part of the temple architecture. These elements provide important information about the wider context of symbolism that forms the background for any analysis of the cosmovision conveyed by Templo Mayor.

Numerous authors have stressed the fact that Huitzilopochtli's temple pyramid represents the *Coatepetl*, the "Serpent Mountain," where the miraculous birth of the god took place. In a way, the whole twin pyramid was considered Coatepec,[48] but in a more limited sense the Coatepetl was only Huitzilopochtli's pyramid while Tlaloc's side had a distinct symbolism, as we shall explain in greater detail later in this chapter. The sculptural elements that denote the Coatepetl are huge sculptures of serpents, which flank the facade of both pyramids. They are fully preserved in Period IVb and permit one to imagine the dramatic power of the building in its original shape. The large platform in front of the twin pyramid is subdivided by large serpent heads. Their magnificently sculptured features show remains of polychromatic painting. Aztec creative power seems to have no limits in the ways in which the characteristics of snakes based on natural observation were combined with purely phantasmal traits. Future research is needed for detailed study of this peculiar synthesis, which was achieved between the observation of nature, symbolism, and artistic expression.

The five serpent heads on the frontal platform have different features according to their location on Tlaloc's or Huitzilopochtli's side. Michel Graulich identifies the head on the southern (Huitzilopochtli's) side as a feathered serpent decorated with emblems of political authority, while the head on the northern (Tlaloc's) side shows two rings that he relates to the mask of Tlaloc. According to Graulich, these serpents reflect the basic dualism of Templo Mayor which seems to have ancient roots in the iconography of Middle Classic period Teotihuacan, Xochicalco, and Cacaxtla.[49] In addition, the excavation revealed two enormous snakes with an undulating body of six meters each, which had the function of limiting the north and south edges of the platform (see pl. 8). Finally, innumerable small serpent heads also are embedded in the outer wall of the pyramid (on its north, east, and south sides).

At the foot of Huitzilopochtli's pyramid, also corresponding to Period IVb, the well-known huge relief stone of Coyolxauhqui was found which symbolizes the reactualization of the myth of the birth of the god at Coatepec and his victory over Coyolxauhqui and her 400 brothers, the centzon huitznahua. In his anger Huitzilopochtli decapitated the goddess; her head and mutilated body rolled down to the foot of the Serpent Mountain, where they came to rest.[50]

The sensational discovery of the big relief stone of Coyolxauhqui initiated the excavation project in February 1978. The dismembered goddess represented on it was immediately identified as Coyolxauhqui, the god's rebellious sister, who plays such an important role in the myth of his miraculous birth. Since numerous previous studies have dealt with this identification, it is not necessary to repeat the myth here;[51] however, it is important to note that this relief stone contains the symbolic reference to the Aztec ethnic group, glorified in their patron god Huitzilopochtli. If the latter came to be intimately identified with the solar deity, Coyolxauhqui belonged to that group of female deities who had close associations with the night, not only the moon but also the stars. Her identification with the moon was first proposed by E. Seler[52] and since then has been repeated by numerous authors; however, a recent iconographic study by C. Aguilera suggests that Coyolxauhqui rather symbolized the Milky Way, which in ancient Mesoamerica was considered the nocturnal counterpart of the sun.[53]

A historical aspect of this myth is that the rebellious sister of Huitzilopochtli is the sorceress Malinalxochitl, founder of the important province of Malinalco and mother of Copil, whose defeat by the Mexica and heart sacrifice came to be mythically related to the foundation of Tenochtitlan.[54] Malinalxochitl and Coyolxauhqui both share elements with the earth and mother goddess Cihuacoatl-Coatlicue. In the myth of the birth of Huitzilopochtli, Coatlicue is the mother of Coyolxauhqui. In some other mythical versions, however, the elder sister (Coyolxauhqui-Malinalxochitl) and the mother (Coatlicue) are considered identical.[55] Curiously, the relief stone does not represent a young woman, but a woman of rather advanced age who has already given birth to children. This circumstance is visible from the iconographic details. This poses some very interesting problems with respect to the symbolism of Templo Mayor and the link that existed between Coyolxauhqui and the ancient earth goddess Cihuacoatl-Coatlicue.

On the whole, some five sculptured images of Coyolxauhqui have been found in the vicinity of Templo Mayor on different occasions, demonstrating that the close tie between Huitzilopochtli and Coyolxauhqui persisted through time.

Since 1786, certain major sculptures were discovered in the immediate surroundings of Templo Mayor, that is at different points of the Zócalo of Mexico City and adjacent streets[56] (see Matos, this volume, fig. 1). Most of these sculptures today form part of the *Sala Mexica* of the National Museum of Anthropology. One of the most outstanding pieces is the colossal head of Coyolxauhqui, sculptured from green stone and characterized by the mark of copper bells on her cheeks.[57] These sculptures include the monumental statue of Coatlicue, which embodies a whole iconographic inventory of the qualities of this ferocious earth and mother goddess (pl. 31), and the equally monumental Yollotlicue, a related goddess who wears a necklace of human hearts instead of skulls. To the same association of ideas belong the representations of the *cihuateteo*, "the divine women" who died in childbirth and were transformed into monsters who threatened to devour humankind.

Other monumental sculptures found in the vicinity of Templo Mayor include the enormous head of the Xiuhcoatl, the fire serpent and weapon used by Huitzilopochtli to defeat his rebellious sister and brothers, and the stone cuauhxicalli in the shape of a fierce jaguar, a recipient for blood and hearts in the context of human sacrifice. Here we might also mention the extraordinary number of magnificent representations of snakes and reptiles exhibited in the Sala Mexica of the Museum of Anthropology which convey such an important message for the underlying concepts of cosmovision. On the other hand, there also exist monuments such as the *Teocalli de la Guerra Sagrada* (a miniature temple symbolizing sacred warfare), and the "Stone of Warriors," or "the Stone of Tizoc" that give a historical dimension to the Templo Mayor. These major monuments were also linked to the legitimation of political power of an expanding conquest state.[58] Finally, we must mention the famous Calendar Stone, which explains in a condensed form the basic structure of the calendar system (it might have been used horizontally and was related to the sun as well as to the earth deity, Tlaltecuhtli).[59]

It is necessary to take these monumental sculptures into account in order to reconstruct the full picture of symbolism at the Templo Mayor and people the temple structrues with these mythical beings or charters. Probably only a small proportion of the major artworks that existed have survived destruction. Curiously, no single statue of Huitzilopochtli has been discovered, neither previously nor during the present excavation. Either they were all destroyed by the Spaniards, precisely because of their importance, or they were hidden away by the Indians, to be lost forever.[60] As we have seen, however, several attributes of the known sculptures refer to the myth of Huitzilopochtli relating the patron deity to Coyolxauhqui as well as to Coatlicue-Cihuacoatl. The chroniclers, particularly Diego Durán, speak of the importance of the cult of Cihuacoatl. Her shrine was a completely dark temple, the Tlillan, an artificial kind of cave where she presided over a multitude of small idols called *tecuacuiltin*.[61] This temple had a very low entrance and was situated right next to Huitzilopochtli's temple. Cihuacoatl had an important priesthood at her service; besides her old priests, also called tecuacuiltin, the maidens dedicated to Huitzilopochtli also served the goddess.[62]

One approach for deeper penetration into the myth surrounding the Templo Mayor is to gain a better understanding of the cult of Cihuacoatl and the complex symbolism of this goddess. Are Cihuacoatl and Coatlicue the same deity? How are they related to Coyolxauhqui-Malinalxochitl, who was designated by some sources as Huitzilopochtli's elder sister while others call her his mother?

An important government functionary in the Aztec state also held the title of Cihuacoatl, "woman serpent." According to some sources, he was a kind of deputy king related to internal civil and religious affairs.[63] Tlacaelel, brother of Itzcoatl,[64] assumed this function after the war against Cuitlahuac and Chalco,[65] and according to Durán and Tezozomoc, he became the real power behind successive Tlatoque (rulers) who were his brothers or nephews. In which way was this political office related to the cult of the earth goddess Cihuacoatl, who was the patroness of the southern lake region of Culhuacan, Xochimilco, Cuitlahuac, and Chalco, but who was also particularly related to the important religious centers of Chalma and Malinalco to the southwest of the Valley of Mexico?

Cecelia Klein argues that it is necessary to connect the study of the religious iconography of Cihuacoatl with a historical approach that takes into account the sociopolitical functions acquired by the cult of this goddess during the fifteenth century.[66] In fact, the importance of the goddess increased after the conquest of the southern lake region, the period in which the office of Cihuacoatl was introduced into Aztec political organization. In a previous section (on military expansion, human sacrifice, and amplifications of Templo Mayor) we have also stressed the significance of the conquest of Chalco for the Mexica in economic, political, and religious terms. Michel Graulich, however, points out that the dual form of government embodied by the Tlatoani and the Cihuacoatl was closely linked to the sky-sun and the earth-water dualisms in pre-Hispanic cosmovision. Antecedents of this duality may be found in the two opposed dignitaries represented on the lintels of Cacaxtla. For the Aztecs, the Tlatoani was the representative of Huitzilopochtli associated to the sun and the sky, deriving his authority from Quetzalcoatl,[67] while the Cihuacoatl represented the female aspects of the earth and darkness, like Tlaloc.[68]

The cult of Cihuacoatl was closely linked to Huitzilopochtli's temple service;[69] however, it was also connected with Tlaloc's priesthood.[70] This is another aspect where the study of ceremonial organization combined with the study of iconography can lead the way to new insights. Here, as in several other points investigated in this chapter, we discover a connection between the cults of Huitzilopochtli, Cihuacoatl, and Tlaloc that must have been explained in mythical terms. Klein suggests that in Aztec mythology Cihuacoatl, in her aspect of the old earth mother Ilamatecuhtli, was considered the spouse of the earth and water god Tlaloc. Both were considered as ugly and very old.[71] The Aztecs were in the process of identifying their patron deity Huitzilopochtli as the son of these ancient lords of the earth and the underworld. Needless to say, if these internal associations between the three main deities which appear in the symbolism of Templo Mayor can be substantiated by further evidence, this constitutes an extremely interesting hypothesis to be followed up in the future.

In our analysis of the monumental architectural and sculptural elements at the

Templo Mayor, we now turn to the site itself. The dualism of Tlaloc's and Huit-zilopochtli's pyramid is further expressed by a number of sculptures that occur sym-metrically. These include various large earthenware braziers; those on Tlaloc's side represent the god with his characteristic attributes, while those on the south side of the pyramid are adorned with a peculiar knot that symbolizes Huitzilopochtli. In the shrine at the summit of the twin pyramid corresponding to Period II, there was dis-covered a sculpture of a Chac Mool placed right in front of Tlaloc's (north) shrine (pl. 52). It corresponds symmetrically to the *techcatl*, the narrow sacrificial stone of black lava situated in front of Huitzilopochtli's (south) shrine. The shape of the latter stone, as well as its use for mass human sacrifices, is amply described by sixteenth-century chronicles. One of the surprises of the excavation was to find this stone situated ex-actly in the place indicated by the historical sources.

The chronicles do not mention the Chac Mool at the Templo Mayor, however, which is the first Aztec sculpture of this type discovered in situ; therefore, it is stimulat-ing to speculate about its original purpose. Other such sculptures are known from Tula or from Chichen Itza and were interpreted as divine messengers related to the rain gods. According to Seler, the recipient carried on the abdomen served to receive pulque, which was offered precisely to the tlaloque as rain, mountain, and pulque gods.[72] One is reminded of the information given by Juan B. Pomar, who describes Tlaloc's statue on the summit of Mount Tlaloc. According to this chronicler, this statue was made of white stone and had human form. It was seated on a quadrangle stone slab, its face directed toward the east. On its head it carried a receptacle hewn from the same stone as the sculpture that was filled with liquid rubber, and in it the Indians offered seed corn of all their sustenance—white, black, red, and yellow maize; different varieties of beans, chili peppers; chian (sage); and *huauhtli* and *michihuauhtli* (varieties of amaranth). These offerings were renewed once a year in a solemn rite that was accompanied by child sacrifices.[73]

M. Graulich has proposed another hypothesis concerning the use of the Chac Mool that does not necessarily contradict the functions in the preceding paragraphs. He suggests that it might have been employed as a sacrificial stone for those victims of the rain gods which, according to the chroniclers, were sacrificed "on the back of" or "on top of" someone else.[74] In this sense there would have existed a functional cor-respondence between the Chac Mool and the techcatl, which constitutes a very in-teresting possibility within the dualism of Templo Mayor. Pasztory also believes that the location of the sculpture in front of the temple doorway and the dish that it holds in its hands suggest this sculpture may have been a sacrificial stone or a receptacle for offerings.[75]

Now we pass on to the period richest in findings, the frontal platform of Period IVb. On Tlaloc's side we find a small altar with two stone frogs (pl. 9). These sculp-tures of animals symbolizing the earth, water, and fertility are true masterpieces of Aztec sculptural art, as are the two eagle heads adorning the temple of the eagles. This latter building belongs to the latest results of the excavation and leads us beyond the main temple on its north side: Beyond Tlaloc's temple, corresponding to Period V, a large patio was excavated that contains a small structure, the facade of which is adorned by two polychromatic eagle heads. Within the same patio, along the north wall of the big temple, three other small structures were revealed, the first one of unspecified use and the second one a stone tzompantli (skull rack) consisting of some 240 grinning stone skulls, each having a slightly different enigmatic expression (pl. 10). Behind this tzompantli, the so-called Red Temple was discovered, which is identical to another red temple excavated earlier on the south side, next to Huitzilopochtli's temple. The most interesting fact about these two red temples is that they contain elements of Classic period Teotihuacan architectural style and thus raise the question of how far this style can be considered a product of the historical consciousness of the Aztecs in an endeavor to emulate the ancient metropolis.

By far the most spectacular findings with respect to historical tradition were discovered in the very final stage of the excavation and are located within the eagle structure to the north of the three small temples (pl. 11). They permit us to get a glimpse of the inner chambers of the temple precinct, leading us beyond the huge twin pyramid. Three large rectangular chambers were excavated. All along their walls run side benches that are decorated with a frieze of warriors wearing plumed headdresses and holding a shield and staff in their hands (pl. 23). Each warrior image contains slightly different details. The figures seem to be walking in a solemn procession, the purpose of which might have been an act of bloodletting or penance. The procession converges on a central emblem consisting of a grass ball into which sacrificial bones and thorns were placed and that was a symbol of self-sacrifice.[76] Above the figures, a band of snakes is depicted consisting of *quetzalcoatl* (feathered serpents), alternating with *xiuhcoatl* (fire serpents), and *mixcoatl* (cloud serpents). This extraordinary polychromatic relief, which is the best preserved painting of the entire excavation (because it was covered by the humid soil just above the phreatic level), is almost identical to a similar side bench known from the Toltec capital of Tula. What is the significance of this correspondence to Toltec art at the Templo Mayor? Who executed these reliefs? What did the Aztecs want to express by copying art styles of past centuries, particularly the Toltec style, which is known to have been so highly appreciated?[77]

In these inner chambers several interesting sculptures were found at strategic locations. Among them were two huge braziers representing the god Tlaloc, executed in a strange baroque style. Almost identical clay braziers are also known from Tula. Further into the structure, flanking the entrance to the second chamber, two clay statues of human size representing eagle warriors were revealed (pl. 53). The clay was covered by a stucco design of feathers painted white to indicate the eagle costume. The stoic face of the warrior gazes out of the beak of the eagle. This statue is a hollow clay doll that had to be assembled from its different parts or limbs. A surprisingly naturalistic impression is achieved that overwhelms the spectator.

After passing through this entrance flanked by the two eagle warriors, we find

1. The Stone of Coyolxauhqui, a huge sculptured disk (11 feet across) depicting the goddess Coyolxauhqui who, according to Aztec tradition, was dismembered by Huitzilopochtli.

2. General view of Templo Mayor archaeological zone looking north. Note the Coyolxauhqui stone on the general platform.

3. General view of Templo Mayor looking east.

4. View of the stairways of the different stages. Note the covering at left that protected the Coyolxauhqui stone during the excavations.

1

2

3

4

5. Stage II, approximately A.D. 1390. Note that the twin temples were in place at this early date.

6. Stage III, A.D. 1441. The stairway with the seven life-size sculptures in situ.

7. Stage III. The seven figures shown in plate 6 have been removed. Note the steepness of the stairways.

5

6

7

8. Stage IVb. Note the undulating serpent (approximately six meters in length) indicating the name of the temple (Coatepec; Serpent Hill).

9. Stage IVb. This "frog altar" located in front of the high stairways is associated with the cult of Tlaloc.

10. Stage VI (approximately A.D. 1500). Altar decorated with more than 240 skulls, possibly indicating the northern region of the Dead, Mictlampa.

11. Stage VI. Eagle head in the balustrade of the warriors' precinct on the north patio of the temple area.

8

9

10

11

12. Offering 61. Note the crocodile head in the lower left corner and the coral remains in the top right corner.

13. Offering 61, lower level. Note the predominance of marine elements, including shells, brain coral, and conch shells.

14. Chamber 3. The two magnificent polychrome containers are shown. In between these containers, note jaguar remains next to masks, stone figures, and copal.

12

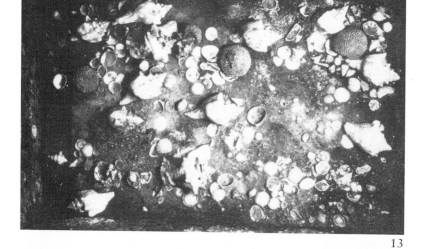

13

14

15. Offering 48. Remains of forty-two children sacrificed in honor of Tlaloc.

16. Chamber 2. Located on the Tlaloc side, this chamber contained masks and figures of Mezcala style with jaguar remains and conch shells.

17. Offering 58. Note the turtle shell and sawfish remains in the middle.

18. Offering H. Located in the interior of the altar of skulls, this offering contained jaguar and wolf remains, bowl of Tlaloc, and flutes.

15

16

17

18

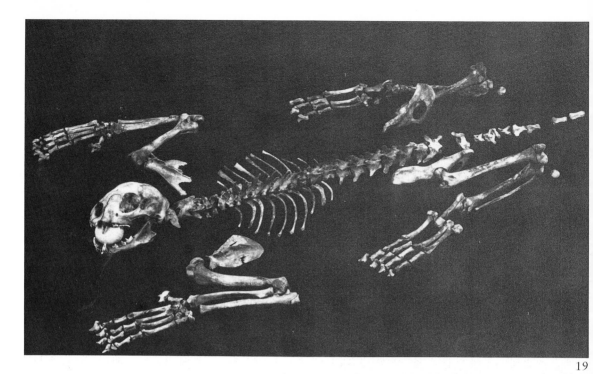

19

19. Jaguar skeleton from chamber 2.

20. Detail of jaguar with large greenstone in mouth.

21. Human skull with knife in mouth. Note the coastal shells above.

22. Different types of skulls found in various offerings.

20

21

22

23

23. Bench from the interior of Eagle Warrior Precinct with image of warrior in procession. Note the undulating serpent above.

24. Vase with image of Mictlantecuhtli, the Lord of Mictlan, the realm of the Dead.

25. Mezcala-style human figure.

24

25

26. Group of fish made of mother-of-pearl. From offering 41.

27. Offering 41. A miniature canoe with fishing instruments and fish inside.

28. A mother-of-pearl necklace with images of serpent heads, frogs, fish, and snake rattles.

29. Sculptures of the Aztec deity Tepeyollotl (Heart of the Mountain) or Xiuhtecuhtli (God of Fire).

30

31

30. Another figure of Tepeyollotl or Xiuhtecuhtli.

31. Coatlicue, Lady of the Serpent Skirt, Mother of the Gods, found in 1790 near the Cathedral of Mexico.

32. Ceremonial knife (tecpatl) with the face of the god. Note the turquoise eyebrow.

32

33

34

35

36

37

38

33. Turtle remains related to fertility and longevity.

34. Coral remains associated with Tlaloc's cult.

35. Crocodile head of offering 7.

36. Shell from the coastal area.

37. Small shell from coastal area.

38. Shell associated with Tlaloc cult.

39. Olmec mask. This is the oldest object (800 B.C.) found in the Templo Mayor.

40. Teotihuacan mask with obsidian eyes.

41. Teotihuacan mask with ear pieces and shell and obsidian eyes.   42–44. Mezcala-style masks.

45

46

47

45. Rear view of Mezcala-style mask (see pl. 44) with painted glyph.

46. Orange ceramic funerary urn from stage IVb.

47. Representations of the Rain and Mountain God Tlaloc.

48. Mixtec figure representing Tlaloc.

48

49

50

49. Ceramic vase representing Tlaloc.

50. Brazier with the face of Tlaloc.

51. Clay urn with face of Tlaloc.

52. Chac Mool in stone with painted costume (stage II).

51

52

53. Eagle warrior in clay ceramic. Found in Eagle Warrior Precinct on the north side (stage V).

54. Chamber II (period IV) with tubular Mezcala-style idols associated with the mountain cult.

53

54

55a–d. Four tubular Mezcala-style idols.

55a

55b

55c

55d

56. Tlaloc-Tlaltecuhtli, in crouching earth-monster position, under base of several monumental sculptures found at Templo Mayor.

57. Two superposed Tlaloc representations, as earth monster Tlaltecuhtli. Note the olin sign at the center.

56

57

that the next passageway was guarded by two life-size statues of Mictlantecuhtli, the lord of the Mictlan, "the land of the dead," or the underworld. They were also made of clay and conjured the realistic presence of the emaciated body of a skeleton.[78] Unfortunately, these figures were more heavily damaged, and it has not been possible to reconstruct them as thoroughly as the eagle warriors. The symbolism of these representations and of the entire place is highly intriguing. Was the cult of the eagle warriors not a cult dedicated to the sun? Where do we find their counterpart, the jaguar warriors? Why do the jaguars not appear inside the temple together with the eagles, as is the case of the sculptures hewn out of rock at the mountain sanctuary of Malinalco? The eagle heads at the shrine of Templo Mayor actually do show stylistic parallels to the sculptures of the same animal at Malinalco.

As we have seen, the entrance to the last chamber was guarded by Mictlantecuhtli, the lord of the realm of the dead. While the reference to the underworld is apparent, its relation to the rain god Tlaloc is not so clear. The chamber is situated at the north side of Tlaloc's pyramid, a fact that bears an interesting correspondence to the notion that the Mictlan was situated geographically to the north.[79] In the ritual calendar, offerings to the dead were brought during the months of May to August, the period between the two zenith passages when the sun's shadow pointed north at noon. With respect to Tlaloc, we have noted previously that he was also considered to be the old lord of the underworld. This fact might explain the relation to Mictlan we find in the above-mentioned buildings on the north side of the temple. As we have pointed out with respect to the ritual cycles, there existed a mythical association between the Mictlan, the north, the calendar, the agricultural year, the night, the rainy season, and the underworld presided over by Tlaloc. The rain god's particular domain was the *Tlalocan*, which was a kind of underworld situated inside the earth. It was perceived as space inside the mountains filled with water. This notion turns out to be fundamental for our interpretation of the offerings, as we shall see below. It is interesting to note that among Nahua groups of the Sierra de Puebla in central Mexico there still survives the belief that Tlaloc reigns over the domain of the dead called *Tlalocan*, which is associated with water and abundance.[80] The famous Tepantitlan murals from Teotihuacan seem to illustrate this same association of ideas dating from the Classic period.[81]

The fact of the imitation of Toltec style in these chambers becomes understandable if one takes into account that Tlaloc was also a god of dynastic succession, an old god related to the ancestors and to past cosmic ages or "suns." The Aztecs regarded him as a Toltec deity;[82] however, we know that within Toltec tradition they subsumed cultural elements going back as far as Teotihuacan. Actually they seem to have made no clear distinction between them. Some authors have suggested that Tlaloc represented the autochthonous civilized peoples of the central highlands (associated to the earth, the night, and the rainy season), in opposition to the newcomers or conquerors, whose symbols were the sky and the sun of the dry season. Yet, this dualistic cosmogonic opposition was in no way invented by the Aztecs but had ancient roots, as is evidenced by the splendid murals from Cacaxtla dating from the eighth century A.D.[83]

The Offerings of Templo Mayor

We may now turn to one of the outstanding aspects of the excavation: the fact that it brought to light more than 100 offering caches containing some 7,000 objects.[84] These offerings belong to all building periods; however, Periods II, IV, and IVb are the richest in these findings.

The confrontation with the excavation results over the past few years, particularly with the material from the offerings, has led me to ask myself increasingly more complex questions about the global symbolism of the Great Temple, which are presented in the following sections as a number of hypotheses. The goal is to integrate the excavation results into a wider understanding of Aztec cosmology and culture but adhering as closely as possible to the messages revealed by the archaeological objects themselves. From the methodological point of view it is fundamental to allow the material remains to speak for themselves, interpreting them in their own terms, and not merely to illustrate from the written sources associations that the temple might suggest. One can extract really new messages from the study of the archaeological data if one keeps this methodological difference in mind. In this sense my analysis of the offerings led me in a new direction.[85] My initial hypothesis to study at Templo Mayor "offerings dedicated to Tlaloc" in contrast to "offerings dedicated to Huitzilopochtli" and to interpret them mainly in terms of their sociopolitical functions was transformed in the course of the study. One of the main conclusions is that the offerings represent an aspect of the Templo Mayor quite *different* from that suggested by its architecture or the monumental sculptures. While architecture, monumental sculpture, and public state rituals were clearly connected to the legitimation of political power within the expanding conquest state, the burial of offerings rather seems to derive from ancient traditions of cosmological thought that were related to political ideology, only in a more indirect way.[86] The focus of my analysis of the offerings thus became concentrated in the field of cosmovision, in certain aspects of the observation of nature and their link to Aztec society and religion.

The offering caches may be classified into three types: (1) those in which the objects are put inside a cache with stucco floor and stone walls, (2) those found inside stone urns covered with a lid, and (3) those placed directly into the structure or the filling of the building.[87] The distribution of these caches seems to be far from fortuitous and coincides with the main axes of the Great Temple. Here, as well as in the architecture, the situation is determined by the existence of the twin pyramid. The offerings are concentrated on the frontal platform, at the point of union of the two pyramids, at a midpoint in front of Huitzilopochtli's or Tlaloc's pyramid, and at the corners of the twin pyramid on the front and rear sides. A number of offerings were also found on the rear side, at the point of union between the two pyramids, and in the middle of each one of them. The richest offerings correspond to Period IVb; on the whole, these are the best preserved.[88] Inside the shrines on top of the twin pyramid, corresponding to Period II, several interesting offerings were also excavated.[89] Yet it is too early to make a completely systematic analysis of the location as well as the content of all the offerings, as the corresponding excavation reports are not yet accessible, and it is hoped that they will soon be published in full extent.[90] The information for the following preliminary classification is taken from several previous publications by Matos; it is complemented by my own observations gathered over the past years.[91]

Evidence of Human Sacrifices, Warfare, and Tribute

As might be expected on the basis of what we know about Aztec cult, there exists ample evidence of human sacrifice at the Templo Mayor. It is important to note that this evidence relates to both Huitzilopochtli and Tlaloc. The most spectacular finding is Offertory Cache 48, which contains eleven polychromatic stone effigies of Tlaloc (pl. 47) placed over an ossuary of more than thirty skulls, long bones, and ribs belonging to children of the age of a few months up to seven or eight years (pl. 15). This cache was found on the northwest corner of the pyramid of Tlaloc and corresponds to the period of Coyolxauhqui (IVb). It represents the only case of complete skeletons found at the Templo Mayor.[92]

A number of other offering caches contain decapitated human skulls, some of which are adorned with eyes made of inlaid semiprecious stones and with noses made of flint knife (tecpatl); some of them carry another tecpatl stuck into their mouths. Still other skulls are worked in such a way that there remains only a gruesome mask (pls. 21, 22). To the complex of human sacrifices also seems to belong the enormous quantity of flint knives that were found in the offerings together with other objects; such tecpatls served as blades for sacrificial knives. Especially interesting are the four caches situated on the rear side of the double pyramid which contain tecpatls decorated with faces (pl. 32). The eyes and mouths were made of inlaid shells and obsidian; the remains of red paint can be discerned on them. They were stuck into a base of copal, which indicates their use in certain ceremonies. Their symbolism was immersed in myth and may have been specifically related to the rite of decapitation.[93]

D. Nagao points out that as a tool for sacrifice, flint was associated with death and destruction. Knives were often depicted in the codices, forming the nose or mouth of Mictlantecuhtli and Tlaltecuhtli, death and earth deities, respectively. Note, however:

> The deeper and more pervasive significance for flint was not with sacrifice and death, but rather with origins and beginnings. . . . Calendrically, *tecpatl* was also associated with beginnings and origins. . . . The flint knife was . . . an important symbol with particular significance for the Mexica nation. . . . It was closely identified not only with the birth of the Mexica nation, but also may have been a symbol of the Mexica people themselves.[94]

In this sense, it is interesting to note that according to a myth related by Durán, "Cihuacoatl's son" had the shape of a flint or a sacrificial knife;[95] If Cihuacoatl-Coatlicue was Huitzilopochtli's mother, then the flint knife might have been directly the symbol of the Aztec patron god. Flint knives, with and without faces, would thus seem to belong to the cult of Huitzilopochtli at the Templo Mayor. To complicate matters further, however, some of the tecpatls found in the excavation show in a stylized way the traces of goggle-like eyes and fangs made of serpents characteristic of Tlaloc! Another one of these flint knives has a series of fangs instead of teeth, reminiscent of Tlaloc as well. The symbolism of these strange tecpatls with faces still needs further investigation.

To the context of human sacrifice also belong the innumerable stone representations of human skulls revealed in the excavation, although it is not always clear to which architectural context they belonged. The most important building in this respect is the stone tzompantli, a small temple on the north side of Tlaloc's pyramid—corresponding to Period V—which contains some 240 stone skulls with grinning faces, each with a slightly different gruesome expression (see pl. 10).[96]

The stone tzompantli and also the real skulls buried in the offering caches give testimony of the practice of human sacrifice and thus reveal indirectly the importance of warfare in Aztec society. They corroborate in general terms the evidence (obtained from historical sources) for the link between military conquests and the great human sacrifices taking place at the Templo Mayor that we analyzed at the beginning of this chapter. The offering caches also contain a multitude of objects that proceed from distant parts of the empire and, most probably, reached Tenochtitlan through tribute.

Another outstanding item among the offerings are hundreds of stone masks. Some of them are very simple in style and have been characterized as "Mezcala" style original to Guerrero. In Cámara II more than fifty such small stone masks were found, some of them bearing glyphs on their rear side (pls. 14, 16, 25, 42–45). It was originally thought that these glyphs might register the place of origin of these masks; however, a recent analysis points to the conclusion that they are funerary masks carrying the personal name of the dead.[97] Cámara II contains many more small stone idols and a beautiful small idol of Tlaloc made of greenstone.[98] The context of the offering is the cult of Tlaloc and it is located on the north side of the temple dedicated to this god.

Other individual stone masks seem to belong to a different context as, for example, the two precious masks that were found in Cache 82 on the south side of the temple. One is made of alabaster and is Mexica in style, while the other one is made of dark greenstone and its style is clearly Teotihuacan (i.e., dating from the Classic period!) (pl. 41). Another beautiful example of a Teotihuacan-style mask made of light greenstone was localized in Cache 20 (pl. 40). The archaeologists have dated it to A.D. 500. This offering belongs to Period IV and is situated at the point of union between the two pyramids at their rear side. It also contains the most famous piece found in the excavation, namely, a truly Olmec mask (pl. 39). Its material, dark green jade, seems to have come from the area located between the modern states of Puebla, Oaxaca, and Guerrero; it was dated to B.C. 800.[99] The same offering contains a great variety of other objects, including a so-called Xiuhtecuhtli, a sculpture of Tlaloc, numerous small idols, flint knives, decapitated skulls, a small alabaster head of a deer, a swordfish, tortoise shells, other kinds of shells, and an enormous quantity of small snails.

The different art styles reflected in a number of objects, particularly the stone masks, point to their specific geographic origin. Most probably the Aztecs acquired these objects by means of tribute. The Olmec mask and the two Teotihuacan masks additionally raise the perturbing question as to how far back the Aztecs had a historical consciousness. Apparently it reached as far back as Teotihuacan or even Olmec times. At any rate it seems that they buried these masks with the understanding that they were particularly valuable ancient objects that enhanced the magical power of the Great Temple.[100] "Antiquity" in this context seems to have been a highly appreciated value (pls. 46, 24). "Center" and "periphery" of the vast realm dominated by the Aztecs were symbolically represented in the offerings; antiquity and historical consciousness were other elements present. As I will argue in the following sections, however, these concepts do not seem to have had a primordially political significance; the offerings expressed, above all, a cosmovision, the delimitation of known space in terms of the observation of nature, and only indirectly reflected also political domination and tribute.

Offerings to Huitzilopochtli

It would seem logical to try to make a basic division between the offerings according to their location on Tlaloc's or Huitzilopochtli's side. A number of caches were situated precisely at the junction between the two pyramids, however, apparently containing elements relating to both deities. On the whole, a sharp distinction between caches dedicated exclusively to either of the two gods has not been observed thus far and, most probably, does not exist. In general terms, the principle of blending of opposites seems to have been at least as important as the distinction between Huitzilopochtli's and Tlaloc's symbolisms.

Among the offerings found on the south side, the following elements might relate in a specific way to Huitzilopochtli. Inside the shrine of the god on top of the pyramid, corresponding to Period II, and next to the sacrificial stone (techcatl), a ceramic vessel in the form of a dog was found. The dog was an animal related to the sun cult, and dogs were sacrificed in the month of Atemoztli, which corresponded to the winter solstice.[101] In the same context several stone vessels, one of alabaster and the other one of obsidian, were excavated; they contain cremated bones and apparently belong to the cult of deified dead rulers. Is it, perhaps, even possible to speak of reminiscences of an ancestor cult? On Huitzilopochtli's side two more ceramic funerary urns were found; both of them are beautifully worked in relief and depict two important deities, Tezcatlipoca and, possibly, Mixcoatl.[102]

Other offerings particularly related to Huitzilopochtli might have been bones of birds (no natural species of an eagle has been identified thus far in the excavation) and small golden bells. As we have stated above, the offerings of decapitated skulls, skulls worked as gruesome masks, sacrificial knives, and flint knives with faces, as well as beautifully worked stone masks (the Olmec one, the two Teotihuacan examples, an Aztec mask, etc.), probably maintain a special relation to Huitzilopochtli. We have also mentioned the possibility that the flint knife was the symbol of Cihuacoatl's son, (Huitzilopochtli?), and in this sense contained complex mythological connotations. Nevertheless, some of the above-mentioned objects were also found on Tlaloc's side in the context of the offerings dedicated to that god; therefore, warfare, human sacrifice, and tribute cannot be considered exclusively of Huitzilopochtli's domain.

Offerings to Tlaloc

The excavation reveals that by far the greatest amount of offerings were related to the cult of Tlaloc; they were found on either side of the twin pyramid. In the following pages we will explore some of the manifold dimensions of this cult and suggest that its symbolism went far beyond the presence of water and rain being inscribed within the wider context of the fertility cult. In this sense I conceive of the offerings as an indicator of the underlying religious ideology at the Templo Mayor. This analysis, in fact, suggests certain new perspectives in the interpretation of Aztec cosmovision and state religion.

The cult of Tlaloc at the Templo Mayor was a cult of human sacrifice. The slaying of human victims was not only related to warfare and to the cult of the sun but also formed an integral part of the water and fertility cult as well. The only ossuary of complete human skeletons excavated at the Templo Mayor is represented by more than thirty skulls and bones of small children buried together with splendid effigies of polychrome Tlalocs within Offertory Cache 48 on the northwest side of Tlaloc's pyramid (pls. 47, 15). One of the main ritual cycles dedicated to Tlaloc that had the purpose of conjuring the coming of the rains was precisely the cycle of child sacrifices that took place during the driest season of the year. The children represented the tlaloque, the servants of the god Tlaloc who were supposed to be dwarfs inhabiting the mountains from where they sent the rains and thunderstorms by hitting big barrels with sticks to produce the sound of thunder. Child sacrifices are not only frequently documented in the written sources from the eve of the Spanish Conquest but also constitute one of the earliest records of human sacrifice in the archaeological context of Mesoamerica.[103] It seems that they were already important at Teotihuacan, having been involved in the building of the Pyramid of the Sun.[104]

The offerings to Tlaloc may be classified, *a grosso modo*, as (1) representations of the god in vessels, sculptures, idols, and relief stones (pl. 50); (2) offerings of animals in sculptures and as natural species; and (3) offerings of certain symbolic objects such as jade beads, which were also specifically related to the god.

A great number of vessels with the effigy of Tlaloc have been excavated; they show different sizes and shapes and are made of stone or ceramic, and most of them show remains of polychromatic painting (pls. 49, 51). All of these vessels depict the characteristic large spectacle-like eyes and the fauces with the fangs, which present a combination of the serpent motif and the fangs of the jaguar. A careful study of the stylistic elements of this variety of vessels is needed. Besides, a great number of small stone idols also show the same typical traits of Tlaloc (pl. 48). Some can easily be identified, while in others the characteristic Tlaloc face is represented in such a stylized way that it is barely recognizable.

The Mountain Cult

For the analysis of these idols, it is necessary to take into account the following circumstances. In Aztec cosmovision, Tlaloc was not only a deity of water and the rains but was, above all, a mountain god. The multitude of tlaloque, which were the manifestation of the god in innumerable local forms, were identified with particular mountains of the landscape. In the Valley of Mexico all mountains had their own names, and cult was rendered to them at the end of the rainy season. The two prominent volcanoes, Popocatepetl and Iztac Cihuatl, as well as Mount Tlaloc to the southeast, were by far the most important deities, and specific festivals were celebrated in their honor. Certain other mountains beyond the valley were also included in Aztec cosmovision and are mentioned in the cult. The Aztecs further conceptualized a close relation between the mountains and the pulque gods, who were innumerable local patron deities such as the tlaloque. In the annual cycle of festivals, this close association could also be observed.

Considering these cosmological concepts, I think that certain small stone idols found in profuse quantities in the offering caches of the Templo Mayor are of particular interest (pls. 14, 16, 54, 55a–d).[105] I am referring to a class of idols that are generally made of rough greenstone and have a height of some fifteen to thirty centimeters. Their bodies are insinuated in an almost abstract way. The broader upper part is constituted by the head, while the slim and pointed lower part is formed by the roughly insinuated legs. In many of these sculptures the volume corresponding to the legs presents a deep vertical groove that produces a superficial division between the legs. In some cases the cut is deep, completely separating the two legs. The general impression evoked is that of an oval or tubular shape. In many of these idols the arms, joined to the body, are hardly traced, while in others they are crossed in front of the upper part of the body. The face shows in a few cases certain attributes of Tlaloc. The sculptures exhibit rests of black paint in combination with red, blue, or yellow colors (pls. 55a–d).

At their discovery, these sculptures were classified by the archaeologists from the

Templo Mayor project as "Guerrero or Mezcala style," and their origin through tribute was assumed.[106] I would like to express my doubts with respect to this premature
classification, however; the term "Mezcala style" in itself is rather vague and does not
denote clearly any specific time period. Since the traits of these idols are extremely
stylized, it is rather doubtful whether they necessarily indicate "Mezcala," that is a
local style from Guerrero, given the fact that similar idols are known from many other
parts of Mesoamerica, including the Zapotec and Mixtec regions of Oaxaca,[107] the
Tlapanecs of Guerrero,[108] and the Maya area of Guatemala and Chiapas. In some of
these groups the idol traits are documented archaeologically as well as ethnographically. The recent ethnographic information is particularly interesting with respect to
the functions of these idols. They form part of local Indian peasant religion in which
the pagan ceremonies take place mainly at mountains and caves that constitute a
sacred landscape around the communities where ethnic resistance was kept alive.

In 1930 L. Schultze-Jena studied in the highland Quiché town of Chichicastenango the use of such idols called *alxik* (little gods of destiny). They were related to
the *Tutek'aj*, a large stone idol situated on the summit of the ritually most important
mountain of the region. The diviner of the community used the small idols as inter-
mediaries in orations and offerings to the *Turuk'aj*. They were carefully wrapped in
a cloth and were kept in the house of the diviner where they received regular offerings. Schultze-Jena suggests that in former times some of these small stone idols were
considered *aj ixim*, "protector of the corn kernels," *aj choch*, "protector of the house,"
aj su'ts, "beings or lords of the clouds."[109] The same author reported in the 1930s the
use of similar idols for the Tlapanecs and Mixtecs living in the mountainous border
area between the modern states of Guerrero and Oaxaca. Their cult clearly relates to
the deities of rain, mountains, and the earth. At the summit of important mountains
such idols are invoked for rain and fertility. They receive offerings at a rudimentary
altar made of natural stones which is called "the House of Rain."[110]

Although a shift in the specific functions of these idols probably took place after the Spanish Conquest, nevertheless it is important to connect the archaeological
objects with recent ethnographic ones. The comparison between different areas of
Mesoamerica is also fundamental. A collection of ninety-one such anthropomorphic
sculptures from Guerrero preserved in the Museo Nacional de Antropología which
are very similar to the ones found at Templo Mayor were studied in 1961 by J. Alcina. In his detailed archaeological analysis, Alcina concluded that, most probably,
these idols represented tutelary deities that might have also been used as personal amulets, as their symbolism was closely connected to fertility, agriculture, and the earth.
Alcina also pointed to the basic similarity of the Guerrero sculptures with the penates
that are archaeologically known from the ancient Mixtecs and, by means of comparison with similar idols from other areas, concluded that they were inscribed within
a fertility cult that reached beyond the borders of ancient Guerrero, even beyond the
borders of ancient Mesoamerica.[111]

Andrés Ciudad Ruíz, in a recent study of similar idols excavated at a late Classic site near Totonicapan, Guatemala,[112] also relates these to the wider context of similar idols found in different parts of Mesoamerica since the pre-Classic period. In the highland Guatemala Quiché area, such small stone or clay idols with extremely stylized traits were called *camahuiles* and were found in profuse quantities at sites dating from the end of the pre-Classic to the late post-Classic period. There also exist numerous ethnographic examples, as the reference to Schultze-Jena shows. Ancient Oaxaca is another region where the cult of small figurines is particularly well documented. At Monte Alban they were found inside tombs and funerary sites dating from Period III throughout Period V; in the last horizon they were known as *penates* and associated with the Mixteca-Puebla style. Ciudad points out that the so-called Mezcala style figurines from Guerrero form only one local variety of this larger group of idols found over a wide area of central and southern Mesoamerica.

With respect to the functions of these small stylized idols, Ciudad proposes that they were related to the cult of the dead, of ancestors and lineages, although he does not exclude their use as tutelary gods or amulets within the cult of fertility and agriculture, as suggested by other authors. Their rather undifferentiated nature permitted their use in multiple aspects of rituals at the peasant level as well as in urban centers.

Finally, I would like to mention here the translation given for the Quiché term of these small idols, camahuil (or *kabavil*), as "deity" or "idol."[113] The name used in Chichicastenango, alxik (mentioned a few paragraphs above) has been translated as "little gods of destiny,"[114] while closely related terms such as *ah-ilix* were rendered as "guardian, protector,"[115] and *alaxic* as "lineage."[116] These terms are interesting in comparison to the names of the small idols used in Aztec cult (see below, *tepictoton* or *tecuacuiltin* below this same page).

I have quoted such detailed comparative material from other parts of Mesoamerica and different time periods because it is my opinion that the oval-shaped stylized idols found at the Templo Mayor should be understood in this perspective. The above-mentioned comparative data—which surely could be complemented by additional information—were not taken into account in what I consider a premature classification of these idols as Mezcala style. It seems that they belong to a type of small sculpture common in many parts of ancient Mesoamerica that was related to the cult of ancestors, tutelary gods, and the earth and fertility in general. The use of these idols had ancient roots in the Mesoamerican past. Although this cult was important, above all, on the community and family levels, it also appears at major urban ceremonial centers. Unfortunately, the exact archaeological extraction of the majority of small idols reviewed above is unknown.[117]

The Templo Mayor is one of the few sites where such idols have been excavated in their original setting. There, these idols were found in a context totally dedicated to the cult of Tlaloc, that is, to the rains, the sea, the mountains, and the earth. We shall analyze this symbolism in greater detail in the following pages. The oval-shaped form and the small, handy size of these sculptures strongly suggest their use in certain ritual functions. Some of them bear an inscription with a glyph on their backs, which might indicate their origin from specific communities. They may have reached Tenochtitlan through tribute; however, more important than their possible origin through tribute seems to have been their ritual function. In this sense, I propose the hypothesis that these idols embodied particular localities, such as villages or mountains. In terms of Aztec cult, this means that they represented a kind of tlaloque, or local spirits of mountains or places. Because their body features are so abstract, one might think that they might have been wrapped in paper garments and insignia corresponding to the rain gods.

One is also reminded of the two Aztec festivals of *Tepeilhuitl* and *Atemoztli*, corresponding to October and December, respectively, when miniature images were made of all the mountains of the Valley of Mexico. We have referred to these ceremonies earlier (section on Cosmovision and the observation of nature). These idols were called *tepictoton* (sculptured figurines; defined earlier) or *ixiptla tepetl* (images of the mountains).[118] Bernardino de Sahagún relates that during Tepeilhuitl "they celebrated feasts in honor of the eminent mountains which existed in all those places of New Spain where the clouds engendered; they made an image in human form of each one of them."[119] These images were formed of *tzoalli*, a dough consisting of maize mixed with other seeds and honey, however; thus the tepictoton can be taken only as an analogy. The small stone idols of the Templo Mayor belong to a whole series of miniature images that were used in the mountain cult.

In this respect, information given by Diego Durán is highly illuminating. Inside the Tlillan, the dark temple dedicated to Cihuacoatl which was situated right next to Huitzilopochtli's pyramid, a multitude of small and larger idols were placed along the walls. Just as in Tlaloc's sanctuary high up on Mount Tlaloc, these idols were representations of mountains. They were called *tecuacuiltin* (sculptured images, statues) and were dressed in paper garments and insignia decorated with liquid rubber.

> When they decided to celebrate any particular feast to these small idols, . . . for it was their day, or because they needed their help, then they fetched them from there [the Tlillan] and carried them in a procession to the mountain or cave which bore their name, and there . . . they brought them their ordinary sacrifices and offerings, invoking that mountain that it should favor them in [their needs]. . . , because of lack of water, a plague or famine, or a future warfare. Having finished the ceremony, they immediately took [the idols] back to the temple and placed them where they usually stood.[120]

It should be noted that the Tlillan or temple to which these small mountain idols belonged, was the shrine of the earth goddess Cihuacoatl and that its architecture was the imitation of a dark cave. Tlillan, in fact, means "the place of blackness," or the "dark place." A strong link is thus established between the rain and mountain gods and the earth goddess Cihuacoatl, who herself figures among the images that were formed of all the mountains of the Valley of Mexico.[121]

Another noteworthy point in this context refers to the Nahuatl term for village or community. It was regarded as *altepetl*, which means "mountain of water" or "mountain filled with water," and the corresponding glyph was, in fact, a mountain with its fauces or a cave on its lower part.[122] Mountains and water symbolized natural forces considered necessary for the life of the community. Since pre-Classic times the mountains were represented as maintaining a special relation to human settlements, and modern ethnographic data from traditional Indian areas still reveal abundantly this link of the mountain as protector and place of origin with respect to the community. These concepts point to the wider context of Aztec cosmovision. As we have seen before, there existed a close association between the springs, the lakes, and the mountains. The clouds gathered around the mountain peaks, a phenomenon that produced thunderstorms and rains. Bernardino de Sahagún relates that the Aztecs conceived of space underneath the earth full of water; these waters proceeded from the Tlalocan, the paradise of the rain god, and came out through springs to form the rivers, the lakes, and the sea. The mountains had the function to retain the waters, such as

> big vessels or mansions filled with water; and it might happen that they break . . . then the water which they enclosed, would pour out and would inundate the earth; for this reason they used to call the villages where the people lived, *altepetl* which means "mountain of water" or "mountain full of water."[123]

A correct understanding of the term *altepetl* is very important since this sociopolitical unit (the village) was situated within the realm of cosmovision, forming part of the cosmic order, the same as the mountains, caves, springs, or the sea. The Aztecs integrated cosmic and human order ideologically into one single construct, and both were considered equally vulnerable to the precarious balance of forces threatening with disaster. As López Austin has stated: "The pyramids expressed symbolically the concept of *altepetl*, or community. It was the mountains that, in their interior, retained water with its vital importance for humanity."[124] According to Van Zantwijk, finally, "the largest pyramidal temple also expressed the religious, sacerdotal vision of the ordering of the universe."[125]

The symbolism of the Templo Mayor as a sacred mountain seems to fall within the same context. The *Cronica Mexicayotl* relates that Tenochtitlan was founded over two rocks that arose above two caves filled with water. The one looking toward the east contained the *tleatl* (water of fire) and *atlatlayan* (water of conflagration); the one facing north contained the *matlalatl* (blue water) and *toxpalatl* (yellow water?), referring to symbolic colors and specific qualities of these primordial waters.[126] In those waters resided, according to Sahagún,[127] "the father and mother of the gods," namely,

93

Huehueteotl, the ancient god of fire and lord of time who occupied the center of the earth. The Mexica built their Great Temple precisely at that place, considered the axis mundi or center of the universe.[128] The temple itself was a sacred mountain covering the subterranean waters like a cave. Within Sahagún's list of the seventy-eight "buildings" or places belonging to the precinct of the Templo Mayor, four sacred springs or wells are mentioned: *Tlilapan*, "place of black water," *Tezcaapan*, place of the water of the mirror," *Coaapan*, "place of the serpent water," and *tozpalatl*, "yellow waters."[129] The exact location of these springs is not indicated. One natural spring that issued near the site of the pre-Hispanic temple was found to be still flowing in 1900, when Batres excavated the area behind the Cathedral.[130]

In this context one should remember that, in fact, the Templo Mayor, as well as the entire island of Tenochtitlan, was very close to the groundwater. Even today the groundwater appears in certain parts of the archaeological site and has made it impossible to dig further below the phreatic level. Naturally, Tenochtitlán, which was situated on an island, was also surrounded by the waters of the lake, in analogy to the disk floating on the sea, which was the Aztec image of the earth. The tradition of building the main temple and axis mundi on top of a sacred cave from which a spring issued seems also to have older antecedents and might date back at least to Classic period Teotihuacan.[131]

The offerings demonstrate that this vision of space—the cult of the mountains, caves, and water—materialized at the Templo Mayor. The importance of this cult in relation to Tlaloc emerges as an aspect of the god that had been known before; however, our sixteenth-century sources do not stress it to the extent that it is visible in the material remains. These traits connect the god with other deities such as *Tepeyollotl* (The Heart of the Mountain), who was visualized in the form of a jaguar. The jaguar was an important religious symbol in Mesoamerica since Olmec times. It is Mexico's fiercest animal and dwells in the tropical rain forest. Since ancient times it was connected to the earth, the rains, and to the night. The starry night was compared to the skin of that animal. The jaguar was also a symbol of physical strength and ultimately of political power. As E. Wolf has pointed out very aptly, "in the complex symbolical language [of Mesoamerica], caves and mountains also denote settlements and towns, . . . and the jaguar [became] a symbol of domination, not only over the sacred orifices of the earth but also over [man].[132]

Several skulls and a complete skeleton of a jaguar were found in several offering caches dedicated to Tlaloc. In the case of the skeleton discovered in Cámara II, its skull carries an egg-shaped jade stone in its mouth (pls. 19, 20). Greenstone and jade were symbols as ancient as the jaguar and denoted the heart as the seat of life and regeneration. They were specifically related to the rain gods. Another skull of a jaguar in Cámara III carries a silex knife in its jaws, thus connecting the animal with the complex of human sacrifice.

Let us return to the symbolism of the center and the sacred mountain. Another class of important offerings revealed in the excavation are rather large idols of a seated god, represented in the naturalistic form of an old man whose face is characterized by a wise and somewhat ironic smile and who wears a headdress of two horns (pls. 12, 29, 30). More than a dozen of these strange figures have been discovered in offering caches on Tlaloc's side as well as Huitzilopochtli's side of the pyramid. These figures were prematurely identified as Xiuhtecuhtli-Huehueteotl, the ancient fire god and lord of time. Several authors have pointed out other possibilities of interpretation. Recently, Debra Nagao has argued that these figures represented Ometeotl-Tonacatecuhtli, the lord of duality and sustenance who thus would have maintained a specific relation to the offerings.[133] Henry B. Nicholson has identified these idols with Tepeyollotl, the above-mentioned jaguar god related to mountains, caves, and the night.[134] Eduard Seler, however, proposed that this enigmatic old deity may have belonged to the mountain and pulque gods.[135]

The fact that these figures have only two teeth was taken as an indication of old age; however, these teeth might also be interpreted as fangs and could thus be considered as attributes of Tlaloc. Another characteristic of these idols is the *tlaquechpanyotl*, a kind of fan they wear at the nape of the neck. These fans were made of amate (bark paper) and were decorated with drops of liquid rubber. They were one of the most typical attributes of the rain gods. The Chac Mool in front of Tlaloc's shrine also wears such a tlaquechpanyotl (pl. 52), and it is depicted on several ceramic vessels representing Tlaloc at the Templo Mayor. Several figures of the same enigmatic old deity were discovered previously, in October 1900, during the excavation by L. Batres at the Calle de las Escalerillas, right next to the present site, and were analyzed by Seler in his highly suggestive study of these findings.[136] On the basis of their attributes (the tlaquechpanyotl and the fangs), Seler identified these figures as mountain gods, or tlaloque.[137] He further claimed that the two horns that stick out from the forehead were another attribute of the rain gods. Among the children sacrificed to Tlaloc during I Atlcahualo, they selected those who had two cowlicks of hair.[138] Seler suggested that these horns might have symbolized the mountain peaks. In the same exhaustive study he discussed a series of other objects found together with these figures in the October 1900 excavation: sacrificial knives made of flint and obsidian, shell trumpets, shells, an enormous amount of jade beads, small relief plates of greenstone representing water deities and serpents, small idols made of copal, and skulls of children, some of which are painted with black color. All these objects clearly relate to the cult of Tlaloc. It is interesting to note that the findings behind the Zócalo of Mexico City gave already at the beginning of this century quite a representative sample of the main objects deposited in the offerings, and their analysis thus is truly complementary to the present excavation.

Seler also included in his study several idols made of copal; these constitute another class of interesting offerings. The traits of these small idols are highly stylized; their only clearly visible attribute is the large fan (tlaquechpanyotl) worn at the nape of the neck. The use of copal idols in Aztec ritual is confirmed by the sixteenth-century written sources. Bernardino de Sahagún describes that during the rites of *VI Etzalcualiztli*, Tlaloc's main festival at the beginning of the rainy season, the priests burned such idols called *copalteteo* or *ulteteo* (gods made of copal, or gods made of liquid rubber).[139]

We may thus conclude that in the context of the offerings of Templo Mayor a variety of small idols have come to light that were all related to the cult of the rain god. These idols were generally made of greenstone, but some also consisted of copal. They either represented the god Tlaloc characterized by the iconography of his face, or they wore certain attributes that identified them as tlaloque. The most important of these attributes was the tlaquechpanyotl. We have taken particular interest in analyzing the oval-shaped idols with stylized traits, which were the most numerous of all. We proposed the hypothesis that these idols embodied specific places and communities representing local spirits conjuring space, mountains, and water. The rather large and important figure of the old seated god with the headdress of two horns may have been connected specifically with the "heart of the sacred mountain" that was the Templo Mayor. According to Duran, there existed a close relationship between these mountain idols and the goddess Cihuacoatl in whose dark temple, the Tlillan—situated right next to Huitzilopochtli's pyramid—they guarded images of all the major mountains of the Valley of Mexico. The latter were used on certain dates in rituals dedicated to these mountains. Inside the sanctuary at the summit of Mount Tlaloc they also kept a multitude of such small mountain images. The rich symbolism of this variety of small stone idols found in the caches at the Templo Mayor needs to be investigated with greater detail in the future. These idols also should be compared to other such idols found in offerings at other temples and sacred places of the Valley of Mexico. These sacred places were primarily mountain shrines, caves, springs, and places at the shore or inside the lake.[140] There is abundant archaeological documentation of this,[141] which must be analyzed systematically with respect to the geography and ecology of the Valley of Mexico.

The cult of mountains, caves, and water is also interesting from other points of view. It is not only one of the most ancient cults that can be traced back to Classic and even pre-Classic times,[142] but it is also the popular cult, which, together with the one of maize and fertility, has survived most stongly in Indian peasant religion to the present day. The former is documented by archaeological data, especially from the great metropolis of Teotihuacan,[143] while the latter can be studied through abundant ethnographic evidence from traditional Indian peasant regions such as Guatemala, highland Chiapas, Oaxaca, the Sierra de Puebla (Nahuas and Totonacs), the Nahuas from Veracruz, or the Nahua and Tlapanec areas in northeastern Guerrero.[144] Some of these popular rites can still be observed in the southern part of the Valley of Mexico and adjoining Morelos, in the vicinity of the great volcanoes.[145] These data reveal a common background of beliefs that is really striking and must go back to an ancient pan-Mesoamerican heritage. Its survival is due to the fact that it has formed, together with the cult of maize and fertility, the nucleus of Indian peasant religion throughout the colonial period and up to the present.

Without elaborating further on this point, I would like to stress that the interpretation of the offerings revealed to me these links of Templo Mayor with such widespread concepts of ancient Mesoamerican religion as the sacralization of mountains, caves, and water. This cosmovision was inspired by and received a continuous reinforcement from the natural environment of Mesoamerica, a volcanic territory with conspicuous mountain peaks where the rain-bringing clouds assemble. Clouds and fog also gather in the steep valleys and canyons of the broken landscape. Caves are another particularly frequent feature of this country; mountains bedecked with caves from which springs issue recall, indeed, images recorded in pre-Hispanic rock paintings, murals, and codices, whose roots go back at least as far as Teotihuacan.

The close association of the Aztec god Tlaloc to mountains as reflected in ritual is further corroborated by the pages of the *Codex Borbonicus* referring to the yearly cycle of festivals. According to Nowotny,[146] this valuable early colonial codex, which reflects an almost purely pre-Hispanic pictographic tradition, constituted a manual for the cult of a specific temple located in the Valley of Mexico. As a manual, the codex selects those ceremonies that took place precisely at this temple, while it neglects others that were of no particular interest for this purpose. These ceremonies show an almost exclusive dedication to the cult of rain, the mountains, and maize. The main deities represented are Tlaloc, Cinteotl, Chicomecoatl, and Cihuacoatl, and the central festival of the manuscript is *Ochpaniztli* as the festival of maize.

The paintings in the Borbonicus for the months of *III Tozoztontli, IV Huey tozoztli, XIII Tepeilhuitl,* and *XVI Atemoztli*—those related to the cult of Tlaloc— show the god with his characteristic attire placed inside a temple situated atop a mountain. This mountain with Tlaloc's temple dominates all the respective pages; it must have been very important and was used as a symbol for the whole cluster of ideas pertaining to the cult of rain and mountains in Aztec ritual (child sacrifices, certain types of offering, the festivals of the tepictoton, etc.).[147]

The *Codex Borbonicus* further reflects another important association of ritual concepts: the Tlaloc imaginary is intimately connected to the cult of maize and agricultural fertility, with the latter expressed by elaborately painted offerings of maize cobs. This linking of the two cults is greatest during the feast of XI Ochpaniztli, where the codex depicts the sacrifice of the maize goddess Chicomecoatl amid a lavish symbolism of maize and fertility, in the presence of the rain gods of the four colors, placed in the four world directions.[148]

In his commentary to the manuscript, Nowotny stressed the fact that Tlaloc is represented with the image of the mountain, but he does not offer any explanation of its meaning.[149] This symbolism becomes coherent once we understand that the mountain cult was an essential aspect of the cult of Tlaloc. Thus the *Codex Borbonicus* provides the most important documentary support to corroborate the interpretation of the role played by the mountains in cosmovision as well as Aztec ritual; it also helps us to understand the presence of the symbolism of mountains in the excavation of the Templo Mayor.

The Cult of Agriculture and Maize

There also was a close connection between Tlaloc as a mountain deity and the popular cult of agriculture and fertility. We have noted that such a relationship is expressed in the pictographs of the *Codex Borbonicus*. The explanation for this circumstance is provided by a myth according to which the tlaloque (or rather the Tlaloque of the four cardinal directions that appear in the *Codex Borbonicus*?)[150] were considered to be the "original owners" of maize and all food plants. Men gained access to their staple food through the cult of Tlaloc. Maize, other plants, and riches were kept in caves inside the mountains.[151]

The *Historia de los Reynos de Culhuacan y México* preserves two myths that explain how men acquired maize from the Tlaloque. According to the first myth,[152] Nanahuatl stole the white, purple, yellow, and red maize from the Tlaloque (the blue, white, yellow, and red Tlaloque), together with beans, amaranth, and sage, that is, all the important food staples. By means of the lightning, Nanahuatl split up the *Tonacatepetl*,[153] where all crops were locked up, and he stole them.[154] The analysis of these myths leads us to the following conclusion. While Huitzilopochtli's pyramid at the Templo Mayor was the Coatepetl—the Serpent Mountain, where according to myth the miraculous birth of Huitzilopochtli took place—Tlaloc's pyramid was the Tonacatepetl, the Mountain of Sustenance, which was mythically related to water and maize; it contained the ritual access to human sustenance.[155]

In this sense, Nagao's identification of the strange seated idols with the headdress of two horns, as Tonacatecuhtli[156] fits very well into the context of this interpretation. His presence would thus stress the fact that Templo Mayor was Coatepetl as well as Tonacatepetl, where resided Tonacatecuhtli, "the Lord of Sustenance."

The second myth related in the *Historia de los Reynos*[157] establishes a connection between the domain of the Tlaloque over maize and the Toltec period. Because of the arrogance of the last Toltec king, Huemac, the Tlaloque withdrew their "precious stones, their quetzal plumes" (i.e., maize) during a period of four years, which caused a great starvation in Tula and led to the downfall of Toltec power. This myth presents the Mexica—who happened to be present at these events taking place at the springs of Chapultepec—as the legitimate successors of the Toltecs. The transition of political power is symbolized by the acquisition of maize, which the rain gods grant at free will. This mythical account is purely fictitious, and there is no direct line of continuity from the Toltec empire to the Aztec state; nevertheless, it reflects the Mexica pretension to appear as the guardians of Toltec cultural heritage. The original owners of man's sustenance were the rain and mountain gods, the ancient patrons of agriculture.[158]

The Presence of the Sea

The next step of our analysis leads us to investigate several other classes of objects contained in the offering caches, which adds further aspects to the symbolism of Tlaloc at the Templo Mayor. These aspects are closely linked to Tlaloc's role as mountain deity and owner of agriculture, as we shall argue below. These offerings are of two basic types. Type A includes small sculptures of fish, snails, snakes, other reptiles, and insects made of common stone, semiprecious stone, jade, obsidian, or mother-of-pearl (pl. 26). These masterpieces of Aztec sculptorial art include a mother-of-pearl necklace composed of more than 180 pieces representing fish, frogs, shells, and serpents (pl. 28). It was found in Cámara II and might have been an adornment worn by a high priest officiating at rain ceremonies. To these offerings also belong two miniature boats (pl. 27). One of these boats contained miniature fishing implements, as well as three fish of mother-of-pearl worked in such a realistic and skillful way that the fish appear to be floating on the water. The texture of the mother of pearl and the reflection of light on the body of the fish insinuate movement of water. This small set of sculptures constitutes one of the most outstanding pieces of art discovered in the excavation.

In addition to these small sculptures denoting the cult of water, the offertory caches contain type B: an enormous variety of real animal remains, such as fish, swordfish, shark teeth, sea urchin, tortoise, crocodiles, conch shells, snails, corals, and a species called *brain coral* (pls. 13, 17, 18, 33–38). This class of offerings is particularly noteworthy and enigmatic; in statistical terms, it probably makes up the greatest proportion of offerings. From the outset of the excavation, I was intrigued by the peculiar presence of these natural remains, and largely to explain these facts, I undertook the present investigation. The question arises as to why the Aztecs accumulated these natural species at the Templo Mayor such as in a museum of natural history. Usually they form different layers in the stone caches: the lowest level is generally formed by sand brought from the sea, and several layers of animals were placed on top, maintaining a certain orientation, mostly toward the east or the west.[159] The objects were not buried in the caches in a casual way but were placed there according to certain basic cosmological concepts.

These enigmatic natural species belonged to the context of the cult of fertility and water; however, they also convey a *notion of space*. In this respect one circumstance is highly significant: it is the *presence of the sea* in the offerings of Templo Mayor. One might have expected that the majority of these animals came from the immediate natural environment—the abundant fauna living in the lakes of the Valley of Mexico. This is not the case, however; the vast majority of them are to be classified zoologically as *marine fauna* that had to be transported to Tenochtitlan over long distances either from the Gulf or Pacific coast. Their exact geographic origin can be determined and is currently being studied by biologists collaborating in the Templo Mayor project.[160] What was the deeper symbolical significance of this strong presence of the sea at the Great Temple?

The natural species as well as the small stone idols (some with place glyphs on their backs) were brought to Tenochtitlan from distant parts of the Aztec empire. The majority of caches containing these objects belong to Period IVb. In the previous building periods only a few offerings were discovered.[161] Their increase during Period IVb may, in fact, be correlated with the expansion of the Aztec empire under Moctezuma I and his successor Axayacatl, who supposedly undertook the enlargements of the frontal platform and facade corresponding to Period IVb.

Almost certainly these numerous offerings from faraway places reached Tenochtitlan through tribute. In the case of the stone objects, the idols might have been brought from the provinces of the Aztec empire (e.g., from Guerrero), although it is also possible that the stone was brought as raw material and was worked by artists in Tenochtitlán. The fact that some of the objects seem to be of foreign origin, however, does not in itself reveal the importance of tribute at the Templo Mayor, nor does it show any specific relation to the worship of Huitzilopochtli; instead, it denotes only the *manner of their possible acquisition*. Some objects could also have come to Tenochtitlan by exchange or long distance trade, which was also closely related to royal power. Naturally, as a consequence of the expansion of their empire, the Mexica were proud to make offerings of exotic objects to which they had gained access by means of imperial domination. Yet, such luxury goods were employed more frequently in the grand ritual dramas—in ostentatious ceremonies, dances, and banquets forming part of the monthly festivals—than in the context of the offerings related to the temple structure.[162] There is no indication that the Templo Mayor offerings provide a representative sample of objects and stylistic elements from all provinces conquered by the Triple Alliance. Some of the objects buried in the temple rather seem to denote the existence of a consciousness of a cultural and historical tradition preceding the Azecs (e.g., the Olmec mask, several Teotihuacan masks, the Toltec braziers, Mixtec and Gulf coast ceramics, etc.).

In contrast to these precious objects of antiquity, the natural species from the Gulf and Pacific coasts conveyed, above all, *a vision of space*. This notion of territoriality was an adequate expression of the limits of the political domain the Aztec empire had reached by expanding toward the tropical lowlands of both shores. It thus reveals the intrinsic dialectics of "center" and "periphery" within the realm of the empire and gives testimony of the presence of the periphery at the capital.[163] As we indicated in the Introduction to this volume, the analysis of center and periphery in the Templo Mayor offerings points to additional elements beyond the notion of socially delimited space. The enigmatic presence of the sea cannot be explained only in terms of political history but it evokes certain general aspects of Aztec cosmovision that were derived from the observation of nature.

Within the symbolism of personifying natural elements there existed a close association between the rains, thunderstorms, mountains, rivers, springs, and lakes, *as well as the sea*. The earth was called *Cemanahuac*, "the place surrounded by water," and was conceived of as a disk or a huge alligator (*cipactli*) floating on the waters. These waters proceeded from Tlalocan, the paradise of the rain god, and came forth through springs to form the rivers, the lakes, and the sea. Tlalocan was, in a way, the conceptualization of space underneath the earth full of water which connected the mountains with the sea. As Sahagún indicates, the ancient inhabitants of Mexico believed that all the rivers proceeded from a place called Tlalocan: "And they said that the mountains were only magic places, with earth, with rock on the surface; that they were only like *ollas* or like houses; that they were filled with the water which was there."[164] Not only do the rivers spring from the mountains, but

> The sea enters within the land, through its veins and channels; [it] penetrates below the [surface of the] earth and [inside] the mountains; and wheresoever it finds its path to come out, it issues from the roots of the mountains or the valleys of the earth; . . . in the way that the big rivers proceed from the sea through secret subterranean channels below the earth.[165]

Large and deep caves were a particularly apt entrance to Tlalocan and were thought to have a subterranean communication to the sea.[166]

The offerings of marine animals thus seem to suggest that by the magic of analogy, the Aztecs wanted to conjure the presence of the sea at the Templo Mayor. The sea was a symbol of *absolute fertility embodied in water*—the Nahuatl term for it was *huey atl* (the "big water," or water in its absolute form).[167] At the same time the sea was the necessary counterpart and complement to the conception of the earth and the sky. Another term for the sea was *ilhuica atl*,[168] which means literally "the heavenly water" or "the water of the sky" (*ilhuicatl*, sky; *atl*, water), that is, the place where sky and the earth meet. Sahagún explains these concepts evocatively by saying that ilhuica atl means

> water that blended with the sky because the ancient inhabitants of this land thought that the sky merged with the water in the sea, as if it were a house where water is the walls and the sky is above them, and therefore they called the sea *ihuica atl* as if saying "water that merged with the sky."[169]

101

In this passage the Spanish version of Sahagún is richer in images than the Nahuatl original, which merely states that ilhuica atl meant "water that reaches the heavens" because it stretched extending to the sky.[170] The earth was surrounded by the waters of the sea; at its extremes, this water was elevated to form the walls on which the sky rested. According to the *Codex Vaticano Latino*, the waters of the sea surrounded like walls the four inferior planes of the sky and formed a support for the nine upper levels.[171]

The same association of ideas is explained in more detail by the *Histoyre du Mechique*, which describes the formation of the earth's surface as the tearing apart of the goddess Tlaltecuhtli, a monstrous being with eyes and predacious mouths at her joints, who floated in a great primordial sea. From parts of her body, hills and valleys, trees and plants were created. Her eyes became springs and caves, and her mouth, rivers and large caverns. While one-half of the monster was transformed into the earth, from the other half the sky was created.[172] This passage from the *Histoyre du Mechique* is extremely important; it appears to be a simplified reference to a much more complex mythical notion. In the concluding remarks of this study we shall return to this image of an opposition and dialectical unity of the earth, the sky, and the sea.

Tlaloc-Tlaltecuhtli-Cihuacoatl-Coyolxauhqui

This leads us to consider a final important aspect of the cult of Tlaloc and to interpret in the archaeological findings those representations where the god appears as Tlaltecuhtli (earth lord) in the crouching earth-monster position with eagle claws and skulls adorning his knees and elbows; he also carries skulls in his hands (pl. 56). Some eight relief stones of this type were found in the excavation,[173] and several more date from previous findings.[174] Several other relief stones from the Templo Mayor portray similar iconographic motifs (pl. 57).

These representations demonstrate that there existed a strong link between Tlaloc and the earth, a circumstance that we have mentioned before with respect to the two aspects of the god derived from Teotihuacan. According to Pasztory, "Tlaloc B" of Teotihuacan was a terrestrial deity linked to the underworld, to caves, darkness, the night, the "night sun," and the jaguar. Precisely these aspects are related to the correct translation of the god's name. Tlaloc, or rather Tlalloc, means "he who has the quality of earth," "he who is made of earth," or "he who is the embodiment of the earth," as Thelma Sullivan has shown in an illuminating analysis of the etymology of the name in relation to the functions of the god.[175] She concluded that Tlaloc was essentially an earth god or may have originally had a dual nature representing earth and water. The earth monster Tlalteotl or Tlaltecuhtli from which the earth's surface and the sky were created also had a dual nature.[176]

The significance of the Tlaltecuhtli representations recently discovered at the Templo Mayor is confirmed by the fact that similar reliefs also form the base of a number of important sculptures belonging within the context of the Great Temple that were found on previous occasions in the vicinity of the precinct.[177] These include the two famous monumental sculptures of the Coatlicue and Yollotlicue exhibited in the *Sala Mexica* of the National Museum of Anthropology (pl. 31). As several authors have noted,[178] Coatlicue, "she with the serpent skirt" and mother of Huitzilopochtli, according to the myth of his miraculous birth, is not the only possible identification for this colossal statue, which in itself constitutes an inventory of philosophical concepts cast into stone. Her identification as Coatlicue is an example of the many preconceived interpretations in Aztec religion that once established are repeated uncritically by generations of scholars. The figure with death and serpent attributes, claws, and fangs may rather represent the voracious earth itself, the earth monster that we find portrayed on so many other sculptures and reliefs.

The mother and earth goddess who symbolizes these destructive as well as regenerative forces of the earth was Cihuacoatl, the same goddess who, according to the historical sources, played such an important role at the Templo Mayor; she was also closely related to Huitzilopochtli's temple service. The specifically Aztec mother goddess Coatlicue seems to have been only another aspect of the more ancient earth mother *Cihuacoatl* ("Woman Serpent"). We have made numerous references in this study to the importance of the cult of this goddess. Her linkage to Tlaloc is not commonly recognized, although we have mentioned the fact that in her dark temple, the Tlillan, the mountain images were kept. She herself figured among the deified mountains represented during the ceremonies of Tepeilhuitl, and certain data indicate that she might have been identified with the Iztac Cihuatl ("White Woman"), the prominent volcano in the southern lake region from where her cult was introduced into the Mexica pantheon.[179] In this context an ethnographic parallel from the modern Quiché of Momostenango, Guatemala, is highly illuminating to prove the depth of the common historical background of Mesoamerican cosmovision from the central Mexican highlands to the Maya area. According to Barbara Tedlock, thanksgiving for the harvest is offered to the earth deity, "mountains-plains" (*Juyubtak'aj*) or the "world" (*mundo*), in December.[180] These modern Quiché harvest ceremonies are linked to the mountain gods as aspects of the earth deity, in a similar way as the Mexica attributed harvest to the tlaloque. The latter were related to the ancient earth goddess Cihuacoatl-Ilamatecuhtli. Among the Quiché, the earth deity's very name, "Mountain-Plains," proves that there exists the same association of cosmological concepts as among the Aztecs.

While rain, mountains, and the earth were closely connected to the seasons and to agriculture in Aztec cosmovision, the Tlaltecuhtli reliefs lead us to consider still broader philosophical concepts. The link between Tlaloc as earth monster and Cihuacoatl becomes evident on the basis of the above-mentioned Tlaltecuhtli representations, which formed such an essential part of the iconography of Templo Mayor. The *Histoyre du Mechique* confirms that the earth monster Tlaltecuhtli and Cihuacoatl really were the same deity. After relating the creation of the earth, the source states that "this goddess [i.e., the earth] sometimes cried out during the night, desiring to eat human hearts, and it did not want to calm down as long as they did not give them [the hearts] to her nor did she want to bear fruit if she was not irrigated with human blood."[181] Other sources discuss in very similar terms the goddess Cihuacoatl, who was a mother goddess related not only to fertility but also to warfare and human sacrifice.[182]

Both Tlaloc and Cihuacoatl were deities of ancient Toltec affiliation. Cihuacoatl was the patroness of Culhuacán, the community with a Toltec dynasty through which the rulers of Tenochtitlán claimed descent. In this sense it seems logical that certain traditions identified Cihuacoatl as the spouse of Tlaloc. Both were considered as ugly and very old. Further, Tlaloc-Tlaltecuhtli and Cihuacoatl-Coatlicue-Ilamatecuhtli, as ancient deities or lords of the underworld,[183] appear to have been the parents of Huitzilopochtli.[184]

Several other iconographic elements at Templo Mayor establish a special relationship to the earth. The so-called greenstone goddess, one of the major sculptures found among the offerings (Cámara V), was identified by Pasztory as a death goddess with fertility aspects.[185] The sculpture is adorned by two glyphs: 2 Tochtli, the symbol of the pulque gods, links her to the fertility deities; the second glyph, 1 Tochtli, is the date of the creation of the earth.[186] The same 1 Tochtli date appears on several Tlaltecuhtli (Tlaloc as earth monster) representations at the base of monuments,[187] as well as on the base of the colossal diorite Coyolxauhqui head. For a number of reasons that cannot be discussed here in detail, Coyolxauhqui seems to be another deity whose customary interpretation (derived from the myth of the birth of Huitzilopochtli) might be disputed on the basis of her iconography at the Templo Mayor. The dismembered female body represented on the famous relief stone does not depict a young woman, as would be the case of Huitzilopochtli's sister, but it shows the wrinkles on the abdomen that characterize mature women who have already given birth. She embodied a Cihuateotl, a woman who had died in childbirth and had become converted into a goddess, a monstrous deity threatening men.[188] Since the same goddesses sometimes appear interchangeably as mothers, wives, and daughters in Aztec religion, one might conclude that from one point of view Coyolxauhqui and Coatlicue-Cihuacoatl are the same. In this respect, the conclusions reached by Pasztory on the iconography of the relief stone are highly suggestive. She points out that the fanged monstrous masks that Coyolxauhqui has at her feet, knees, and elbows are characteristic of earth monster images, that "their presence relates Coyolxauhqui to those emblems of darkness and chaos," and that "indeed, the entire design of the body appears to be an asymmetrical profile representation of an earth monster" (pl. 1).[189] E. Calnek suggested that the monument, which was located at the base of Huitzilopochtli's stairway and did not have any counterpart on Tlaloc's side, may have marked the conceptual center of Tenochtitlan, the point of convergence of conquest and sacrifice.[190] Might it possibly denote another aspect of the earth monster, related to both Cihuacoatl and

Tlaloc-Tlaltecuhtli, which received the human victims that were thrown down from the summit of the pyramid and was at the same time the symbolical center of the temple precinct? In the same sense, M. Graulich also interprets the monumental relief stone as an altar dedicated to the earth where the latter received its nourishment (*tlaquaian*, i.e., human sacrifices). These sacrifices of captives were intended not only to guarantee the movement of the sun but also to maintain the eternal duality between sun and earth, day and night, and dry season (*tlachinolli*) and rainy season (*atl*). Thus it was necessary to conduct wars (*atl tlachinolli*) and to sacrifice captives to nourish the sky and the earth. While the heart sacrifice was appropriate for the sun, decapitation was a fertility rite directed to the earth.[191]

CONCLUSIONS

The present study leads me to the following conclusions, which I propose here as a series of hypotheses:

1. The iconography of Cihuacoatl-Coatlicue-Coyolxauhqui, as well as the Tlaltecuhtli representations on relief stones, indicates that on the mythological level Templo Mayor, the sacred mountain, was the earth itself, the earth as a voracious monster devouring human victims and blood. At the same time, the earth contained regenerative forces that linked it to agricultural growth and fertility in general. Matos has suggested that it was particularly the large frontal platform of the twin temple where the majority of offerings are buried, which was believed to symbolize the earth.[192] The natural environment of the Valley of Mexico was also reflected symbolically in this cosmovision since Templo Mayor was conceived of as the sacred mountain resting upon the earth (i.e., the island of Tenochtitlan) which like a disk floated in the waters of the primordial sea. In fact, in the lake region the groundwater was (and still is) situated near the surface, evoking the impression of the subterranean space filled with water.

2. The offerings of Templo Mayor are inscribed within this cosmovision and should be analyzed in this context. Rather than being restricted to the god Tlaloc, they were brought to the earth itself. In a way, Tlaloc was also simply another male aspect of the earth. As a counterpart and yet intimately related to the earth symbolism, the content of the offerings denoted the presence of water in its manifold manifestations through the cult of the mountains and the sea. Pluvial water filled the inside of mountains and caves, where it was retained during the dry season to be conjured by ritual during the rainy season. Beyond the recurring cycles of the dry and rainy seasons, the sea was the absolute embodiment of fertility and life. Ilhuica atl, "the heavenly waters," was the place where sky and earth meet. Another term for it was huey atl, "the big water," or water in its absolute form. As we have seen, the *Histoyre du Mechique* describes the creation of the earth's surface as the tearing apart of the goddess Tlaltecuhtli-Tlalteotl; while one-half of the monster was transformed into the earth, from the sky was created the other half.

3. This basic symbolism of water, the earth, the sky, and the sun[193] seems to reveal certain basic philosophical concepts that have ancient roots in Mesoamerican culture. It may be correlated with Classic and early post-Classic iconographic motives ranging from the central highlands (Teotihuacan, Xochicalco, Cacaxtla) down to the Maya area (Palenque, etc.),[194] although this latter point still needs further exploration. There is abundant archaeological, ethnohistorical, and ethnographic documentation which needs to be brought together in a systematic, comparative way. This material points to an ancient cult centered around the sacralization of the earth and water which, perhaps, acquired the need of mass human sacrifices only in the last, Aztec period. Among the Mexica warrior elite, the earth assumed truly monstrous traits—claws and fangs, devouring maws, and human skulls as adornment. This frightening image was an adequate expression of the ideological necessities of the Aztec conquest state.

The reference to mountains and the sea, however, denoted a fertility symbolism that seems to be present in central Mexico at least since early Classic times. The offerings at the Templo Mayor form an integral part of this cosmovision and thus reveal the time depth as well as spatial dimensions of ancient symbols derived from Mesoamerica's common cultural heritage. We may speak of a *natural philosophy* based on the dialectical conception of the necessary harmony between the earth, the sky, and the water (the sea) that was guaranteed by ritual.

4. We may also conclude that the symbolism of the temple structure, with its major monuments and the offerings studied in this chapter, is an aspect of Aztec religious symbolism fundamentally different from that of the great public rituals that took place at the same temple. The former must be analyzed in terms of the basic concepts of cosmovision; its bond to the social structure and political organization was not so direct as was that of the great public rituals, which directly expressed the ideological pretensions of the Aztec warrior elite. If I have used the term "natural philosophy" in reference to these cosmological concepts, however, it implies that there also existed a "social" dimension to these concepts, since philosophy of nature is the product of a specific evolutionary level of early civilizations in which the relation to the natural environment (geography, climate, ecology, technology, and agriculture) came to be expressed in terms of abstract philosophical concepts. Even though we may detect such abstract formulations in Aztec cosmovision, at the same time the presence of deified principles of nature was still all-encompassing. These deities were not so much a matter of abstract philosophical speculation but they embodied, above all, the practical concern of ritual, or magic acts intended to exercise control over the forces of nature.

5. A final observation is that this philosophy of natural elements analyzed here formed part of Aztec state cult corresponding to the last period of expansion of that conquest state. This means that the cult of water, mountains, and the earth was imbued with ideological elements through which the Aztecs pursued to legitimate their political domination. The monumental art of the second half of the fifteenth century

clearly expressed this imperial vision and claim to legitimacy. A cosmovision of ancient cultural roots was integrated into Mexica state cult.

POSTSCRIPT

In contrast to the pre-Hispanic situation, the cult of water, mountains, and the earth, which survived after the Spanish Conquest and can be studied in recent ethnographic data from traditional Indian communities, lost this integration into the state cult. From an expression of elite culture, it was transformed into the cult of Indian peasant communities and thus lost its articulation with the wider coherent ideology of an autonomous society.

In spite of the fundamental transformations that took place in Indian communities during the colonial period up to modern times, it is revealing to study in contemporary ethnographic data this basic attitude to the natural environment, which has preserved to an astonishing degree elements of the ancient coherent cosmovision that we have tried to reconstruct in this study. In this perspective, I shall quote here in full extent material that was collected by Tim Knab in an anthropological field investigation among the Nahua of San Miguel in the Sierra de Puebla.[195] Knab records:

> The earth, the most holy earth, santisima tierra, *talticpac wan talocan*, is the source of life for the people of San Miguel. As they themselves say:
>
> > We live HERE on the earth (stamping on the mud floor)
> > we are all fruits of the earth
> > the earth sustains us
> > we grow here, on the earth and lower
> > and when we die we wither in the earth
> > we are ALL FRUITS of the earth (stamping on the mud floor).[196]
>
> However, the necessary counterpart to the earth is the sky and the sun. The latter is identified with Christ, "the virgins, the moon, the saints, the stars, all of which together keep the darkness of the underworld, talocan, at bay, providing their santisima luz, both day and night so that man does not wither and die in the earth."
>
> > We eat of the earth
> > then the earth eats us.
>
> Without the light of the sky man cannot live, just as he cannot live without the earth. Man in this sense must live in harmony between the worlds of the earth and the sky. Maintaining this relationship with the sky and the earth is essential for man's well being on the surface of the earth.[197]

Referring himself to the cardinal directions, Knab reports that

In the east is the great lake of the underworld that meets this side of the surface of the world and the sky where the *atagat*, man or lord of the water, resides with his sometimes wife the *asihuaw*, water woman, who sometimes also resides on the other side of the world in the west in the *sihuawchan* or house of the women. In the deepest depths of this part of the underworld at the bottom of the great underworld lake or sea is where the atagat and asihuaw live. All of the supernaturals associated with the water reside within their domain. This place is a paradise with abundant water for all and rich fields beneath the waters from which all waters issue forth to the surface of the world. . . . The center of talocan, talocan melaw or the true talocan is where the señores talocan reside who rule over the entire underworld. . . . The center of talocan is in a very real sense not only the center of the under-world but, in that it controls and so to speak possesses the earth, wind and rain necessary for man's existence, the center of the surface of the earth with which it is analogous.

Not only is the form and structure of talocan analogous with that of the surface of the earth and the sky but also the structure of relationships that must be maintained. All three worlds are interdependent in a very real sense in that man by maintaining his relationships with the underworld and the sky is at the same time maintaining the underworld and the sky. The offer-ings, for the underworld are the sustenance and maintenance of both the sky and the underworld. The relationship is however reciprocal in that earth, wind, water and light are necessary for the sustenance of man.[198]

These concepts regarding the attitude of their natural environment, taken from a modern Nahua peasant community of central Mexico, prove to be extremely helpful in illustrating and clarifying the natural philosophy that formed the background of the Aztec Templo Mayor. This cosmovision had ancient roots in the past of Mesoamerican civilization. The richness of this material gives an idea of the possi-bilities that this type of study—integrating archaeology, ethnohistory, and modern eth-nography into a critical unitary approach—may offer for future research.

Notes

1. The term "cosmovision," borrowed from the common Spanish and German usage, denotes the structured view in which the ancient Mesoamericans combined their notions of cos-mology relating to time and space into a systematic whole. This term is thus somewhat more specific than the English terms "cosmology" and "worldview." Recently, several specialized pub-lications in the English language have made use of the term "cosmovision." (See Anthony F. Aveni and Gary Urton, eds., *Ethnoastronomy and Archaeostronomy in the American Tropics*, *Annals of the New York Academy of Sciences*, vol. 385 [New York: The New York Academy of Sciences, 1982]; Tichy, Franz, ed., *Space and Time in the Cosmovision of Mesoamerica*, in *Lateinamerika-Studien*, vol. 10 [Munich: Wilhelm Fink Verlag, 1982].)

2. "Ideology" forms an important concept of the approach used in this study. It denotes a system of symbolic representation that serves the function of legitimizing and justifying the existing order of society. In this sense, a distinction should be made between "objective social reality" and the "explanation" given of that reality. In societies that have experienced the rise

of social classes and the state, ideology serves the end of mystification of the established social order based on inequality. The "false conscience" that is created of reality also encompasses the relation to nature and to natural phenomena that are being reinterpreted in social terms. (See Johanna Broda, "Astronomy, Cosmovision and Ideology of pre-Hispanic Mesoamerica," in *Ethnoastronomy and Archaeoastronomy in the American Tropics*, Anthony F. Aveni and Gary Urton, eds., p. 81.)

3. Pedro Carrasco and Johanna Broda, eds., *Economía Política e Ideología en el México Prehispánico* (Mexico: Nueva Imagen-Centro de Investigaciones Superiores del INAH, 1978); Johanna Broda, "Ideology of the Aztec State and Human Sacrifice," in *Societies in Transition: Essays in honor of Pedro Carrasco*, Roger Joseph, Frances F. Berdan, Hugo G. Nutini, eds. (in press).

4. Johanna Broda, "Aspectos Socio-económicos e Ideológicos de la Expansión del Estado Mexica," in *Economía y Sociedad en los Andes y Mesoamérica*, José Alcina Franch, ed., *Revista de la Universidad Complutense* XXVIII (117) (Madrid: Universidad Complutense de Madrid, 1982a): 73–94. Johanna Broda, "Ideology of the Aztec State."

5. Charles Gibson, "Structure of the Aztec Empire," in *Handbook of Middle American Indians*, vol. 10, part I (Austin: University of Texas Press, 1971), p. 379.

6. Diego Durán, *Historia de las Indias de Nueva España*, 2 vols.; Angel Ma. Garibay, ed. (México: Editorial Porrúa, 1967), vol. II; pp. 211–214.

7. Hernando Alvarado Tezozómoc, *Crónica Mexicana* (México: Editorial Leyenda, 1944), pp. 86–90.

8. Durán, *Historia*, II: 235–237.

9. Durán, *Historia*, II: 175.

10. Broda, "Aspectos Socio-económicos e Ideológicos . . .": 84–87.

11. Durán, *Historia*, II: 333–347.

12. Durán, *Historia*, II: 340.

13. Durán, *Historia*, II: 439–444, 485–490.

14. See Johanna Broda, "Tlacaxipehualiztli: A Reconstruction of an Aztec Calendar Festival from Sixteenth Century Sources," *Revista Española de Antropología Americana* (Madrid) 5 (1970): 197–274; Johanna Broda, "Los Estamentos en el Ceremonial Mexica," in Pedro Carrasco, Johanna Broda, et al., *Estratificación Social en la Mesoamérica Prehispánica* (Mexico: SEP-INAH, 1976), pp. 37–66; Johanna Broda, "Relaciones Políticas Ritualizadas: El Ritual Como Expresión de Una Ideología," in *Economía Política e Ideología en el México Prehispánico*, Pedro Carrasco and Johanna Broda, eds. pp. 219–255; Johanna Broda, "Estatificación Social y Ritual Mexica: Un Ensayo de Antropología Social de los Mexica," *Indiana* (Berlin) 5 (1979): 45–82; Johanna Broda, "Aspectos Socio-económicos e Ideológicos"; Johanna Broda, "La Fiesta Azteca del Fuego Nuevo y el Culto de las Pléyades," in *Space and Time in the Cosmovision of Mesoamerica*, Franz Tichy, ed., *Lateinamerika-Studien*, vol. 10 (Munich: Wilhelm Fink-Verlag, 1982b), pp. 129–158. Johanna Broda, "Ideology of the Aztec State."

15. See note 2.

16. Miguel León-Portilla and Eduardo Matos Moctezuma, *El Templo Mayor*, Mexico: Bancomer, S.A., 1981.

17. *Pictorial manuscripts: Codex Borbonicus, Codex Magliabecchi, Codex Tudela, and Codex Vaticanus A. Annals and anonymous Interpretations of Codices: Historia de los Mexicanos por Sus Pinturas, Histoyre du Mechique, Anales de Cuauhtitlán, and Historia Tolteca Chichimeca. Chroniclers:* Bernardino de Sahagún, Diego Durán, Motolinía (Toribio de Benavente), Francisco de las Navas, Juan B. Pomar, Hernando Alvarado Tezozómoc, Juan de Tovar, Gerónimo de Mendieta, and Juan de Torquemada. We have mentioned here only the

most important sources on pre-Hispanic central Mexican religion on the eve of the Spanish Conquest. For more details and bibliographical references, see my publications on the Aztec festivals (see note 14).

18. Broda, "Las Fiestas Aztecas de los Dioses de la Lluvia": 298–299; Fray Bernardino de Sahagún (FC): *Florentine Codex: General History of the Things of New Spain*, 13 parts, Arthur J. O. Anderson and Charles E. Dibble, eds., transl., Monographs of the School of American Research, no. 14 (Salt Lake City: The School of American Research and the University of Utah, 1951–1982): II: 26, 89.

19. Johanna Broda, "Astronomy, Cosmovision and Ideology"; Johanna Broda, "La Fiesta Azteca del Fuego Nuevo;" Johanna Broda, "Cíclos Agrícolas en el Culto: Un Problema de la Correlación del Calendario Mexica," in *Calendars in Mesoamerica and Peru: Native American Computations of Time,* Anthony F. Aveni and Gordon Brotherston, eds. (Oxford: BAR International Series 174, 1983), pp. 145–165.

20. For the Teotihuacan evidence, see Esther Pasztory, *The Iconography of the Teotihuacan Tlaloc*, Studies in Pre-Columbian Art and Archaeology, no. 15 (Washington, D.C.: Dumbarton Oaks, 1974); "Artistic Traditions of the Middle Classic Period," in *Middle Classic Mesoamerica*, A.D. 400–700, Esther Pasztory, ed. (New York: Columbia University, 1978), pp. 108–142; Esther Pasztory, "The Aztec Tlaloc: God of Antiquity," in *Studies in Memory of Thelma D. Sullivan*, J. Kathryn Josserand and Karen Dakin, eds. (Oxford: BAR International Series, in press); and Doris Heyden, "Caves, Gods and Myths: World-View and Planning in Teotihuacan," in *Mesoamerican Sites and World Views*, Elizabeth Benson, ed. (Washington, D.C.: Dumbarton Oaks, 1981), pp. 1–40.

21. Pasztory, "Artistic Traditions"; "Iconography of the Teotihuacan Tlaloc"; "Aztec Tlaloc."

22. Cecelia Klein, *The Face of the Earth: Frontality in Two-Dimensional Mesoamerican Art.* Outstanding Dissertations in the Fine Arts (series). (New York and London: Garland, 1976); "Who was Tlaloc?" [*Journal of Latin American Lore* 6(2) (1980): 155–204].

23. Pasztory, "Iconography of the Teotihuacan Tlaloc": 10–20.

24. The Aztec Tlaloc's relationship to the earth was noted previously by Thelma D. Sullivan ("Tlaloc: A New Etymological Interpretation of the God's Name and What it Reveals of His Essence and Nature," in *Atti del XL Congreso Internationale Degli Americanisti*, Roma and Genova, 1972, vol. II [Genova: Casa Editrice Tilgher, 1974], pp. 213–219), and Klein (*The Face of the Earth*).

25. Klein, "Who was Tlaloc?": 167, 168, 179–198.

26. Broda, "Las Fiestas Aztecas de los Dioses de la Lluvia": 323.

27. Michel Graulich ("Templo Mayor, Coyolxauhqui und Cacaxtla," *Mexicon* [Berlin] V[5] [1983]: 91–94) establishes a remarkable parallel between the symbolism of these serpents and the iconography of the late Classic sites of Xochicalco and Cacaxtla.

28. Fray Alonso de Molina (*Vocabulario en Lengua Castellana y Mexicana* [Mexico: Editorial Porrúa, 1970]): *tonalco*, "estío, parte del año," "el tiempo que no llue"; *tonalla*, "esto, tiempo seco, quando no llueue" (p. 149); *xopan*, "verano"; *xopaleuac*, "cosa muy verde" (p. 161).

29. The Roman numerals refer to the sequence of the months within the yearly cycle as indicated by Bernardino de Sahagún. According to this chronicler, the first month of the year was *I Atlcahualo*. This terminology is used here for the purpose of better orientation concerning the place of a month in the sequence of the eighteen monthly periods, but it does not imply any judgment concerning the beginning of the year. The latter item still constitutes an unresolved problem within the investigation on the pre-Hispanic calendar (Broda, "Cíclos Agrícolas en el Culto," 148). I have followed Karl Anton Nowotny ("Die Aztekischen Festkreise,"

Zeitschrift für Ethnologie [Braunschweig] 93(1, 2) (1968): 84–106) in adopting this system of numeration by Roman numerals.

30. Broda, "Las Fiestas Aztecas de los Dioses de la Lluvia": 272–276; Broda, "Ciclos Agrícolas en el Culto."

31. Durán, *Historia*, I: 82.

32. Broda, "Las Fiestas Aztecas de los Dioses de la Lluvia": 277–279.

33. Constantine G. Rickards, "The Ruins of Tlaloc, State of Mexico," *Journal de la Société des Américanistes* (Paris) 21 (1929): 197–199; Charles Wicke and Fernando Horcasitas, "Archaeological Investigations on Monte Tlaloc, Mexico," *Mesoamerican Notes 5* (1957): 83–96.

34. Sahagún (FC), II: 42.

35. These terms are derived from Molina (see note 28). A similar division in the calendar of central Mexico (in the *xiuhpohualli*, or sun calendar) was proposed by Pedro Carrasco ("Las Fiestas de los Meses Mexicanos," in *Mesoamérica: Homenaje al Dr. Paul Kirchhoff*, Barbro Dahlgren, ed. [Mexico: SEP-INAH, 1979], pp. 52–90) and Carmen Aguilera ("Xolpan y Tonalco. Una Hipotesis Acerca de la Correlacion Astronómica del Calendario Mexica," *Estudios de Cultura Nahuatl*, [Mexico: UNAM] 15 [1982: 185–208]).

36. This does not mean that the rites of either of the two basic divisions were exclusively dedicated to the same symbolism. The child sacrifices belonged to the dry season because they were intended precisely to conjure the coming of the rains.

37. Broda, "Las Fiestas Aztecas de los Dioses de la Lluvia": 282–298; "Ciclos Agrícolas en el Culto": 152–154.

38. Cecelia Klein, "Rethinking Cihuacoatl: Aztec Political Imagery of the Conquered Woman." Paper presented at the XLIII International Congress of Americanists (Vancouver, 1979, unpublished).

39. Pasztory, "Artistic Traditions": 132.

40. With respect to Classic Period Teotihuacan, Pasztory suggests that "the sun god in the underworld was probably represented by the net jaguar. The net jaguar is shown in water and fertility context in mural painting, which suggests the underworld during the rainy season" (Pasztory, "Artistic Traditions": 132). The motif of the net jaguar leads us back to the previously mentioned distinction between Tlaloc A and Tlaloc B suggested by Pasztory (*Iconography*) and Cecelia Klein ("Who was Tlaloc?" *Journal of Latin American Lore* 6[2] [1980]: 155–204), thus establishing the connection between certain aspects of the god Tlaloc and the solar cult.

41. Esther Pasztory, "The Xochicalco Stelae and a Middle Classic Deity Triad in Mesoamerica," in *Actas del XXIII Congreso Internacional de Historia del Arte*, vol. I (Granada, 1973), pp. 185–215. See note 44.

42. Graulich ("Templo Mayor") analyzes in the mural paintings of Cacaxtla a whole complex of ideas associated with the basic dualism of the dry and the rainy seasons. He suggests that the earth-water and sky-sun dualisms evident in Aztec iconography derive from roots that can be studied at Teotihuacan, Xochicalco, and Cacaxtla. These basic structures of cosmovision were also related to political structure, to the dualistic form of government that was represented among the Aztecs by the *tlatoani* (the sun) and the *cihuacoatl* (the earth) but that we also find in the murals of Cacaxtla as the two dignitaries, the first one dressed as a raptorial bird and his counterpart dressed as a jaguar.

43. See the interesting interpretation proposed by M. Cohodas for the iconography of the Panels of the Sun, Cross, and Foliated Cross at Palenque (Marvin Cohodas, "The Iconography of the Panels of the Sun, Cross, and Foliated Cross at Palenque: Part II," in *Primera Mesa Redonda de Palenque, Part I*, Merle Greene Robertson, ed. [Pebble Beach, Calif.: The Robert

Louis Stevenson School, 1974], pp. 95–107 and "The Iconography of the Panels of the Sun, Cross, and Foliated Cross at Palenque: Part III," in *Segunda Mesa Redonda de Palenque, Part III*, Merle Greene Robertson, ed. [Pebble Beach, Calif.: The Robert Louis Stevenson School, 1976], pp. 155–176). See note 16.

44. Pasztory interprets a similar theme in the iconography of stelae 1 to 3 from Xochicalco in the sense that they represent the death and rebirth of the sun (maize) in the underworld during the yearly agricultural cycle (Pasztory, "Xochicalco Stelae"). A parallel theme may be found at Palenque, in the temple of the Cross, the Inscriptions, and the Foliated Cross dating from the seventh century, the same as Xochicalco. According to M. Cohodas's interpretation, the iconography of the carved tablets belonging to the three temples may depict the three stages of the sun's yearly cycle corresponding to the dry and the rainy seasons and to the birth of maize (Cohodas, "Iconography," parts II and III). Cohodas bases his interpretation on an analogy with modern ethnographical data gathered by R. Girard. The Chortis living near the ancient Classic center of Copan (Honduras) still practice esoteric ceremonies based on the sun's yearly course in relation to the dry and rainy seasons and to the agricultural cycle (Rafael Girard, *Los Mayas Eternos* [Mexico: Libro Mex, 1962]). We thus seem to be dealing with fundamental concepts of Mesoamerican cosmovision that have ancient roots and a distribution from the central highlands down to the Maya area and have survived in some elements up to the present day. Ethnographic data from the important agricultural ceremonies taking place on the 2–3 May in the traditional Nahua area of northeastern Guerrero (Citlala, Ostotempa, Ameyaltepec, etc.) also corroborate this fact. The "fiesta de la Santa Cruz" (feast of the Holy Cross) is the most important surviving festival that preserves pre-Hispanic elements related to the solar year, the petition for rain during the peak of the dry season, and the beginning of the agricultural cycle (Broda, "Cíclos Agrícolas en el Culto": 153).

45. Broda, "Cíclos Agrícolas en el Culto": 156, 157.

46. These were illnesses related to the cold humid mountain climate, such as rheumatism and dropsy (Broda, "Las Fiestas Aztecas de los Dioses de la Lluvia": 255).

47. Broda, "Las Fiestas Aztecas . . . ": 300–306, 312–318, 321, 322; "Cíclos Agrícolas en el Culto": 155–157.

48. Coatepec, "at the place of the Serpent Mountain," "on the Serpent Mountain" (Fray Bernardino de Sahagún [HG]: *Historia General de las Cosas de Nueva España*, 4 vols. Angel María Garibay, ed. [Mexico: Editorial Porrúa, 1956]: Book III: 271–273).

49. Michel Graulich, "Templo Mayor": 91–94.

50. Sahagún (HG): Book III, chapter 1.

51. Carmen Aguilera, *Coyolxauhqui: Ensayo Iconográfico.* Cuadernos de la Biblioteca, Serie Investigación, no. 2. Biblioteca Nacional de Antropología e Historia (Mexico: INAH, 1978). Eduardo Matos Moctezuma, "Los Hallazgos de la Arquelogía," in Miguel León-Portilla and Eduardo Matos Moctezuma, *El Templo Mayor* (Mexico: Bancomer, S.A., 1981a), pp. 103–284; E. Matos, *Una Visita al Templo Mayor de Tenochtitlan.* (Mexico: INAH, 1981b); Miguel León-Portilla, *México-Tenochtitlan: Su Espacio y Tiempo Sagrados* (Mexico: INAH, 1978); M. León-Portilla, "Los Testimonios de la Historia," in M. León-Portilla and E. Matos, *El Templo Mayor*: 33–102.

52. Eduard Seler (GA), *Gesammelte Abhandlungen*, 5 vols. (Graz-Austria: Akademische Druck-und Verlagsanstalt, 1960a): II, pp. 966 ff.

53. In the most detailed study that has been undertaken of the iconography of this relief stone, Carmen Aguilera (*Coyolxauhqui*: 75) identifies Coyolxauhqui as a Cihuacoatl (a woman who died in childbirth and became converted into a goddess). The Cihuateteo were mother goddesses whose basic attributes were derived not from the earth but from the sun and the stars.

According to Aguilera, Coyolxauhqui belonged to the group of *tzitzimime*, "astral bodies that shine in the night." (Hernando Alvarado Tezozómoc, *Crónica Mexicayotl*, Adrián León, transl., Instituto de Investigaciones Históricas [Mexico: UNAM, 1949], 260.) "She was a Cihuacoatl, an astral deity . . . that accompanies the sun and dwells in the air" (Aguilera, *Coyolxauhqui*: 105). In this sense Aguilera concludes that Coyolxauhqui was related to the ancient goddess of Toltec affiliation, Cihuacoatl, whose main attributes were also the nocturnal fire or astral light and that identified her with the Milky Way (ibid., 142, 146, 150).

54. Durán, *Historia*, II: 38.

55. Sahagún (FC): III: 1–5; Tezozómoc, *Crónica Mexicayotl*, 34–35; Durán, *Historia*, I: 131. It seems that these kingship terms could be used interchangeably in Aztec society (see Rudolf Van Zantwijk, "Los Seis Barrios Sirvientes de Huitzilopochtli," *Estudios de Cultura Nahuatl* [Mexico: UNAM] 6 [1966]: 177–185).

56. Eduard Seler, "Die Ausgrabungen am Orte des Haupttempels in Mexiko" (1901), in *Gesammelte Abhandlungen*, vol. II (Graz-Austria: Akademische Druck-und Verlagsanstalt) (1960b), pp. 767–904; Eduardo Matos Moctezuma, ed., *Trabajos Arqueológicos en el Centro de la Ciudad de México (Antología)* (Mexico: INAH, 1979), map: "Herencia Arqueológica de México-Huitzilopochtli."

57. Coyolxauhqui's name means precisely, "She With the Copper Bells."

58. See the analysis of Aztec monumental sculpture presented by Richard F. Townsend (*State and Cosmos in the Art of Tenochtitlan*, Studies in Pre-Columbian Art and Archaeology, no. 20 [Washington, D.C.: Trustees for Harvard University, 1979], pp. 15–22, 37–70), and Esther Pasztory (*Aztec Art* [New York: Harry N. Abrams, 1983], pp. 146–150).

59. Carlos Navarrete and Doris Heyden ("La Cara Central de la Piedra del Sol: Una Hipótesis," *Estudios de Cultura Nahuatl* [Mexico] 11 [1974]: 355–376, proposed that the central figure of the Calendar Stone was the Earth Lord, Tlaltecuhtli. Klein (*Face of the Earth*), on the other hand, suggested that the face represented the night sun, which, precisely, shared some iconographic details with the earth deities.

60. Huitzilopochtli, "el gran ausente" in the symbolism of the sculptures found in the recent excavation, might have been mainly represented by a *bulto*, a sacred bundle incorporated into a statue as shown on an early colonial codex from Mexico City (Archivo General de la Nación, Ramo Inquisición, vol. 37, México). According to a recent investigation by Robert Moreno de los Arcos, the bundles of the Aztec patron deities were saved from the Spaniards and hidden away by the Indians during the sixteenth century. Included with these bundles was that of Cihuacoatl! (Moreno de los Arcos, personal communication). For a preliminary report on this investigation entitled *Historia de la división Parroquial de la Ciudad de México: 1524–1974*, see Roberto Moreno de los Arcos, "Los Territorios Parroquiales de la Ciudad Arzobispal, 1325–1981," *Gaceta Oficial del Arzobispado de Mexico*, XXII (9–10) (1982): 152–173.

61. *Tecuacuiltin*, "sculptured images, statues" ("imagen de bulto, estatua") (Durán, *Historia*, I: 313).

62. Durán, *Historia*, I: 125–133.

63. Rudolf Van Zantwijk, "La Paz Azteca. La Ordenación del Mundo por los Mexica." *Estudios de Cultura Nahuatl* (Mexico) 3 (1962): 101–135.

64. Durán, *Historia*, I: 125–132.

65. Miguel Acosta Saignes, "Los Teopixque: Organización Sacerdotal entre los Mexica." *Revista Mexicana de Estudios Antropológicos* (Mexico) 8 (1946): 177–178.

66. Klein, "Rethinking Cihuacoatl."

67. Durán, *Historia*, II: 302, 507.

68. Durán, *Historia*, I: 125–126; Graulich, "Templo Mayor"; Anneliese Mönnich, *Die*

Gestalt der Erdgöttin in den Religionen Mesoamerikas, Ph.D. thesis (Berlin: Freie Universität Berlin, 1969), p. 103. The latter is a detailed comparative study of the earth goddess in ancient Mesoamerica.

69. Durán, *Historia*, I: 131.

70. According to Klein ("Rethinking Cihuacoatl": note 37), the association between the high priest Cihuacoatl and the temple of Tlaloc can be inferred on the basis of (1) the synthesis that certain priestly insignia show between elements of Tlaloc and Cihuacoatl, (2) the probability that Cihuacoatl was considered the wife of Tlaloc (Klein, "Who was Tlaloc?": 175, 198), and (3) certain functions of the high priest Cihuacoatl at Tlaloc's temple (*Codex Magliabecchi* 79). We might add that the figure of Cihuacoatl—whom the glossary of the Codex Borbonicus calls *papa mayor* (high priest)—played an important role in the annual cycle of festivals, which according to this codex centered around the cult of Tlaloc, the rains, and maize. The details of this important role are not yet fully understood, however. For other interesting details of the iconography of Cihuacoatl, see Aguilera (*Coyolxauhqui*: 144–156), who stresses several other aspects of this goddess: her relation to the night sky and to the stars, particularly the Milky Way.

71. Klein, "Who Was Tlaloc?": 197.

72. Seler (GA), II: 820.

73. Juan Bautista Pomar, "Relación de Tezcoco," in Pomar-Zurita: *Relaciones de Tezcoco y de los Señores de la Nueva España*. Colección de Documentos para la Historia de México, vol. 2 (Mexico: S. Chávez Hayhoe, 1941), p. 15.

74. Michel Graulich, "Quelques Obervations sur les Sculptures Mesoamericaines Dites 'Chac Mool.'" Unpublished manuscript, n.d.

75. Pasztory, *Aztec Art*: 144.

76. Fifty-two panels of the same type relief were already found during the excavation of the *Calle de Las Escalerillas* in 1900. Twenty-one of these are today preserved in the National Museum of Anthropology and History; the rest apparently were lost. They were studied by H. Beyer and identified as high-ranking warriors with their corresponding emblems, led by their ruler wearing the guise of the god Tezcatlipoca (Hermann Beyer, "La Procesión de los Señores" [1955], in *Trabajos Arqueológicos en el Centro de la Ciudad de Mexico*, Eduardo Matos Moctezuma, ed. [Mexico: SEP-INAH, 1979], pp. 149–166). Recently, Cecelia Klein ("The Ideology of Autosacrifice at the *Templo Mayor*," in *The Aztec Templo Mayor*, Elizabeth H. Boone, ed. [Washington, D.C.: Dumbarton Oaks, 1986]) has suggested that the chambers with the warrior reliefs were actually assigned to ceremonies of penance and ritual bloodletting. In this precinct Aztec noble dignitaries fulfilled priestly functions that were fundamental to legitimization of their political office.

77. In the same sense, the Chac Mool figure in the front of Tlaloc's shrine constituted, according to Pasztory, a conscious imitation of Toltec art (Pasztory, *Aztec Art*: 144).

78. The direct experience of the different stages of the excavation process during which these highly enigmatic sculptures were discovered has enabled me to mentally reconstruct the inner arrangement of these chambers. I would like to thank Francisco Hinojosa from the Templo Mayor Project for many fruitful discussions at the site.

79. Pedro Carrasco, "Las Fiestas de los Meses Mexicanos," in *Mesoamérica: Homenaje al Dr. Paul Kirchhoff*, Barbro Dahlgren, ed. (Mexico: SEP-INAH, 1979), p. 56.

80. See the interesting ethnographic and linguistic field material gathered by Tim Knab, quoted in detail at the end of this chapter (see notes 195–198, below).

81. Pasztory, *The Iconography of the Teotihuacan Tlaloc*; Heyden, "Caves, Gods and Myths."

82. Pasztory, "The Aztec Tlaloc"; Sullivan, "Tlaloc"; Klein, "Who was Tlaloc?"

83. Graulich, "Templo Mayor": 92.

84. Matos, "Los Hallazgos de la Arqueología"; Matos, *Una Visita al Templo Mayor*; Eduardo Matos Moctezuma, "El Templo Mayor: Economía e Ideología," in *El Templo Mayor: Excavaciones y Estudios*. Eduardo Matos Moctezuma, ed. (Mexico: INAH, 1982a), pp. 109–118.

85. I first formulated the hypothesis of this particular linkage of the cult of Tlaloc and Templo Mayor as reflecting an ancient cosmovision relating to water, mountains, and the sea, in my paper entitled "El Culto Mexica de los Cerros y del Agua," (*Multidisciplina* [Mexico: Escuela Nacional de Estudios Profesionales Acatlan—UNAM] 3, no. 7 [1982c]: 45–56). Further reference is made to a paper I presented in 1983, at the Dumbarton Oaks Symposium on "The Aztec Templo Mayor." I wrote that paper following completion of the present more exhaustive investigation; therefore, it constitutes a somewhat condensed synthesis of the present investigation. The Dumbarton Oaks paper was submitted for publication prior to the final revision of the present manuscript, however; thus the reader will find cross-references as well as parallelisms in both essays.

86. Only after completing this investigation, I came to know about Debra Nagao's study on *Mexica Buried Offerings: A Historical and Contextual Approach* (Oxford: BAR International Series 235, 1985). This study deals with a comparative investigation of offertory caches in different regions of Mesoamerica from pre-Classic through post-Classic times and includes material from the Templo Mayor available in publication before 1982. Nagao analyzes the content, arrangement, and distribution of these offerings placed into caches buried in the earth or in ceremonial structures and distinguishes between offerings within an architectural context and burial offerings. This study is extremely useful in its comparative approach, "contextual" analysis and thorough interpretation. Although our objects are not the same, Nagao's comparative archaeological material from different periods, she confirms the conclusion reached in the present investigation that the offerings at the Templo Mayor are votive offerings brought to the earth and were inscribed within the context of an ancient cult of the earth (see Nagao, *Mexica Buried Offerings . . .* : 77–85). In future research it should be possible to integrate more fully the conclusions reached by both studies. In the present essay I have only incorporated a few references to Nagao's study after having completed the final version of my manuscript.

87. Matos, *Una Visita al Templo Mayor*: 189.

88. Thirty-three caches were recovered; see Eduardo Matos Moctezuma, "El Simbolismo del Templo Mayor," in *The Aztec Templo Mayor*, Elizabeth H. Boone, ed. (Washington, D.C.: Dumbarton Oaks, 1987. Pages 185–210.), and Eduardo Matos Moctezuma, this volume (text and site map).

89. Matos, *Una Visita al Templo Mayor*: 141.

90. Thus far one volume of the excavation reports has been published. (Eduardo Matos Moctezuma, ed., *El Templo Mayor: Excavaciones y Estudios* [Mexico: INAH, 1982a]; the second volume is in preparation. Two other volumes contain the reedition of earlier useful studies on Templo Mayor (Eduardo Matos Moctezuma, ed., *Trabajos Arqueológicos en el Centro de la Ciudad de México* [Antología] [Mexico: SEP-INAH, 1982b], as well as an anthology of all the texts of sixteenth-century chroniclers referring to Templo Mayor (Barbara Dahlgren, Emma Pérez-Rocha, Lourdes Suáres Díez, and Perla Valle de Revueltas, eds., *Corazón de Copil* [Mexico: INAH, 1982]). Finally, a volume containing maps and sketches of the site has been published (Eduardo Matos Moctezuma, ed., *El Templo Mayor: Planos, Cortes y Perspectivas*. Dibujos Victor Rangel [Mexico: INAH, 1982b]).

91. Matos, "Los Hallazgos de la Arqueología"; Matos, *Una Visita al Templo Mayor*;

115

Matos, "El Templo Mayor: Economía e Ideología." I particularly want to thank Eduardo Matos Moctezuma for the facilities he provided to me over the years enabling me to consult the excavation in situ. Without this generous and encouraging assistance, it would not have been possible for me to undertake the present investigation.

92. Juan Alberto Román Berrelleza, "La Ofrenda No. 48 del Templo Mayor: Un Caso de Sacrificios Infantiles," in *The Aztec Templo Mayor*, Elizabeth H. Boone, ed. (Washington, D.C.: Dumbarton Oaks. 1987. Pages 131–143.), presents a case study of this offering cache with skeletons of infants.

93. See *Codex Borgia* 13, p. 32, where a multitude of such tecpatls with faces are represented. According to Karl Anton Nowotny's interpretation (*Codex Borgia*, Commentary, Facsimile Edition [Graz-Austria: Akademische Druck-und Verlagsanstalt, 1976]), this page of the *Codex Borgia* refers to temple rites and to the mystical effects of the sacrifice by decapitation. From the decapitated body of the victim sprout innumerable tecpatls, and the heart is also represented by a tecpatl (Nowotny, *Tlacuilolli*: 31, table 14).

94. Nagao, *Mexica Buried Offerings*: 63, 64.

95. Durán, *Historia*, I: 130; Sahagún (HG), I: 46–47.

96. Unfortunately, we will never know whether there existed another stone tzompantli on the south side of Huitzilopochtli's temple as in the case of the two so-called red temples that were excavated, symmetrically distributed, on both the north and the south sides of Templo Mayor. The area on the north side, where the other tzompantli might have stood, could not be duly excavated.

97. Personal communication by Guillermo Ahuja from the Templo Mayor Project, whose research has dealt with Cámara II.

98. Guillermo Ahuja, "Excavación de la Cámara II," in *Templo Mayor: Excavaciones y Estudios*, Eduardo Matos Moctezuma, ed. (Mexico: INAH, 1982a), pp. 191–212; Carlos González, "Materiales de Estilo Mezcala en el Templo Mayor," in *The Aztec Templo Mayor*, Elizabeth H. Boone, ed. (Washington, D.C.: Dumbarton Oaks, 1986).

99. Matos, *Una Visita al Templo Mayor*: 196.

100. See Nagao, *Mexica Buried Offerings*: 73, 74, where this topic is analyzed in a very suggestive way.

101. Fray Francisco de las Navas, *Calendario de Fray Francisco de las Navas, de don Antonio de Guevara y Anónimo Tlaxcalteca*, Colección Ramírez, Opúsculos Históricos, vol. 21; Colección Antigua, vol. 210; Archivo Histórico del INAH, Museo Nacional de Antropología e Historia, unpublished manuscript (n.d.), pp. 93–203; Pedro Carrasco, "Las Fiestas de los Meses Mexicanos": 56, 57.

102. Carmen Aguilera, "Iztac Mixcoatl en la Vasija del Templo Mayor," in *Memoria del Primer Coloquio de Historia de la Religión en Mesoamérica y Areas Afines*, Barbro Dahlgren, ed., Instituto de Investigaciones Antropológicas (Mexico: UNAM, in press).

103. One of the early examples comes from Cacaxtla, a late Classic site built into the hillside in front of Cerro Xochitecatl, Tlaxcala. Next to the main plaza with the spectacular mural of the battle scene, burials of some eighty decapitated infants were excavated. (Personal communication by Diana López de Molina, INAH, who was in charge of that excavation.) Because of its location, with a magnificent view on the volcanoes (Popocatepetl and Iztac Cihuatl), Cacaxtla might very well have been a site dedicated to the mountain cult.

104. According to Leopoldo Batres (*Teotihuacan, Ciudad Sagrada de los Dioses* [Mexico: Imprenta de Hull, 1906], p. 22), skeletal remains of children were found at the four corners of each body of the Pyramid of the Sun in 1906. If we are to trust the information given by this author, this circumstance surely was connected with the fact that the pyramid was built on top

of a large tunnel-shaped cave from which a spring issued (see Doris Heyden, "An Interpretation of the Cave Underneath the Pyramid of the Sun in Teotihuacán, Mexico," *American Antiquity*, 40[2] [1975]: 131–147).

105. The caches containing the greatest number of these idols are Cámara II (Ahuja, "Excavación de la Cámara II": 191–212), Offering Cache 41, as well as several others (see Matos, this volume, list of offering caches).

106. See Matos, "Economía e Ideología": 118. A geologic analysis of the provenience of the greenstone material of these idols is currently under way. (Personal communication by Carlos González; see also Gónzalez, "Materiales de Estilo Mezcala".)

107. Seler (GA), II: 64–66.

108. Leonhard Schultze-Jena, *Bei den Azteken, Mixteken und Tlapaneken der Sierra Madre del Sur von Mexiko, Indiana*, vol. III (Jena: G. Fischer-Verlag, 1938).

109. Leonhard Schultze-Jena, *La Vida y las Creencias de los Indígenas Quichés de Guatemala*, in *Biblioteca de Cultura Popular*, vol. 40, Antonio Goubaud Carrera and Herbert D. Sapper transl. ([Guatemala: Ministerio de Educación Pública, 1947], pp. 56–59; figs. 2, 34). See also Johanna Broda, "El Culto Mexica de los Cerros y del Agua," *Multidisciplina*, Escuela Nacional de Estudios Profesionales, Acatlan (Mexico: UNAM) 3, no. 7 (1982c): 48, 51.

110. For this extremely interesting material, see Schultze-Jena, *Bei den Azteken, Mixteken und Tlapaneken*: 65–67, 140–142, tables XVI–XVIII.

111. José Alcina Franch, "Pequeñas Esculturas Antropomorfas de Guerrero, México," *Revista de Indias* (Madrid) XXI (1961): 296, 328, 331–338.

112. Andrés Ciudad Ruíz, "Comentarios a la Religiosidad Popular en el Altiplano Guatemalteco Durante la Época Prehispánica: Los Camahuiles de Cerámica," *Mayab*, Sociedad Española de Estudios Mayas (Madrid), no. 2 (1986).

113. Munroe Edmonson, *Quiché-English Dictionary*, Middle American Research Institute, publication no. 30 (New Orleans: Tulane University, 1965), p. 105.

114. Munroe Edmonson, *The Book of Counsel: The Popol Vuh of the Quiché Maya of Guatemala*, Middle American Research Institute, publication no. 35 (New Orleans: Tulane University, 1971), p. 213, note 178.

115. Wolfgang Cordan, *Das Buch des Rates* (Düsseldorf-Köln, 1962).

116. Robert M. Carmack, *Evolución del Reino Quiché* (Guatemala City: Editorial Piedra Santa, 1979), p. 84; Ciudad Ruíz, "Comentarios a la Religiosidad Popular."

117. This is the case of the collection of ninety-one sculptures analyzed by Alcina Franch ("Pequeñas Esculturas Antropomorfas": 299) and of the majority of examples reviewed by Ciudad Ruíz ("Comentarios a la Religiosidad Popular"). The camahuiles Ciudad excavated at the site of Agua Tibia near Totonicapan, Guatemala, belong to the late Classic period.

118. Broda, "Las Fiestas Aztecas de los Dioses de la Lluvia": 300, 314.

119. Sahagún (HG), II: 13: 125.

120. Durán, *Historia*, I: 126 (English transl. by J. Broda).

121. See text earlier in this chapter (section on cosmovision and the observation of nature). The tepictoton, the tzoalli images of the mountains made during the month of Tepeilhuitl, also included an image of the goddess Cihuacoatl (Durán, *Historia*, I: 165). One might consider that Cihuacoatl was, in fact, identified with the "white woman," the volcano Iztac Cihuatl. According to Sahagún, the goddess was dressed in white garments (HG, I: 47). In the illustrations of the deities in Book I of the *Historia General* of Sahagún, we find the representation of *Iztac Cihuatl Coatlicue* (!), dressed completely in white (HG, I: 64). This extremely interesting point needs further exploration.

122. See *Historia Tolteca-Chichimeca* (Paul Kirchhoff, Lina Odena Güemes, and Luís

Reyes García, introductory study, transl. and notes [Mexico: INAH, 1976], pp. 1, 2, 22, 19–25), to quote only a few examples.

123. Sahagún (HG), XI: 12: 344 (transl. by J. Broda).

124. Alfredo López Austin, *Hombre-Dios. Política y Religión en Mundo Nahuatl*, Instituto de Investigaciones Históricas (Mexico: UNAM, 1973), p. 62.

125. Rudolf Van Zantwijk, "The Great Temple of Tenochtitlan: Model of Aztec Cosmovision," in *Mesoamerican Sites and World Views*, Elizabeth P. Benson, ed. (Washington, D.C.: Dumbarton Oaks, 1981), p. 73.

126. Tezozómoc, *Crónica Mexicayotl*: 63; Luís Reyes García, "La Visión Cosmológica y la Organización del Imperio Mexica," in *Mesoamérica: Homenaje al Dr. Paul Kirchhoff*, Barbro Dahlgren, ed. (Mexico: INAH), p. 35.

127. Sahagún (FC), VI: 19.

128. Mircea Eliade, *Tratado de Historia de las Religiones* (Mexico: Biblioteca Era, 1975), pp. 328–345; David Carrasco, "Templo Mayor: The Aztec Vision of Place," *Journal of Religion* (London) 11 (1981): 275–297.

129. See Sahagún (HG), II: 234, 236, 238, 241; (FC), II: 167, 168, 171, 174, 178.

130. Edward Calnek ("Myth and History in the Founding of Tenochtitlán," unpublished manuscript, 1977), quoted by Pasztory ("The Aztec Tlaloc," in press).

131. See Heyden ("Caves, Gods and Myths": 1–40) for an analysis of the cave underneath the Pyramid of the Sun. Heyden also reviews interesting comparative material. Recently, archaeologists from the present Teotihuacán Project of INAH have discovered a second cave in the vicinity of the Pyramid of the Sun, which was associated with astronomical observations.

132. Eric Wolf, *Sons of the Shaking Earth* (Chicago: University of Chicago Press, 1959), pp. 72, 73.

133. Debra Nagao, "The Planting of Sustenance: The Symbolism of the Two-Horned God in Mexica Offerings from the Templo Mayor," *Res-Anthropology and Aesthetics* (Cambridge: Peabody Museum, Harvard University) 10 (1958b): 5–27.

134. Henry B. Nicholson and Eloise Quiñones Keber, *Art of Aztec Mexico: Treasures of Tenochtitlan*, catalog of an exhibition at the National Gallery of Art (Washington, D.C., 1983), pp. 88–89.

135. Seler (GA), II: 851–854.

136. See Seler ("Ausgrabungen," 852 ff.). Seler's analysis of the findings in the vicinity of Templo Mayor that were discovered in 1900 by L. Batres (Leopoldo Batres, "Exploraciones Arqueológicas en las Calles de las Escalerillas" [1902], in *Trabajos Arqueológicos en el Centro de la Ciudad de México*, Eduardo Matos Moctezuma, ed. [Mexico: SEP-INAH, 1979], pp. 61–90) is a pioneer study containing many suggestive interpretations on the Templo Mayor that can be applied to the present excavation as well. It continues to be today the longest original interpretation of objects excavated at Templo Mayor that has been published so far. It also remains a source of inspiration for contemporary authors, like so many other parts of Seler's collected writings (*Gesammelte Abhandlungen* [GA]). Due credit is not always given for this inspiration, however.

137. Seler (GA), II: 849–853.

138. Sahagún (FC), II: 42.

139. Sahagún (FC), II: 80; Broda, "Las Fiestas Aztecas de los Dioses de la Lluvia": 290.

140. Broda, "Las Fiestas Aztecas de los Dioses de la Lluvia": 269–315.

141. Personal communication by Carlos Hernández Reyes, INAH. See also José Luís Lorenzo, "Las Zonas Arqueológicas de los Volcanes Iztaccihuatl y Popocatepetl," *Dirección de Prehistoria*, publication no. 3 (Mexico: INAH, 1957), pp. 15–53; Heyden, "Caves, Gods

and Myths"; Guillermo Bonfil Batalla, "Los que Trabajan con el Tiempo," *Anales de Antropología* (Mexico: UNAM) V (1968): 99–128.

142. An example of a sacred cave is depicted on the pre-Classic rock carvings of Chalcatzingo, Morelos; it shows a great open earth monster from which speech scrolls issue (Heyden, "Caves, Gods and Myths").

143. Heyden, "Caves, Gods and Myths."

144. Evidence for this cult is found in the following studies: *Guatemala* (Girard, *Los Mayos Eternos*; Schultze-Jena, "Leben, Glaube und Sprache der Quiché von Guatemala," *Indiana*, vol. I [G. Fischer-Verlag, Jena, 1933]; Oliver LaFarge and Douglas Byers, *The Year Bearer's People*, Middle American Research Series, publication no. 3 [New Orleans, 1931]; E. Michael Mendelson, "A Guatemalan Sacred Bundle," *Man* [London] 170 [1958]: 7; Nathaniel Tarn and Martin Prechtel, "Eating the Fruit: Sexual Metaphor and Initiation in Santiago Atitlan," paper presented at the *XVIII Mesa Redonda de la Sociedad Mexicana de Antropología* [Chiapas: San Cristobál, 1981]); *Highland Chiapas* (Evon Vogt, "Some Aspects of the Sacred Geography of Highland Chiapas," in *Mesoamerican Sites and World-Views*, Elizabeth Benson, ed. [Washington, D.C.: Dumbarton Oaks, 1981], pp. 119–143; Calixta Guiteras-Holmes, *Perils of the Soul: The World View of a Tzotzil Indian* [New York: The Free Press of Glencoe, 1961]; Gary Gossen, "Temporal and Spatial Equivalents in Chamula Ritual Symbolism," in *Reader in Comparative Religion: An Anthropological Approach*, William Lessa and Evon Z. Vogt, eds. [New York and London: Harper and Row, 1972]), pp. 135–149; Ulrich Köhler, *Čonbilal Č'ulelal. Grundformen Mesoamerikanischer Kosmologie und Religion in einem Gebetstext auf Maya-Tzotzil*, Acta Humboldtiana, Series Geographica et Ethnographica, no. 5 [Wiesbaden: Franz Steiner-Verlag, 1977]; William R. Holland, *Medicina Maya en los Altos de Chiapas*, Serie de Antropología Social, no. 2 [Mexico: Instituto Nacional y Indigenista, 1978]); *Oaxaca (*Elsie Clews Parsons, *Mitla, Town of the Souls and Other Zapotec-Speaking Pueblos of Oaxaca, Mexico* [Chicago: University of Chicago Press, 1936]; Julio de la Fuente, "Las Ceremonias de la Lluvia entre los Zapotecos de Hoy," in *XXVII Congreso Internacional de Americanistas, Actas de la Primera Sesión*, vol. III [Mexico, 1939], pp. 479–481, and *Yalalag. Una Villa Zapoteca Serrana*, Museo Nacional de Antropología, Serie Científica, no. 1 [Mexico, 1949]; Pedro Carrasco, "Un Mito y Una Ceremonia entre los Chatinos de Oaxaca," in *A William C. Townsend en el XXV Aniversario del I.L.V.* [Mexico, 1960], 43–48]; *Sierra de Puebla* (Tim Knab, *Words Great and Small: Sierra Nahuat Narrative Discourse in Everyday Life* [unpublished manuscript, copyright 1983]; Alain Ichón, *La Religión de los Totonacas de la Sierra*, Colección SEP-INI, no. 16 [Mexico: Instituto Nacional Indigenista, 1973]); *Nahuas from Veracruz* (Luís Reyes Garcia, ed., *Der Ring aus Tlalocan. Mythen und Gebete, Lieder und Erzählungen der heutigen Nahua in Veracruz und Puebla* [Quellenwerke zur Alten Geschichte Amerikas, vol. 12, Berlin, 1976]; Hildeberto Martínez and Luís Reyes García, "Culto en las Cuevas de Cuautlapa en el Siglo XVIII," *Comunidad* [Mexico: Universidad Iberoamericana], V[27] [1970]: 541–551); *Nahuas of Northeastern Guerrero* (Schultze-Jena, "Bei den Azteken"; Mercedes Olivera, "Huémitl de Mayo en Citlala: Ofrendas para Chicomecoatl o para la Santa Cruz?" in *Mesoamérica: Homenaje al Doctor Paul Kirchoff*, Barbro Dahlgren, ed. [Mexico, SEP-INAH, 1979], pp. 143–158; Ma. Teresa Sepúlveda, "Petición de Lluvias en Ostotempa," *Boletín INAH* [Mexico: INAH] II [4] [1973]; 9–20; Cruz Suárez Jácome, "Petición de Lluvia en Zitlala, Guerrero, *Boletín INAH* [Mexico: INAH] Epoca III [22] [1978]: 3–13; Catherine Good E., *Haciendo la Lucha: Arte y Comercio Nahua* [Mexico: Fondo de Cultura Económica, in press]; and *Tlapanecs of Northeastern Guerrero* (Schultze-Jena, *Bei den Azteken*; Marion Oettinger, quoted by Heyden, "Caves, Gods and Myths," 28).

145. See Bonfil Batalla, "Los que Trabajan con el Tiempo": 101, 103; Lorenzo, "Las

119

Zonas Arqueológicas": 16–53; Heyden, "Caves, Gods and Myths": 27; William Madsen, *Christo-Paganism: A Study of Mexican Religious Syncretism*, Middle American Research Institute, publication no. 19 (New Orleans: Tulane University, 1957), p. 160.

146. Karl Anton Nowotny, "Herkunft und Inhalt des Kodex Borbonicus," in *Codex Borbonicus: Bibliotheque Nationale de l'Assemblee Nationale, Paris (4120)*, facsimile edition (Graz-Austria: Akademische Druck-und Verlagsanstalt, 1974), p. 19.

147. *Codex Borbonicus: Bibliotheque Nationale de l'Assemblee Nationale, Paris (4120)*, commentary by Karl Anton Nowotny, facsimile edition (Graz-Austria: Akademische Druck-und Verlagsanstalt, 1974), pp. 23–26, 32, 35.

148. *Codex Borbonicus*: 23, 29, 30, 31, 32. A distinction is made between Tlaloque and tlaloque; both forms represent the plural of the name of the god Tlaloc but correspond to a conceptual distinction between these multiple manifestations of the god. The tlaloque were the innumerable small servants of Tlaloc, while the Tlaloque were the fourfold manifestation of the rain god corresponding to the four quarters of the universe.

149. Nowotny, "Herkunft und Inhalt": 19.

150. See note 148.

151. According to the chronicler of Oaxaca, Francisco de Burgoa (*Geográfica Descripción de la Parte Septentrional del Polo Artico de América*, 2 vols., Publicaciones del Archivo General de la Nación, XXV–XXVI [Mexico: Talleres Gráficos de la Nación, 1934], I: 341–342), the pre-Hispanic gods who controlled water, seeds, and fruits lived in caves. Modern ethnographic data from Oaxaca also reveal caves full of corn and riches (Parsons, *Mitla*: 421; Heyden, "Caves, Gods and Myths": 27). Similar myths are recorded ethnographically as far south as the Pipiles (Nahuas) of El Salvador (Leonhard Schultze-Jena, *Mythen in der Muttersprache der Pipil von Izalco in El Salvador, Indiana*, vol. II [Jena: G. Fischer Verlag, 1935], pp. 60, 345). See also Karl Anton Nowotny (*Rituale in Mexiko und im Nordamerikanischen Südwesten*, Jahrbuch für Geschichte von Staat, Wirtschaft und Gesellschaft Lateinamerikas, vol. 8 [Cologne: Böhlau Verlag, 1970], p. 22). See note 154.

152. Walter Lehmann, ed., *Die Geschichte der Königreiche von Colhuacán und Mexiko*, Quellenwerke zur Alten Geschichte Amerikas, vol. I (Stuttgart: Verlag Kohlhammer, 1938), pp. 339–340.

153. Tonacatepetl, "the mountain of sustenance"; Tonacayotl, "human sustenance" or "the fruits of the earth" ("mantenimiento humano" or "los frutos de la tierra") (Molina, *Vocabulario*, 149r).

154. We are following here the translation by Günter Zimmermann, which corrects Walter Lehmann's previous translation (see Nowotny, *Rituale*: 13). According to Lehmann's erroneous version, the Tlaloque themselves stole the maize from the Tonacatepetl: "netlalhuilo in tlaloque . . . namoyallo in tlalloque intonacayotl" (Lehmann, ed., *Die Geschichte der Königreiche*: 340). According to Zimmermann, maize is stolen *from* the Tlaloque, its original owners. A similar myth was recorded by Schultze-Jena among the Pipiles (Nahuas) of El Salvador. According to this myth, the tepehua, "the rain boys" or "owners of the mountains," also stole the maize from inside a mountain. The smallest of them, Chijchin, split the mountain (Schultze-Jena, *Mythen in der Muttersprache*: 60, 345; Nowotny, *Rituale*: 22; Broda, "Las Fiestas Aztecas de los Dioses de la Lluvia": 257).

155. Richard F. Townsend ("Pyramid and Sacred Mountain," in *Ethnoastronomy and Archaeoastronomy in the American Tropics*, Anthony F. Aveni and Gary Urton, eds., Annals of the New York Academy of Sciences, vol. 385 [New York: The New York Academy of Sciences, 1982], pp. 48, 61) was the first to propose this identification of Tlaloc's side of the double pyramid, with the Tonacatepetl or cosmic mountain of sustenance. See also my analy-

sis of the myth of the Tonacatepetl according to the *Historia de los Reynos de Colhuacan y Mexico* (Broda, "Las Fiestas Aztecas de los Dioses de la Lluvia": 257).

156. See Nagao, "The Planting of Sustenance."

157. Lehmann, ed., *Die Geschichte der Königreiche*: 375–382.

158. Broda, "Las Fiestas Aztecas de los Dioses de la Lluvia": 256–260.

159. There exist parallels for this practice not only in modern ethnographic material from the Tarahumara Indians in northwestern Mexico (Georg Grünberg, personal communication) but also in the distant Andean region, where the Inca ruler Pachacuti had sand brought from the Pacific coast in Peru up to Cuzco to fill the sacred plaza with it. (I am grateful to Steven A. Wegner for this highly suggestive information.) This comparative material needs to be explored further.

160. Matos, ed., *El Templo Mayor: Excavaciones*: 143–184.

161. Thirty-three offering caches were excavated in Period IVb. The offerings of later periods are poorly preserved because of the destruction. (See Matos, this volume.)

162. See Johanna Broda, "Tlacaxipehualiztli"; Broda, "Los Estamentos;" Broda, "Estratificación Social y Ritual;" Broda, "La Fiesta Azteca del Fuego Nuevo;" Broda, "Ideology of the Aztec State" where such grand ritual dramas are analyzed in detail.

163. D. Carrasco, "Templo Mayor": 287–289; D. Carrasco, this volume.

164. Sahagún (FC), XI: 247.

165. Sahagún (HG), XI: 344, 345 (transl. by J. Broda). In this passage, the Spanish version of Sahagún is more evocative than the Nahuatl original. This passage from Sahagún finds a modern ethnographic parallel among the Nahuas of northeastern Guerrero. Catherine Good recently informed me that people from Oapan told her that if an important well near their village dried up as a result of the extreme drought of that year (March 1984), the most appropriate remedy would be to fetch water from the sea and bring it into contact with the well! Oapan is situated on the Río Balsas and is two or three days walking distance from the Pacific coast. The inhabitants of Oapan and several other neighboring villages are today artisans and merchants of amate (bark-paper) paintings, ceramics, and carved wooden masks who sell their products to tourists in Acapulco and other resorts. (For an anthropological study of this region, see Good, *Haciendo la Lucha*.)

166. The chronicler Diego Durán gives the etymology of "path below the earth" or "long cave" (Durán, *Historia*, I: 81) for the name of Tlaloc. Although this is not correct linguistically, it is interesting because of its meaning (see Sullivan, "Tlaloc" and Heyden, "Caves, Gods and Myths").

167. In Oapan, Guerrero, the term *inan atl* (the mother of the water) is applied to the sea (Catherine Good, personal communication). Besides these ethnographic data from the Nahuas in Guerrero, some really astonishing fragments of information refer to this same complex of cosmological ideas among the Chinantecs of Usila. (The Chinantla is a region situated in the northeastern part of Oaxaca.) According to field material gathered by R. Weitlaner and C. A. Castro between 1943 and 1953, "marine fauna is re-created in the imagination of the usileños who dream with its supernatural images. Among the most common beliefs we find that at the peak of Cerro Rabón there exist four big lagoons and six or seven small ones. At this place a very strong wind is blowing accompanied by lightnings. In those lagoons live "sea animals" like sharks and whales. Only the "brujos" (shamans) may come near such a miraculous place. Another case refers to a water serpent that appears as the guardian of springs. The Chinantecs believe that the rainbow is a marine serpent (Roberto J. Weitlaner and Carlo Antonio Castro, *Usila* [*Morada de Colibríes*]. *Papeles de la Chinatla* VII, Serie Científica, no. 11, Museo Nacional de Antropología [Mexico, 1973, transl. by J. Broda]). Martínez and Reyes

García relate that the Nahuas of Huatusco, Córdoba, Orizaba, and Zóngolica (Veracruz), believe that inside the mountains (*tepetl*) there live small beings of blue color called *tipeyolohtle*, "heart of the mountain." These beings "make the water that boils in the sea, rise to the sky in order to bring the rains." For this reason they are called *tlatsinihkeh*, "tronadores," or "those who produce thunder and lightning" (Martínez and Reyes García, "Culto en las Cuevas": 544). The richness of this material gives an idea of the possibilities for future research!

168. Molina, *Vocabulario*: 37v.

169. Sahagún (HG), XI: 344 (transl. by J. Broda).

170. Sahagún (FC), XI: 247.

171. Alfredo López-Austin, *Cuerpo Humano e Ideología*, 2 vols., Instituto de Investigaciones Antropológicas (Mexico: UNAM, 1980), I: 64–65.

172. "Histoyre du Mechique," in *Teogonía e Historia de los Mexicanos*, Angel María Garibay, ed., Colección Sepan Cuántos, no. 37 (Mexico: Editorial Porrúa, 1965), p. 108.

173. Personal communication by Eduardo Matos Moctezuma.

174. See Leopoldo Batres, "Exploraciones en las Calles de las Escalerillas"; Seler, "Die Ausgrabungen am Orte."

175. Derived from the adjective *tlallo*, "full of earth," "covered with earth," "made of earth" (Sullivan, "Tlaloc": 215).

176. "Histoyre du Mechique," in *Teogonía e Historia*, Angel Ma. Garibay, ed.: 105.

177. These sculptures are the monumental Coatlicue, the *Yollotlicue*, the skeletal greenstone goddess found by Batres in 1900, a monumental feathered serpent with a human face emerging from its jaws, as well as a female monster, Cihuacoatl. These sculptures are now in the Mexican National Museum of Anthropology (Pasztory, *Aztec Art*: 151–162; pls. 100, 101, 109, 113, 116, 117). See also Seler ("Die Ausgrabungen am Orte": 742–841), who referred to these sculptures in his pioneer study (in 1901) on the findings at the Templo Mayor. See also Klein (*Face of the Earth*: 54–152), who presents an analysis of the iconography of Tlaloc in relation to the earth monster Tlaltecuhtli, to Coatlicue-Cihuacoatl and other deities.

178. See Seler ("Die Ausgrabungen am Orte": 787–794); Ignacio Alcocer, *Apuntes sobre la Antigua México-Tenochtitlan* (Mexico: Instituto Panamericano de Geografía e Historia, 1927); Justino Fernández, *Coatlicue: Estética del Arte Indígena Antiguo*, Instituto de Investigaciones Históricas (Mexico: UNAM, 1959); Klein (*Face of the Earth*: 57, 58); and Pasztory (*Aztec Art*: 159).

179. See note 121.

180. Barbara Tedlock, "Earth Rites and Moon Cycles: Mayan Synodic and Sidereal Lunar Reckoning," in *Ethnoastronomy: Indigenous Astronomical and Cosmological Traditions of the World*, John B. Carlson and Von Del Chamberlain, eds. (Washington, D.C.: Smithsonian Institution Press, in press). See also Barbara Tedlock, *Time and the Highland Maya* (Albuquerque: University of New Mexico Press, 1982).

181. "Histoyre du Mechique," in *Teogonía e Historia*, Angel Ma. Garibay, ed.: 108.

182. Durán, *Historia*, I: 130; Sahagún (HG), I: 46–47.

183. This "underworld" was certainly different from that of Mictlan; rather, it was related to Tlalocan, which also was a realm beyond the world of the living and was located inside the earth. For comparative modern ethnographic material, see Knab (*Words Great and Small*), Martínez and Reyes García ("Culto en las Cuevas de Cuautlapa"), and Reyes García, ed. (*Der Ring aus Tlalocan*).

184. Klein, "Who was Tlaloc?": 197–198.

185. Pasztory, *Aztec Art*: 156.

186. A somewhat different interpretation of this sculpture was given by Alfredo López-Austin, "Iconografía Mexica. El Monolito Verde del Templo Mayor," *Anales de Antropología* (Mexico: UNAM) XVI (1979): 135–153.

187. This glyph (1 Tochtli) appears on the bottom of the monumental Coatlicue and Yollotlicue, the large skeletal greenstone goddess, and the feathered serpent with a human face emerging from its open jaws (see note 177) (see also Pasztory, *Aztec Art*: 151–162; pls. 100, 101, 109, 113, 117).

188. Aguilera, *Coyolxauhqui*: 75.

189. Pasztory (*Aztec Art*: 155). For another detailed interpretation of the monumental relief stone and its iconographic elements, see Aguilera (*Coyolxauhqui*) (see also notes 53 and 70). Aguilera and Graulich both conclude that Cihuacoatl and Coyolxauhqui really were the same deity (see Michel Graulich, *Mythes et Rites des Vingtaines du Mexique Central Préhispanique*, 3 vols., Ph.D. thesis, Université Libre de Bruxelles, 1979–1980, vol. II, pp. 543–546); however, different authors have stressed different aspects in the complex character of the goddess Cihuacoatl.

190. Personal communication by Edward Calnek to E. Pasztory (*Aztec Art*: 155).

191. Graulich, "Templo Mayor": 93.

192. Eduardo Matos Moctezuma, personal communication.

193. The aspects of sun and the sky as represented by Huitzilopochtli have not been explored further in this investigation because they have few indications in the offerings. In studying the full symbolism of Templo Mayor, however, it is important to take into account the basic sky-sun and earth-water dualisms that existed on many different levels. A brief but very suggestive interpretation was offered recently by M. Graulich on this point ("Templo Mayor").

194. See notes 40 to 44 and Pasztory ("Xochicalco Stelae"), Graulich ("Templo Mayor"), and Cohodas ("Iconography," parts II and III). See also Girard (*Los Mayas Eternos*), whose interpretation has been somewhat pioneer in this field. His ethnographic fieldwork still awaits due critical evaluation.

195. I would like to thank Tim Knab for granting access to this unpublished text. The Sierra de Puebla is today a "region of refuge" where traditional Indian culture has been preserved to a high degree. The Nahuas of San Miguel cannot be considered direct descendants of Mexica culture; nevertheless, we are dealing with a Nahua group of the central Mexican highlands who, in the sixteenth century, definitely were culturally related to the Nahuas of the Valley of Mexico. Similar notions of Tlalocan are reported by Martínez and Reyes García ("Culto en las Cuevas de Cuautlapa") for the Nahuas of Huatusco, Córdoba, Orizaba, and Zóngolica of Veracruz. See also Reyes García, ed. (*Der Ring aus Tlalocan*) with respect to myths dealing with Tlalocan from the Nahuas of Veracruz and Puebla.

196. Knab, *Words Great and Small*, manuscript: 3–4.

197. Ibid., 5–6.

198. Ibid., 17, 18, 19–20.

Myth, Cosmic Terror, and the Templo Mayor

DAVÍD CARRASCO
University of Colorado
Boulder, Colorado

One of the last narrative views of the Great Aztec Temple before it was partially dismantled by cannon fire by the Spaniards comes from Díaz del Castillo, sergeant in Cortés's army who has given us a hair-raising account of human sacrifice at the ceremonial capital. During the ferocious Spanish siege of the capital of Tenochtitlan, the Aztecs made a desperate sacrifice of Spanish soldiers to their sun and war god Huitzilopochtli, whose shrine sat on top of the Templo Mayor located in the heart of the city.

> When we retreated near to our quarters and had already crossed a great opening where there was much water, the arrows, javelins and stones could no longer reach us. Sandoval, Francisco de Lugo and Andreas de Tapia were standing with Pedro de Alvarado each one relating what had happened to him and what Cortes had ordered, when again there was sounded the dismal drum of Huichilobos and many other shells and horns and things like trumpets and the sound of them all was terrifying, and we all looked towards the lofty Pyramid where they were being sounded, and saw that our comrades whom they had captured when they defeated Cortés were being carried by force up the steps and they were taking them to be sacrificed. When they got them up to a small square in front of the oratory, where their accursed idols are kept, we saw them place plumes on the heads of many of them and with things like fans in their hands they forced them to dance before Huichilobos and after they had danced they immediately placed them on their backs on some rather narrow stones which had been prepared as places for sacrifice, and with some knives they sawed open their chests and drew out their palpitating hearts and offered them to the idols that were

124

there, and they kicked the bodies down the steps, and the Indian butchers who were waiting below cut off their arms and feet and flayed the skin off the faces, and prepared it afterwards like glove leather with the beards on, and kept those for the festivals when they celebrated drunken orgies and the flesh they ate in chilmole.[1]

This shocking description of Aztec ritual killing presents one of the dominant popular images we have of Aztec religion as a tradition of high pyramids, dismal drums, bloodthirsty priests, and eerie settings with cannibalism added for flavor. A more careful look at this description, in terms of familiarity with the Aztec mythic tradition, reveals important clues to the Aztec sense of "orientation" in their cosmos.[2] This text alone shows that the Aztecs seek a vital sense of power at their Great Temple. They act against the growing disequilibrium in their world through aggressive ritual action at their sacred center. They attempt to revitalize themselves at a time of deep crisis by climbing their temple with captive warriors, and, after ceremonial dancing and singing, killing them on an "altar" and throwing their bodies down the steps. Then they dismember and flay their victims, followed by ritual cannibalism. Aztec history and myth tells us that the practice of temple and mountain ascent to revitalize the world through ritual killing was a time-honored tradition.[3] A closer look at Díaz del Castillo's description will reveal that this apparently "barbaric" action and place had mythic significance expressive of the commitment of the Mesoamerican urban tradition to cosmic rejuvenation through ritual killing.

At the outset of this chapter on Aztec strategies for orientation and control, it is important to say that this horrific image is often juxtaposed with the opposite view of Aztec religion and character. Scholars such as Miguel León-Portilla, George Kubler, Burr Brundage, and Esther Pasztory, as well as Richard Townsend,[4] have explored with remarkable insight the philosophical, architectural, and artistic accomplishments of the Aztecs and their neighbors. The fractured image that results from a total view of Aztec life raises questions of the most profound and emotional sort. For instance, how could a people who conceived of and carved the uniquely marvelous calendar stone and developed one of the most accurate calendrical systems of the ancient world[5] spend so much time, energy, and wealth in efforts to obtain and sacrifice human victims for every conceivable feast day in the calendar? Why did a people so fascinated by and accomplished in sculpture, featherwork, craft industries, poetry, and painting[6] become so committed to cosmic regeneration through the thrust of the ceremonial knife? The Aztec image that glares at us through the texts is an image of startling juxtapositions of Flowers, Song/Blood, Cut.

In spite of this frenzied paradox, the "place" of the Great Temple and its ritual traditions remains central and vital in any serious interpretation of the Aztec world. This is especially true when we realize that the Templo Mayor was not only the sacred center of an urban polity but was also the architectural and symbolic end product in a long process of Mesoamerican urbanism. It is particularly important to highlight the urban character of this place and its ceremonial traditions, following the ground-breaking work of Pedro Armillas, Gordon Willey, Paul Kirchhoff, and Pedro Carrasco,[7] who have illuminated the outlines of complex city-state societies that controlled Mesoamerican history for two millennia. The social and symbolic world of the Aztecs and their temple tradition consisted of a collection of small local states called *tlatocayotls*. These city-states consisted of small, agriculturally based, politically organized territories under the control of a city that was the seat of government, ceremonial action, and the home of the ruling class, which claimed descent from the gods. Conflict, warfare, and human sacrifice at major temples dominated the social order of the Aztec world. The Templo Mayor and the city of Tenochtitlan were the paramount expressions of this pattern of organization through control of over 400 towns in thirty-eight provinces that constituted the Aztec empire. The paradigmatic influence of Tenochtitlan is reflected in Edward Calnek's judgment that "Prior to the conquest, it had been the largest and most highly urbanized of all Mesoamerican cities"[8] and the insight of Paul Wheatley that the traditional city, in general, was "the style center of the traditional world,"[9] which set the pattern of social, economic, ritual, and political life. The clues to the Aztec method of dominating this social and symbolic pattern which are reflected in this text provide the point of departure for this contribution to the multidisciplinary exercise on the significance of the Templo Mayor in Mesoamerican religion and society.

HISTORY OF RELIGIONS AND MESOAMERICA

We may come to a greater understanding of the Aztec sense of orientation and control in their world by focusing on the Aztec mythic vision of place, that is, the way they conceived the origin and character of their cosmos and society and their pressured role within it. As a number of studies have shown, by knowing a culture's mythic structure[10] and vision of its own place and position in the cosmos, we come to know the central paradigms of orientation and control in that culture. Jonathan Z. Smith explains the importance of knowing a people's vision of place this way: "The question of the character of the place upon which one stands is the fundamental symbolic and social question. Once an individual or culture has expressed its vision of its place, a whole language of symbols and social structure will follow."[11]

Smith's statement and work become an excellent point of departure into the Aztec case when we join it to the insights revealed in the wider studies by Mircea Eliade and Paul Wheatley on sacred places, ceremonial centers, and ritual repetition. It is especially in Eliade's work on the history of sacred centers that we see more clearly how a language of symbols and social structure will follow from such a vision.[12]

In such works as *The Myth of the Eternal Return*, *Myth and Reality*, and *Patterns in Comparative Religions*, and especially in his essay "Cosmogonic Myth and Sacred History,"[13] Eliade shows that myths of origin constitute a "primordial sacred history," which, brought together by the totality of significant myths, "is fundamental because it explains and, by the same token, justifies the existence of the world, of man, and of society. This is the reason that a mythology is considered at once a true history, it relates how things came into being, providing the exemplary model and also the justification of man's activities." What seems clear in a number of cross-cultural and particular studies in ancient and modern cultures is that this "primordial sacred history" contained in the myths provides the cosmological setting, the sacred context for action, and the exemplary models for the ritual activities that constitute the ceremonial, political, and social world of ancient people. The word "primordial" is especially important here because it refers to an original, authoritative, unquestioned structure of reality. Whether we utilize the terminology of Cornelious Loew, "cosmological conviction";[14] Rene Berthelot, "astro-biological thought";[15] or Jonathan Z. Smith, "utopian cosmology,"[16] traditional Aztec myths have at least four authoritative characteristics relevant to Mesoamerican cosmology, history, and vision of place. These myths (and especially the myth of Huitzilopochtli's birth and the myth of the creation of the fifth sun) (1) enjoy a primordial, authoritative prestige throughout the empire; (2) provide exemplary models for the proper relationship between humans and the cosmos; (3) contain dramatic strategies for rejuvenation of the world at all levels; and (4) appear as influential forces even in opaque fragments and forms that do not seem to have explicit connections to myths but that carry implicit mythic significance. According to Eliade, the major ordering principle for this pattern of archetype and repetition is the Cosmogonic Myth, the Great Story of universal creation, which is the exemplary model for all subsequent creations that result in the order and renewal of all elements of the world. The cosmogonic myth is the story of the birth of the cosmos through heroic and exuberant deeds by supernatural beings. It provides the setting and the pattern for creative action and proper conduct in all levels of reality, both terrestrial and celestial.

My strategy in this chapter will be to penetrate the Azec vision of place exemplified in the Templo Mayor through drawing the lines of coincidence between Aztec mythology, as understood in the light of Eliade and Wheatley's work, and the two dimensions of orientation at Templo Mayor reflected in the opening quotation— ceremonial space and ritual death. Specifically, I will approach this coincidence through direct interpretation of two major mythic episodes in the Aztec tradition, the myth of Huitzilopochtli's birth at the mountain of Coatepec and the cosmogonic myth of the creation of the Fifth Age at the sacred city of Teotihuacan. I will relate these mythic traditions to the evidence associated with the excavation of Templo Mayor, to illustrate how the Aztec vision of place was directed not only toward founding and maintaining a magnificently ordered cosmos held firmly at the capital through miniaturization of religious archetypes but also directed, through the expansion of these archetypes, toward controlling peripheral communities by integrating them forcefully within the Aztec world.

127

I must note the tentative nature of the essay presented in this chapter because the Templo Mayor was not only a paradigm of the Mesoamerican world, but continues to be, for modern scholars, at least two other things—a puzzle and a scandal. It is a puzzle because it contained so many bits, pieces, parts, and shapes of the Aztec world arranged according to a plan that we have still only vaguely discerned. There are an enormous number of questions raised by the groups of masks, rebuildings, child sacrifices, strange deity images, Toltec symbolism, pervasiveness of Tlaloc imagery, and absence of Huitzilopochtli. It will take decades to figure out the full design of this puzzle. The scandal of the Templo Mayor resides in its pre-Columbian use as a theater for large numbers of human sacrifices of warriors, children, and slaves. Although we have been aware of this shocking practice for almost half a millennium, the scholarly community has been remarkably hesitant to explore the evidence and nature of large-scale ritual killing in Aztec Mexico. Something repulsive, threatening, and apparently mind-boggling about the increment in human sacrifices has confounded theologians, anthropologists, and other scholars in their consideration of Aztec ritual.[17] The exemplary, puzzling, and scandalous nature of this temple and the excavation demand an approach similar to the one articulated by Peter Brown in his essay on imaginative curiosity:

> We must ask ourselves whether the imaginative models that we bring to the study of history are sufficiently precise and differentiated, whether they embrace enough of what we sense to be what it is to be human, to enable us to understand and to communicate to others the sheer challenge of the past.[18]

In my view, the imaginative models of the history of religions do provide a useful approach to the "sheer challenge of the Aztec past" and its great temple.

CITY AND SYMBOL

Only in the last thirty years have scholars begun to focus intensely on the urban character of the ancient Mexican world. During this time relatively little attention has been given to the relationship between cosmological archetypes and the great capital cities that directed and dominated Mesoamerican cultural life for nearly 2,000 years. One of the most significant developments in this regard has been the work of an urban ecologist Paul Wheatley, who has developed a general model of how traditional cities were organized as symbols of cosmic order. In three important works of scholarship, *The Pivot of the Four Quarters: A Preliminary Enquiry into the Origins and Character of the Ancient Chinese City*, "City as Symbol," and "The Suspended Pelt: Reflections on a Discarded Model of Spatial Order,"[19] Wheatley has shown that in the seven areas of primary urban generation (China, Mesopotamia, Mesoamerica, Peru, southwestern Nigeria, the Indus Valley, and Egypt), that is, where cities were first created, a special kind of symbolic consciousness was utilized to organize space and human action. The great capitals of the earliest urban societies were laid out as symbols of cosmic order and destiny. Drawing directly from the insights of Mircea Eliade and others in his studies of the mythic influences in archaic civilization, Wheatley has illuminated the manner in which the royal and sacerdotal elites who ruled these capitals developed complex processes of control over the ecological complexes of ancient society. Two sentences from Wheatley's chapter "The Ancient Chinese City as a Cosmo-Magical Symbol" illustrate the religious character of this control:

> Underpinning urban form not only in traditional China but also throughout most of the rest of Asia, and with somewhat modified aspect in the New World, was a complex of ideas to which Rene Berthelot has given the name astro-biology. . . . This mode of thought presupposes an intimate parallelism between the mathematically expressible regimes of the heavens, and the biologically determined rhythms of life on earth, (as manifested conjointly in the succession of the seasons and the annual cycles of plant regeneration).[20]

Wheatley calls this attitude "cosmo-magical thought," thought that dwells on the imitation of complex and detailed archetypes, and he has shown how it was expressed in at least three aspects of spatial organization that contributed to the prestige of capitals as the sacred pivots of the universe.

More specifically, the ancient ideal type city was a sacred space oriented around a quintessentially sacred center in the form of a temple or temple pyramid. This pivot of the community partook of the "symbolism of the center," meaning that it was believed to be the center of the world, the point of intersection of all the world's paths, both terrestrial and celestial. The central structure was an axis mundi, "regarded as the meeting point of heaven, earth, and hell," or "the point of ontological transition between the spheres." The priestly elites who planned and directed the construction of their ceremonial centers often attempted to align their causeways, sections of city, or major buildings with the cardinal compass directions of the universe, "thus assimilating the groups' territory to the cosmic order and constructing a sanctified living space or within the continuum of profane space." These four highways, sections, or structures enforcing the sanctification of the central place were centripetal and centrifugal guides, pulling the sacred and social energies into the center and diffusing the supernatural and royal powers outward into the kingdom. Another aspect of urban sacred space was manifest when a ceremonial center, or one or more of its major buildings, represented through the image, design, and interrelationship of parts a cosmological concept or mythological episode. In this instance, a correspondence between stone image and celestial action was achieved in the appearance of a ceremonial building.

Recently a brilliant analysis of Aztec art, *State and Cosmos in the Art of Tenochtitlan* by Richard Fraser Townsend, demonstrates the Aztec version of this parallelism in a fresh way. Focusing on the "imperial monumental ensemble" of Tenochtitlan, Townsend reveals how ritual attire, sculpture, commemorative monuments, and Nahuatl metaphors expressed a "living structural affinity between the natural and social orders" of the universe. Townsend's study shows how various examples of art, architecture, and numerous ceremonial objects were dramatic ways by which the "Aztec state validated itself by expressing its indissoluble connection with the sacred universe." It is evident in Townsend's elegant rendering of Aztec art the degree to which a commitment to a parallelism between heavens and earth was embedded in Aztec religion. As we shall now see, the Aztec capital and its ceremonial center, especially the myths and architecture of the Templo Mayor, exemplified this pattern of cosmomagical organization in a distinct manner.[21]

THE CENTER OF THE WORLD

The Aztec vision of their city and empire was largely derived from their cosmology, which contained a number of spatial and temporal archetypes, that is, exemplary models of a "transcendental" or celestial origin that appears in the myths, sacred histories, sculpture, and picture books. The Aztecs, like many Mesoamerican communities, conceived of their world as a land surrounded by water, Cemanahuac.[22] At the center or navel, tlalxico, stood their capital city, Tenochtitlan. Through this center flowed the vertical cosmos, which consisted of a series of thirteen layers above and nine layers below the earth. Each celestial layer was inhabited by a deity, a sacred bird, and a specific cosmological influence and color.[23] The nine underworld layers were hazard stations for the souls of the dead, who, through the aid of magical charms buried with the bodies, went on a quest for eternal peace at the lowest level, called *Mictlan.*

The special location of the Aztec capital in this vertical cosmos is referred to in an Aztec poem:

> Proud of itself
> Is the City of Mexico-Tenochtitlan
> Here no one fears to die in war
> This is our glory
>
> This is Your Command
> Oh Giver of Life
> have this in mind, oh princes
> Who could conquer Tenochtitlan
> Who could shake the foundation of heaven?[24]

The city was eulogized as a proud, fearless, and glorious place, an invincible center that linked the world of fearless warriors with the universal god, the "Giver of Life."[25] Conceived of as the "foundation of heaven," Tenochtitlan was the point of union between the celestial powers and the underworld. It joined the many parts of the cosmos together. In Aztec thought it had to be unshakable, for if it was disturbed and conquered, the cosmos would collapse.

How Tenochtitlan gained this special position as the cener of the world is told in the Aztec foundation myth, a version of which is embroidered on the flag of modern Mexico. According to their sacred history, the Aztecs emerged from *Chicomoztoc* (the "Seven Caves"), which was on an island surrounded by a lagoon. Their patron deity Huitzilopochtli appeared in a dream to their shaman priest, commanding him to lead the people south to a place where the god would appear in the form of a great eagle perched on a blooming nopal growing from a rocky island in the middle of a lake. The Aztecs traveled south and beheld the omen, realizing that this was to be the place of their future city, which according to the divine promise would become "the queen and lady of all the others of the earth, and where we will receive all other kings and lords and to which they will come as to one supreme among all the others."[26] The Aztecs rejoiced at the sight of their new land and enthusiastically built the first shrine to the patron god Huitzilopochtli—a shrine made of reeds and wood.[27] This original shrine became the Templo Mayor.

Another version of the foundation story reveals the fuller character of Tenochtitlan as the center of vertical space. Following the sighting of the eagle, one of the Chichimec priests dived into the lake and disappeared. Believing that he had drowned, his companions returned to their camp. Soon he returned to report that beneath the lake he talked with Tlaloc, the old god of the earth, and had received permission for the Aztecs to settle there. The city's existence was thereby sanctified by both the forces of the earth and the sky.

From these stories we can see that Tenochtitlán was conceived not merely as the new settlement but also as the royal city of the world to which the various royal authorities would visit "as one supreme among all the others." This special prestige is reflected in the frontispiece of the *Codex Mendoza*, which is an image of the foundation myth. It pictures the eagle, nopal, stone, and lake image above a large Aztec shield with seven eagle down feathers and seven arrows attached to it. This is the ideogram for "Place of Authority," and the painted image can be read, "The Aztecs have arrived in Tenochtitlan, the place of authority."[28] The persistence of Tenochtitlan's status as the center for royal authority in central Mesoamerica is demonstrated by the fact that when Cortés wrote his second letter in 1520 to the emperor of Spain, he reported that "all the Lords of the Land, who are vassals of the said Moctezuma have houses in the city and reside therein for a certain time of year."

During the next 200 years of Tenochtitlan's existence, an elaborate ceremonial center was constructed around the original shrine. This sacred precinct increased in size about 440 meters on each of its four sides. It is an example of miniaturization and expansion woven together. While the entire ceremonial center constituted an enlargement of the original hierophany at that location, the entire space was organized as a smaller image of the entire universal order. It contained numerous structures, including schools for the nobility (*calmecac*), a series of large and small temples, a giant skull rack, a ball court, and administrative structures, all surrounded by a three-meterhigh wall called the *coatepantli*, or serpent wall. Into this ceremonial center poured pilgrim, king, noble, merchant, warrior, sacrificial victim, architect, ally, and enemy.

It was here that the spectacular human sacrifices took place, often at night before glowing torches and throngs of participants and onlookers. The Aztec world was integrated here. One of the most obvious examples of the integration of religious forces within the capital was the special temple built by Moctezuma II for the purpose of housing the images of deities from towns and cities throughout the Aztec empire. All supernatural powers were imprisoned into the center of the empire in order to integrate the divine forces of the realm.

HUITZILOPOCHTLI AND THE TEMPLO MAYOR

Earlier in this chapter I pointed out the value of identifying a people's vision of place, in particular the mythic dimensions of that vision. We learn a great deal about the Aztec mythic vision from the *teocuicatl*, or divine song about Huitzilopochtli's birth,[29] for this story was the sacred history about the Great Temple, the god, and ritual sacrifice. At the beginning, in the middle, and at the end of this song, we see that the place of Huitzilopochtli's birth, called Coatepec (Serpent Mountain), is the center of the Aztec vision of place. A closer look at the story and its relation to the evidence from the excavation shows the temple of Tlaloc and Huitzilopochtli was an *imago mundi*, an image of the Aztec world.

In order to gain an interpretive perspective on these complexities, I intend to read the myth in five parts that reveal the dramatic progression of an amazing conflict, the intertwining of Aztec myth, the concept of sacred space, and the justification of massive human sacrifice: (1) the cosmological setting of the story; (2) the miraculous pregnancy of Coatlicue, the Mother Goddess; (3) the ferocious preparation for war by the 400 children at the periphery of the Aztec world; (4) Huitzilopochtli's birth and massive killing of his siblings; and (5) the historical epilogue. In this manner, the reader can gain a sense of order and religious meaning in the myth.

The Cosmological Setting

"The Aztecs greatly revered Huitzilopochtli, they knew his origin, his beginning, was in this manner . . . " the narrative begins.

It is important to note the cosmological setting for the action in the myth because it establishes in part the nature of Huitzilopochtli's religious significance. We are immediately told that the Aztecs had great reverence for the god and remembered "his origin, his beginning" in detailed form. The combination of reverence and creation reflects the cosmogonic prestige of the story. This is not just a story about the god—it is the story of his creation. As the narrative continues, we hear of two major places of religious significance in the Aztec landscape—Coatepec, or Serpent Mountain, and Tula,[30] which was the capital of the Toltec empire. The action to come, we are told, takes place near Tula on the great mountain. This location of the action repeats a pattern in many Mesoamerican sacred histories in which the movement from action in the heavens to action on earth passes through, or in relation to, the paradigmatic kingdom of Quetzalcoatl, whose seat of power and authority was in Tollan, also called *Tula*. The proximity to the Toltec tradition is a sine qua non of Aztec authority, as my previous work on Quetzalcoatl demonstrated. In terms of the history of religions, this combination of Coatepec, Tula, and the prestige of origins reflects what has been called a "mythical geography," a geography that is fundamentally important because of its mythic prestige and symbolic capacity to sanctify action and individuals associated with it. In this case, the Aztec poets have created a prestigious space for Huitzilopochtli's birth by linking the Toltec capital, source of the sanctity of kings and cultures, with Coatepec, the source of their own god, and then casting this linkage in the setting of "in illo tempore." At the center of this landscape, at the axis mundi, where the origin of Huitzilopochtli was revealed, the Mother of the Gods, Lady of the Serpent Skirt, is sweeping the temple. She is identified as the mother of "the four hundred gods of the south" especially one, Coyolxauhqui, by name.

The Miraculous Pregnancy of Coatlicue, the Mother Goddess

The narrative continues: "there fell on her some plumage."

Following the narration of the cosmological setting comes a short episode of the miraculous impregnation of the Mother Goddess by a small ball of "fine feathers" that fell from above (pl. 31). This variation on the theme of a conception by divine intervention raises the question regarding the Mesoamerican pattern of the creation of gods. In this case, the divine element descends from above, replicating what Lopez Austin calls the "process of the descent of divine semen into the earthly sphere to create new beings."[31] It is again significant that the meeting point of heaven, in the form of the fine feathers, and the earth, in the form of the Mother Goddess, is the hill Coatepec.

The Four Hundred Children Prepare for War

The narrative continues: "they were very angry, they were very agitated, as if the heart had gone out of them. Coyolxauhqui incited them, she inflamed the anger of her brothers, so that they should kill her mother."

The third and longest episode in the myth details the ferocious preparation for war at the periphery of the Aztec empire and the march to Coatepec. The episode is one of dramatically shifting scenes between center and periphery, important dialogue between the unborn Huitzilopochtli and his mother and uncle, and a crescendo of motion leading to the ascent of the mountain. The entire action is laced with a ferocity of divine warriors cultivated by Coyolxauhqui. The episode reveals, among other things, the martial ideal par excellence of the Aztec warrior who builds himself up into

133

a berserk mode of being through ritual array and communal incitement. It is also revealing that this berserk response to the pregnancy at the temple on the mountain begins at the periphery of the mythical geography and moves toward the center.[32] This is especially important for the meaning of this geographic arrangement for the increment in human sacrifice that took place at the Templo Mayor.

The episode begins with the report that the 400 gods of the south were insulted by Coatlicue's pregnancy, and Coyolxauhqui exhorts them, "My brothers, she has dishonored us, we must kill our mother," and the inquiry of who fathered "what she carries in her womb." The scene abruptly shifts to the mountain, where Coatlicue becomes very frightened and sad of the threat by her children. Then, amazingly, Huitzilopochtli, still in her womb, calms her with the promise, "Do not be afraid, I know what I must do." The action then shifts back to the four hundred gods of the south who decide to kill their mother because of this disgrace. "They were very angry . . . very agitated . . . Coyolxauhqui incited them . . . she inflamed them." They respond to this mountain anger by attiring themselves "as for war." While they dress and groom themselves as warriors, one of the 400, named *Cuahuitlicac*, sneaked to Coatepec and reported every movement and advance toward the hill to Huitzilopochtli, who, still speaking from the womb, instructed his uncle, "Take care, be watchful, my uncle, for I know well what I must do." The text bears repeating at this point:

> And when finally they came to an agreement, the four hundred gods determined to kill, to do away with their mother, then they began to prepare, Coyolxauhqui directing them. They were very robust, well equipped, adorned as for war, they distributed among themselves their paper garb, the anecuyotl, the nettles, the streamers of colored paper, they tied little bells on the calves of their legs, the bells called oyohaulli. Their arrows had barbed points. Then they began to move.

As they move, the informing uncle reports their advance to Huitzilopochtli, who listens carefully from the womb, "Now they are coming through Tzompantitlan . . . Coaxalpan . . . up the side of the mountain . . . now they are on the top, they are here," Coyolxauhqui is leading them.

Huitzilopochtli's Birth

The narrative continues: "Huitzilopochtli was born . . . he struck Coyolxauhqui, he cut off her head . . . Huitzilopochtli pursued the four hundred gods of the south, he drove them away, he humbled them, he destroyed them, he annihilated them."

The entire song has been building toward this dramatic devastation, not just of the sister Coyolxauhqui, but of the enitre warrior population that attacks the mountain. When Coyolxauhqui arrives at the top of the mountain, Huitzilopochtli is born

134

fully grown, swiftly dresses himself as a great warrior, and dismembers his sister with a serpent of fire. It is important to note that the text is specific not only about her head being cut off, but about her body falling to pieces as it rolled down the hill.

It is important to insert here the archaeological discovery of the great Coyolxauhqui stone in 1979. Electrical workers excavating a pit beneath the street behind the national Cathedral of Mexico City uncovered a massive oval stone more than three meters in diameter with the mint condition image of an Aztec goddess on it. The image consisted of a decapitated and dismembered female goddess whose blood was depicted as precious fluid. Her striated head cloth, stomach, dismembered arms, and legs were circled by serpents (see pl. 1). A skull served as her belt buckle. She had earth-monster faces on her knees, elbows, and ankles. Her sandals revealed a royal figure and the iconography shows that this figure was the goddess Coyolxauhqui.[33] Placed alongside the myth we are discussing, this stone is a vivid window to the Aztec sense of place because we know from Sahagún that the Templo Mayor was called *Coatepec* by the Aztecs and consisted of a huge pyramid supporting two temples—one to Huitzilopochtli and one to Tlaloc. Two grand and steep stairways led up to the shrines. What is truly remarkable is that the stone was found directly at the base of the stairway leading up to Huitzilopochtli's temple. On both sides of the stairway's base, completing the bottom of the stairway's sides, were two large grinning serpent heads (pl. 8). The image is clear. The Templo Mayor is the architectural image of Coatepec, or Serpent Mountain, and just as Huitzilopochtli triumphed at the top of the mountain, while his sister was dismembered and fell to pieces below, so Huitzilopochtli's temple and icon sat triumphantly at the top of the Templo Mayor with the carving of the dismembered goddess directly below (see pl. 3). As Broda and others have revealed, the Templo Mayor was also a replica of Mount Tlaloc, the exemplary space of the cult of the rain god.

In fact, most interpretations of this myth end with the dismemberment of Coyolxauhqui and the realization that the Templo Mayor and the architectural arrangement of Huitzilopochtli's temple and the Coyolxauhqui stone replicated this cosmogony; however, a further reading of the myth holds a major key to the significance of this mythic place.

Following Coyolxauhqui's dismemberment, there is a total reversal in the location of berserk, ferocious action—onto the person of Huitzilopochtli. Before, it was Coyolxauhqui who generated the ferocity of battle and transmitted it to her siblings. Now it is Huitzilopochtli who embodies enormous aggression and attacks. We are told again and again about his aggression, but most importantly that he attacks and sacrifices all the other deities in the drama. *It is a myth not just about one sacrifice but about a sudden increment in human sacrifices to include all warriors who come to the Templo Mayor–Coatepec.* Consider the text. Huitzilopochtli "was proud" and drove the 400 off the mountain of the snake, but he did not stop there. "He pursued them, he chased them like rabbits, all around the mountain . . . four times." Here we see reference to the symbolic number four representing directions, but also perhaps to the four previous cosmogonic ages. The text is emphatic regarding this ritual combat and the aggressions of the god: "with nothing could they defend themselves. Huitzilopochtli chased them, he drove them away, he humbled them, he destroyed them, he annihilated them." The text does not end there but continues to portray this ritual aggression in more vivid terms: "they begged him repeatedly, they said to him, 'It is enough.' But Huitzilopochtli was not satisfied, with force he pushed against them . . . and when Huitzilopochtli had killed them, when he had given vent to his wrath, he stripped off their gear [their ornaments]." The aggression of Coyolxauhqui and her 400 siblings dissolved before this one great warrior, who did more than defeat and kill them, he obliterated their existence. Finally, he takes their costumes, their symbols and "introduced them into his destiny, he made them his own insignia." In this act of symbolic possession, Huitzilopochtli transforms their obliteration into his own power, integrating the ritual array, the spiritual forces of their costumes into his own design. This is a remarkable act of paradigmatic value because, as the excavation has shown, so many objects from conquered and allied communities were literally integrated into the base of the Templo Mayor.

The Historical Epilogue

The narrative continues: "the Aztecs venerated him, they made sacrifices to him . . . and his cult came from there, from Coatepec, the Mount of the Serpent."

The myth ends with a direct reference to the paradigmatic role which this action played in Aztec religion. We are told that Huitzilopochtli was a "prodigy" who was conceived miraculously, "he never had any father," and that sacrifices were made to him in exchange for his rewards. In this final section, we are taken out of the mythic realm of the story into the historical purpose of the divine action—to practice the religion of Huitzilopochtli and his manner of birth. As at the beginning, we are solidly placed on the peak of Coatepec, which is identified as the origin of not only the god, but his cult.

The narrative ends: "and his cult came from there, from Coatepec, the Mountain of the Serpent, as it was practiced from most ancient times."

What we learn from this Aztec statement about myth, sacred space, and sacrifice is that *Coatepec was the mythic place where a god was born who sacrificed—not sacrificing just one god, but ferociously sacrificing an abundance of gods as his first act of life*. We are also instructed that this place and action was the source of a cult, a religious practice of many sacrifices, many ascents, and many ritual combats.

Reference to the practice of this cult appears in the reports of Diego Durán, whose informants told him that the events at Coatepec were performed every year in the national festivals of the Aztecs during the month of *Panquetzaliztli*. This ceremony was highlighted by a foot race called *Ipaina Huitzilopochtli* (the haste, velocity, or swiftness of Huitzilopochtli). His comments reveal the relation of the myth just recounted and the theme and activity of the ceremony:

> Thus was named this commemorative celebration because while the god was alive he was never caught, never taken prisoner in war, was always triumphant over his enemies, and, no matter how swift he goes none ever caught up with him. He was the one who caught them. Therefore this feast honored his speed.[34]

It is as though the swiftness of pursuit and execution of the last episode of the myth of Huitzilopochtli's birth becomes the model for this attitude in the ritual. The Templo Mayor and its parts and related actions located at the heart of the city and empire represent the dramatic cosmic victory of Huitzilopochtli and the Aztecs over celestial and terrestrial enemies.

Remembering the opening quotation of this chapter, we can now see that much more than just the butchering of Spaniards was taking place when they ascended the Great Temple, dressed in plumes, forced to dance in symbolic ecstasy, and sacrificed before being thrown down the steps of the temple. A ritual repetition was being carried out to reenact a mythic beginning, a ferocity, and a new conquest.

The Map of Cortés

We can see in this discussion of the Aztec ceremonial center the direct mythic influences on spatial orientation and the integration of kingship, sacrifice, and a number of elements of Aztec religion associated with the Templo Mayor. Order and orientation were prescribed by celestial beings and earthly hierophanies. We can also see opaque mythic influences on the ceremonial center in the recent interpretations by Anthony Aveni concerning the astronomical alignments of the Templo Mayor. Again, the symbolism of the center appears to be the fundamental organizing principle. Aveni and Sharon Gibbs have shown that a valuable clue to the Templo Mayor's location in time and space appears in the map of Tenochtitlán done by Cortés's cartographer during the conquests. The map shows the island city divided by four causeways emerging from the main ceremonial precinct which contained European-style palaces, ceremonial structures, a skull rack, and the Great Temple. Even though the two-towered pyramid is erroneously located on the west side of the ceremonial center, its actual location is indicated by a circular face drawn between the twin towers. As the sixteenth-century friar Motolinia discovered in his research on Aztec religion and the festival of the flaying of men, *Tlacaxipehualiztli*, "This festival takes place when the sun stood in the middle of uichilobos, which was at the equinox and because it was a little out of straight, Moctezuma wished to pull it down and set it right."[35] The facial image in the map is most likely the rising sun, which, according to Aveni and Gibbs, would have risen between the twin temples at seven degrees, six minutes south of east on the equinoctial date. This map, text, and astronomical alignment indicate a more profound alignment in Aztec society, that is, the alignment between the five key elements of the sacred king who lines himself up with the temple, the sun, the horizon, and the ritual of renewal. This coherence of authority, sacred space, star, ritual killing, and horizon is organized by the location, height, and prestige of the Templo Mayor. To understand the ritual significance of this social and symbolic alignment, we must note that the festival also combined the springtime festival of the god with the military initiation of young warriors. It was a great beginning of a fertility cycle and the life of warriors, signaled by the sun rising between the twin temples. Both Tlaloc and Huitzilopochtli's powers were renewed by the dramatic correspondence of the temple, king, star, and human sacrifice.

THE NEW FIRE CEREMONY AND THE TEMPLO MAYOR

It is difficult to overestimate the paramount role of the Templo Mayor in the ceremonial and social life of the Aztec empire. Its status as the axis mundi of the Aztec world was expressed in the mythology of Huitzilopochtli and in the ritual activity of the scores of festivals dedicated to Aztec deities. Aztec kings, warriors, musicians captives, the populace at large took their major point of orientation in geographic and symbolic space to be Coatepec. Although it has hardly been recognized before, even the spatial focus of the New Fire Ceremony, which took place once every fifty-two years, concentrates on the Templo Mayor. Consider the following discussion of this festival of cosmic renewal.

On an evening in the middle of November 1507, a procession of fire priests with a captive warrior "arranged in order and wearing the garb of the gods" advanced from the city of Tenochtitlán toward the ceremonial center on the Hill of the Star. During the days prior to this auspicious night, the populace of the Aztec world participated together in the ritual extinction of fires; the casting of statues and hearthstones into the water; and the clean sweeping of the houses, patios, and walkways. Book VII of the *Florentine Codex*, entitled *The Sun, the Moon, the Stars, and the Binding of the Years*, tells us that in anticipation of this fearful night, women were closed up in granaries to avoid their transformation into fierce beasts who would eat men, pregnant women donned masks of maguey leaves, and children were pinched and nudged awake to avoid being turned into mice while asleep. For on this one night in the calendar round of 18,980 nights the Aztec fire priests celebrated "when the night was divided in half," the New Fire Ceremony, which ensured the rebirth of the sun and the movement of the cosmos for another fifty-two years. This rebirth was achieved symbolically through the heart sacrifice of a brave warrior specifically chosen by the king. We are told that when the procession arrived "in the deep night" at the Hill of the Star, the populace climbed onto their roofs and "with unwavering attention and necks craned toward the hill became filled with dread that the sun would be destroyed forever." It was thought that if fire could not be drawn, the demons of darkness would descend to eat men. As the ceremony proceeded, the priests watched the sky carefully for the movement of a star group known as *Tianquitzli* (marketplace), the cluster we call the *Pleiades*. As it made a meridian transit, signaling that the movement of the heavens had not ceased, a small fire was started on the outstretched chest of a warrior. The text reads, "When a little fire fell, then speedily the priests slashed open the breast with a flint knife, seized the heart, and thrust it into the fire. In the open chest a new fire was drawn and the people could see it from everywhere." The populace cut their ears, even the ears of children in cradles, the text tells us, "and spattered their blood in the ritual flicking of fingers in the direction of the fire on the mountain." Then the new fire was taken down the mountain, carried to the pyramid temple of Huitzilopochtli in the center of the city of Tenochtitlán, where it was placed in the fire holder of the statue of the god. Then messengers, runners, and fire priests who had come from everywhere took the fire back to the cities where the commonfolk, after blistering themselves with the fire, placed it in their homes, and "all were quieted in their hearts."[36]

In reflecting on this famous passage about the New Fire Ceremony, I want to follow the lead of Giovanni Morelli and use an "a-centric" perspective. Morelli, a nineteenth-century art historian, developed a successful method for distinguishing original masterpieces from copies by focusing his eyes not on the most obvious characteristics of a painting in order to identify its master but "on minor details, especially those considered least significant in the style typical of the painter's own school."[37] Instead of looking at the smiles of Leonardo's women or the eyes of Perugino's characters, which were usually raised to heaven, Morelli studied the earlobes, the fingernails, and the shapes of fingers and toes. This method, the Morelli method, used minor details to gain a picture of the whole.

This passage, which contains only a few variants in sixteenth-century accounts, is extraordinarily thick and complex. It has the obvious meanings related to astronomy, calendars, ritual theatres, human sacrifice, and even child rearing. Coursing through it all is a thread, actually two threads, partly hidden, which not only tie the description together but also provide a clue to the underlying social and symbolic purpose of the ritual. These threads are the flow of Moctezuma's authority through all aspects of the ritual and the presence of the Templo Mayor as the axis mundi of the New Fire Ceremony.

The presence of these threads is more evident when we retrace *just* the physical actions of the description. The drama begins with Moctezuma in Tenochtitlan, even though in this account he is not mentioned at the beginning. Elsewhere in this volume, however, we are told that months before the New Fire Ceremony, Moctezuma ordered a captive be found whose name contained the word *xihuitl* (turquoise, grass, or comet)—a symbolic name connoting precious time. The procession of deity impersonators moves along a prescribed passageway, presumably seen and heard by masses of people before arriving at the Hill of the Star. In Motolinia we are told that Moctezuma "had special devotion and reverence for the shrine and the deity" on the Sacred Hill. Assembled in the ceremonial center, the group of priests and lords, sharing a heightened sense of expectation and fear, seek another procession—the procession of the stars through the meridian. Once recognized, the heart sacrifice is carried out, the new fire is lit amid universal rejoicing and bleeding, and the fire is taken to the Templo Mayor, presumably with Moctezuma on hand to see its blaze. Then in what I see as the most meaningful social and symbolic gesture, messengers, priests, and runners who have "come from all directions" to the Templo Mayor take the fire back to the towns and cities of the periphery. In Motolinia we are told that the fire was taken back to the temples only "after asking permission from the great chief of Mexico."[38]

Focusing my eyes on the minor details of Moctezuma's role and the Templo Mayor as the shrine to which the New Fire is taken in order to be dispersed to the populace, I see a skillful symmetry reflecting the Aztec commitment to the interconnection of their world. By "symmetry" I mean the orderly arrangement of symbolic components around an axis. This symmetry consists of five elements: (1) the cosmic mountain (in this text there are two, the Hill of the Star and the Templo Mayor), (2) astronomical events, (3) human sacrifice, (4) agricultural renewal, and (5) sacred kingship. I see the center of this symmetry to be interplay between the king's flow of authority and the axis of Aztec society, the Templo Mayor. This interplay constitutes what the University of Chicago scholar of social thought Ed Shils calls a "center," by which he means "the point of points in a society where its leading ideas come together with its leading institution to create an arena in which events that most vitally affect its members lives take place."[39] What is taking place in the New Fire Ceremony is the integration of the leading idea—Moctezuma's authority—with the leading institution —the Templo Mayor—with the cosmic renewal integrated by an astronomical event.

FOUR QUARTERS AND THE CENTER

One of the most influential archetypes in Mesoamerican culture is reflected in the image of the horizontal cosmos, which appears in the *Codex Fejérváry-Mayer*. Here and elsewhere we see that the cosmos was conceived of as having five parts, with four quadrants called *nauhcampa* (the four parts) extending outward from the central section. Each quadrant was associated with specific names, colors, and influences. Although the pattern varied from culture to culture, a typical Mesoamerican version was as follows: east—Tlalocan (place of dawn)—yellow, fertile, and good; north—Mictlampa (region of the underworld)—red, barren, and bad; west—Cihuatlampa (region of women)—blue, green, unfavorable, and humid; south—Huiztlampa (region of thorns)—white; and center—Tlalxico (navel)—black. The waters surrounding the inhabited land in the middle were called ilhuica atl (the celestial water), which extended upward in a vertical direction merging with the sky and supported the lower level of heaven.[40]

This pattern of five cosmological spaces became the organizing principle for a multiple of supernatural, political, tributary, and economic concepts in central Meso-american society. For instance, the most popular and widespread deity in central Mesoamerica was Tlaloc, the fertilizing rain god. Tlaloc was often conceived of in quintuple forms called the *Tlaloques*, each assigned to one of the sacred directions. The pictorial image of these gods is almost a replica, in terms of design, of the pictorial image of the cosmic regions.[41] The power of this spatial concept extended into Aztec images of cosmological time. For instance, one of the finest pieces of Mesoamerican religious sculpture is the Calendar Stone, more accurately called the *Piedra del Sol*, because it is a carved image of the cosmology depicting the five ages, or "suns," of the universe. In the center of the stone, the cosmic eras are divided into the pattern of a central space called the "Fifth Sun" surrounded by four previous eras, again duplicating the design of cosmic space. We have what Miguel León-Portilla calls the "spatialization of time."[42] In this case, the spatial and temporal structure of the universe has been reduced to the carving on a single giant stone.

Tenochtitlán's prestige as the center of horizontal space is reflected in a number of ways. It is clear from the archaeological evidence and several maps of the city (e.g., see Matos, this volume, figs. 1 and 3) that it was divided into four sections (quadrants) by four major highways that crossed at the base of the Templo Mayor and drove straight out of the ceremonial precinct connecting the city with the mainland.[43] These avenues, carefully aligned to conform to major celestial events, determined the direction of the city's main streets and canals. What is equally important to note is that within this urban replica of cosmological space there were smaller microcosms. Each of the city's four quarters, as Edward Calnek has demonstrated, was a replica of the larger design in that each quarter had its own central temple complex housing the deities of the groups who inhabited that section.[44] A marketplace and administrative center were part of the central precinct of each quarter. Each quarter had its own sacred pivot, reproducing the pattern that dominated the city as a whole. Further, within each quarter the many barrios had their own local ceremonial precinct, repeating the symbolism of the center.

According to one primary source, this spatial order was dictated by the deity who founded the city, Huitzilopochtli. The text reads that the god ordered the priest to "divide the men, each with his relatives, friends and relations in four principal barrios, placing at the center the house you have built for my rest."[45] The divine command is to lay out the new settlement on the model of the horizontal cosmos of the four directions, assimilating the city to the form of the four quadrants that constituted the cosmos.

Recent research in the historical chronicles by Johanna Broda suggests that the Azec practice of cardinal orientation went far beyond the ordering of urban space to include the ordering of parts of the tribute systems that sustained the entire population of Tenochtitlan. In her seminal article, "El tributo en trajes guerreros y la estructura del sistema tributarios mexica,"[46] Broda utilizes the abundant, although partial, evidence concerning tribute patterns of warriors' uniforms sent to Tenochtitlan to demonstrate that the Mexica organized their tribute system into five great regions corresponding to the five major directions (north, west, south, east, and center) in order to conform to their view of cosmic order. She speculates that the influence of cosmomagical thought extended into the palatial structure of Moctezuma, which, the *Codex Mendoza* reveals, was divided into five principal rooms. This codex also shows that the apex of Aztec government consisted of Moctezuma at the center of power with four counselors assisting his royal judgments. It appears, then, that the Aztec perception of their universe as a four-cornered universe significantly influenced not only the spatial structure of their city but also the order of their tribute system, the image of the royal palace, and the balance of their government. This process of miniaturization and duplication on the vertical level has been ably discussed by Rudolf van Zantwijk, who writes about Azec cosmology and Aztec temple: "The principal subdivisions of an entity are repeated within the subdivision themselves. The universe is divided into sky, earth and underworld and each of these three shows a similar tripartite subdivision."[47]

One great contribution toward understanding these mythical dimensions of the Templo Mayor comes from the 100 plus *ofrendas*, offering boxes full of valued objects, including seashells, masks, deity images, knives, human skeletons, necklaces, marine animals, and sculpture (see pls. 12–18), and other items. The significance of these treasures goes far beyond their being evidence of tributary offerings paid to the temple in the capital. When we explore what Matos calls the "language" of these offerings, we realize that the Templo Mayor was not just a place of valuable containers, it was the quintessential container itself, of tribute, cosmology, and myth. It was a monument of the integration of geographic, historical, and supernatural space and time.

Perhaps the most important example of this aspect of the Templo Mayor as center of the universe are the texts that tell how representatives from different cities and towns cast precious stones into the temple base on the occasion of the enlargements. This practice can be partly understood by reference to a similar act of founding told in Fustel de Coulanges's *The Ancient City*. On the occasion of the marking off of Rome's boundary by the circular trench cut by the plow, members of all the communities that were to be integrated into the city brought clods of earth from their homelands and cast them into the open trench. This signified the integration of the many "lands" and the deities of those lands into the new center.[48] Another significance in this act of ritual throwing is the relocation of the powers associated with many axes into a new axis of the world that contains the powers of many central places. It is a distinctive trait of the Mesoamerican world that a similar act of integration would be accomplished by the casting of precious earth in the forms of valuable stones from the peripheral communities. The Templo Mayor is the precious center into which were placed the many precious parts of land and sea.

Matos's other point about these offerings deserves reiteration and development from the perspective of the history of religion. Consider again the location of the offerings boxes. They are placed at the cardinal points of the temple, in the middle of the four sides, at the corners and the point of union of the twin temples (see Matos, this volume, fig. 3). At every powerful cosmological point, offerings are buried that connect that terrestrial space to cosmological influences, marking the lines of parallelisms between heaven and earth. The rich sense of alignment we noted in the astronomical orientation of Templo Mayor is enlarged in the alignments of offering, architecture, and cosmology. In a sense, temple and offerings constitute a miniature map of the cosmic order. We have the replication of the symbolism of the center and cardinal axiality in a more detailed precise way than simply the reference to the four powerful directions of the universe.

In Cosmic Darkness: The Birth of the Fifth Sun

This discussion of the influences of Aztec cosmology and cardinal axiality on the spatial organization of the capital, in relation to the Templo Mayor, enhances our understanding of the pervasiveness of mythic thought in Tenochtitlan. In retrospect, we have already learned that this pervasiveness was also specifically lodged in the action of human sacrifice, as revealed in the relationship between the myth of Huitzilopochtli's birth and the sculptural image and location of the Coyolxauhqui stone, plus the evidence in text and archaeology of human sacrifice at the Templo Mayor. We see that the question of the increment in human sacrifice is partially answered through the discovery within the myth that Huitzilopochtli kills not just one goddess, but that he annihilates all the deities—his sacrificial aggression extends to the killing of all the divine beings. This significant discovery appears to be Aztec specific; that is, the mythic structure of massive sacrifices seems to be particularly Aztec. As a historian of religions, sensitive to Mircea Eliade's emphasis on the overriding prestige of cosmogonic myth, however, I am encouraged to search out the texts further to see if any prior inkling or similar pattern appears in more ancient or more pervasive cosmogonic episodes in Mesoamerica. In fact, when we carry out this exercise in search of origins, we find that the cosmogonic imperative for incremental massive sacrifice has an even greater primordiality of surprising proportions. Equally important, the movement of retrieval from the specific Aztec cosmogony of massive sacrifice to the more general and probably ancient Mesoamerican paradigm was a movement made by the Aztecs themselves. That is, the prologue that accompanies the text of Huitzilopochtli's birth in Sahagún's Book III tells us to move in the direction of prior cosmogony that unfolded in the ancient city of Tenochtitlan. Within this act of mythic retrieval, we discover not only the presence of a locative view of the cosmos, in which all things are in their place, but also the indications of an apocalyptic view of the universe in which order, place, and stability cannot be achieved.

143

This movement and discovery is suggested in the short but rich prologue to the sacred song of Huitzilopochtli's birth commented upon earlier in this chapter. Prior to the statement of Aztec reverence for "the beginning" of Huitzilopochtli, we are told that the entire chapter of Book III of the *Florentine Codex* is concerned not with Huitzilopochtli's beginning but with "how the gods had their beginnings."[49] This statement about the creation of the gods is accompanied by the acknowledgment that "where the gods began is not well known." This ignorance of place, indicating either a non-Aztec or older tradition, is in sharp contrast to the specific place and proximity of Coatepec and Tula, which organized the mythic geography of Huitzilopochtli's birth. Then reference is made to the prestigious capital of Teotihuacán (abode of the gods), as the location of the primordial gathering of the gods in the cosmogonic darkness. What is immediately interesting about this is that, as in the myth of Huitzilopochtli, a gathering of gods takes place to bring forth "the sun," and this creation involves the destruction of all the gods. The text suggests the weight of this creative-destructive process was in the minds of the deities, for they "debated who would bear upon his back the burden of rule, who would be the sun." The scene is impressive in its cosmogonic opaqueness. In the darkness, the deities have gathered in the great ceremonial center to struggle together to create a new universe. Then the prologue to Huitzilopochtli's story ends with the remarkable statement that "all the gods died when the sun came into being. None remained who had not perished."[50]

The discovery made in the Huitzilopochtli myth appears once more—the massive killing of gods brings about, or is part of, the cosmogonic act of creation—only in this episode, it is not just the birth of one god that matters, it is the passage from darkness, potentiality, and chaos into the brilliant light of the universe, actuality, and cosmological order that is accomplished. The larger universe within which Huitzilopochtli, Coyolxauhqui, the Centzonhuitzhahua, and the Fifth Age existed, is what is created in Teotihuacán.

This short prologue tells us that even in the Aztec mind, a *primordiality behind Tenochtitlan's primordiality* was the authentic stage of origin. Fortunately, we have a long and vivid account of this cosmogonic act in Book VII of the *Florentine Codex*. Turning to its details, we learn about the character and drama of this primordial condition. The more detailed version of the cosmogonic prologue to Huitzilopochtli's birth tells us that for fifty-two years following the end of the four ages, the world was in darkness. "When no sun had shown and no dawn had broken," the gods gathered at Teotihuacan to create a new age. They asked, "Who will carry the burden? Who will take it upon himself to be the sun, to bring the dawn?" Following four days of penance and ritual, all the gods gathered around a divine hearth where a fire had been burning for the duration. Two gods, *Nanauatzin* (the pimply one) and *Tecuciztecatl* (lord of snails), prepared to create the new sun by hurling themselves into the fire. After they dressed themselves for the ceremonial suicide, Tecuciztecatl approached the fire several times but became frightened. Then Nanauatzin was ordered to try. The text begins:

> "Onward thou, O Nanauatzin! Take heart!" And Nanauatzin, daring all at once, determined-resolved-hardened his heart, and shut firmly his eyes. He had no fear; he did not stop short; he did not falter in fright. . . . All at once he quickly threw and cast himself into the fire; once and for all he went. Thereupon he burned; his body crackled and sizzled. . . . Tecuciztecatl . . . cast himself upon the fire. . . . It is told that then flew up an eagle, which followed them. It threw itself suddenly into the flames, it cast itself into them. . . . Therefore its feathers are scorched looking and blackened—smutted—in various places, and singed by the fire. . . . From this event it is said, they took . . . the custom whereby was called and named one who was valiant, a warrior.[51]

It is important that within this cosmogonic myth the story of the creation of warriors stands out as the primary act of creation. On one hand, Nanauatzin's daring, hard heart, and surrender to the fire is the paradigmatic attitude of the primal warrior; on the other hand, the first inklings of creation are the emergence of the eagle, who dives back into the fire, scorching himself, and the jaguar, which becomes marked and darkened by the divine fire. When we remember that the two great orders of warrior knights in Aztec society were the eagle and jaguar knights, it appears that the Aztecs drew directly from this tradition to legitimize the religious significance and power of their soldiers. The text continues:

> Then the gods sat waiting to see where Nanauatzin would come to rise—he who fell first into the fire—in order that he might shine as the sun; in order that dawn might break. When the gods had sat and been waiting for a long time, thereupon began the reddening of the dawn; in all directions, all around, the dawn and light extended. And so, they say, thereupon the gods fell upon their knees in order to await where he who had become the sun would become to rise. In all directions they looked; everywhere they peered and kept turning about. Uncertain were those whom they asked. Some thought that it would be from the north that the sun would come to rise, and placed themselves to look there; some did so to the west; some placed themselves to look south. They expected that he might rise in all directions, because the light was everywhere. And some placed themselves so that they could watch there to the east.[52]

This original confusion about the sun's place of emergence in the glowing dawn reveals the lack of clear orientation that existed in the cosmos prior to the appearance of the sun above the horizon. It is with the sun's clear appearance and passage that the universe becomes organized. The text continues:

145

Thus they say that those who looked there to the east were Quetzalcoatl: the name of the second was Ecatl: and Totec . . . and the red Tezcatlipoca . . . . And when the sun came to rise, when he burst forth, he appeared to be red; he kept swaying from side to side.[53]

This is the cosmic condition facing men in the Fifth Age of the Aztecs. The sun is "swaying from side to side," unable to achieve stability, or find its place, or initiate a creative movement. Even at the mythic level, the level at which cosmological order was achieved, the sun has a profound difficulty finding its place and orienting the world.

This unstable and threatening situation demands still more exertion from the gods because the sun and moon "could only remain still and motionless." The gods then commit themselves to a course of action that will have a terrible paradigmatic influence on the Toltec and Aztec societies: they decide to sacrifice themselves to ensure the motion of the sun. "Let this be, that through us the sun may be revived. Let all of us die." Then *Ecatl* (the wind god), a guise of Quetzalcoatl, "arose and exerted himself fiercely and violently as he blew. At once he could move him, who thereupon went on his way."[54]

It is remarkable that upon finding the cosmogonic background for Huitzilopochtli's story we arrive at the same discovery. Creation of the cosmos in Aztec and pre-Aztec Mesoamerica is directly tied to the sacrifice, not of one or a few deities, but to the increment in sacrifice that begins with one courageous warrior and spreads to annihilate all the gods who have gathered at the divine center of the world. The unstable cosmos that is created depends on massive ritual killing and an increment in divine death.

The cosmic pattern of massive sacrifices to energize the sun is repeated in a subsequent episode in which terrestrial warfare and human sacrifice is created by the gods to ensure their nourishment. In one version, the god Mixcoatl (cloud serpent) creates five human beings and 400 Chichimec warriors to stir up discord and warfare. When the masses of warriors pass their time hunting and drinking, the god sends the five individuals to slaughter them. In this account, war among human beings is created to ensure sacrificial victims for the gods.

CENTER AND PERIPHERY

Until now we have seen abundant evidence that the Aztec city was structured by a series of meanings and activities associated with what Mircea Eliade calls the "Symbolism of the Centre." It is becoming clearer to me that the usual way in which some historians of religions conceive of the category of the center does not constitute a thorough interpretive approach for understanding the Templo Mayor's history and meaning. A people's vision of place reflects the intertwining of symbol and society, ontology, and history. In this regard, it is vitally important, in the Aztec case at least, not just to be aware of the integrating powers of the axis mundi but also to acknowledge and interpret the impulses of expansion of a sacred center and the political and symbolic results. We have seen how this process of the expansion of Aztec's sacred space paralleled the development of Tenochtitlan from the spot of the nopal (cactus plant) to the shrine of Huitzilopochtli and spread to the four quadrants of the city and eventually the organization of tribute payments for the empire. But we have also seen evidence that distant, peripheral communities, that is, the centzon huitznahua (Coyolxauhqui's 400 brothers) played a major role in the symbolism of the Templo Mayor. This suggests that it is necessary to understand the historical, social, and symbolic tension that developed between the centripetal character of the capital and the centrifugal tendencies of the capital. For instance, Edward Shils has shown that great centers are ruled by elites whose authority has

> an expansive tendency . . . a tendency to expand the order it represents towards the saturation of territorial space . . . the periphery. Rulers, simply out of their possession of authority and the impulses which it generates, wish to be obeyed and they wish to obtain assent to the order they symbolically embody.[55]

These impulses of expansion will inevitably lead to involvement in peripheral and competing traditions of value, meaning, and authority. This sometimes results in tentative arrangements of power and authority between the center and the periphery. Peripheral systems and their symbols may be weaker within a hierarchy of an empire; nevertheless, they have the potential to threaten the center with disbelief, reversal, and rebellion. It is within this kind of situation that W. B. Yeat's famous line has direct relevance: "Things fall apart; the centre cannot hold." Although I cannot discuss the Mesoamerican pattern in detail here, it appears that ancient Mexican kingdoms were sometimes arranged similarly to what Stanley Tambiah in his study of Southeast Asian kingdoms calls "pulsating galactic polities," that is, kingdoms in which the capital cities were in constant tension and antagonism with the surrounding allied and enemy settlements. In these pulsating kingdoms, the "exemplary centers" are frequently deflated by rebellion and disputes with unstable factions who threatened to bring about processes of disintegration on a large scale. This resulted in the periodic relocation of capital cities and an eccentric and unstable understanding of authority.[56] My own study of Mesoamerican urbanism has led me to the formulation of "eccentric periodicities," that is, periods of stability lasting for extended periods ending in dramatic and near-total collapses. Then, after a period of recovery, a new period of stability organized by a regional capital in a different location takes place only to give way to disintegration and rebellion. In my view, the pulsating pattern in Mesoamerica fluctuated at different times and places between a slow and ponderous rhythm, and a more rapid rhythm of fusion and fission.

I consider this point important, because it suggests not only that centers dominate and control peripheries but also that peripheries influence and sometimes transform centers, even a center so aggressive and dominant as Tenochtitlan. I apply the category of periphery, in relation to center, in three ways: spatial, social, and symbolic. The Aztec periphery refers to distant spaces and geographies, to social order and prior civilizations, and to the masses of people whose religious sensibility and symbolism differed from the elite structures of power and authority. With this pattern in mind, we can reconsider the evidence uncovered at the Great Temple to see the impact of peripheral territories on the capital city. We will see that threats from the Aztec past and the competing traditions of their contemporary world transformed the Templo Mayor and the city it sanctified. As we shall see, this pattern of social organization, combined with the mythic structure of incremental human sacrifice, provides a rich interpretive framework for understanding the scandal of Templo Mayor.

Symbols from the Periphery

As noted previously, the Templo Mayor was the symbolic center of the great tribute network of the Aztec empire (see pls. 13–16). It was not only the material expression of Aztec religious thought but was also the symbolic instrument for the collection and redistribution of wealth and goods from all over the empire. The social world that the Aztecs strove to control consisted of small local states called *tlatocayotls*.[57] These city-states consisted of small, agriculturally based, politically organized territories under the control of a city that was the seat of government, ceremonial center, and home of a ruling class that claimed descent from the gods. Conflict and warfare were constant, and the conquest of one tlatocayotl by another resulted in the imposition of significant tribute on the conquered people. As the Aztec conquests proceeded to incorporate scores of these city-states into their empire, tribute payments to Tenochtitlan became enormous. The city's prestige and wealth depended to a large degree on these enormous amounts of tribute payments that flowed into the capital and ensured economic superiority for the royal house, the nobles, and the common citizen. Significantly, over 100 offerings of symbolic tribute have been uncovered at strategic points around the base of the pyramid, at every stage of its construction. These offerings contain seashells (see pls. 12, 13, 26, 27), finely carved masks (see pls. 44–47), statues of deities, sacrificed humans and animals (see pls. 35, 38, 21, 22), knives (see pl. 32), and jewelry. Professor Broda's intense analysis of these materials reveals, among other things, the "sacred landscapes" symbolized in the offerings dedicated to Tlaloc. From my perspective, the fertility-mountain-earth-mother complex she has illuminated reflects the Aztec conception of periphery—the lands, labors, and religious beliefs of the masses of people located beyond the city and, in many cases, beyond the core of the Aztec empire. Over 80 percent of these objects are from distant and frontier provinces under Aztec domination. Their presence in the heart of the city dis-

148

plays the attempt to integrate valued and symbolic objects from the periphery of the Aztec state into the foundation of the central shrine as a means of sanctifying the conquests and the expansion of Aztec sacred social order. For instance, a number of offerings contain large and small shells (see pl. 13), usually oriented toward the south, which were brought from the distant seacoasts. They represent the powers of fertility associated with the great bodies of water. These powers are also represented in the crocodiles (see pl. 38) and swordfish buried at the temple. Another meaning of these burials relates to the fact that the Aztecs called the terrestrial world Cemanahuac, which means the land surrounded by water. In this light, the offerings of the shells and marine objects demonstrate the Aztec desire to incorporate the edges of their world into the sacred shrine and constitute a symbolism of center and periphery. The fertility symbols from the periphery were buried at the center.

This integration of peripheral places is elaborated in one of the most impressive discoveries to date, the offering of over fifty finely carved masks in one burial in front of Tlaloc's shrine (see pl. 16). These masks have noble, frightening, awe-inspiring faces that were carved in many different settlements under Aztec domination. They display different artistic styles (see pls. 42–44), emphasizing different facial features, and were apparently offered as special tribute to the Great Temple for some auspicious ceremonial event during the latter part of the fifteenth century. They are signs not only of offering but also of subjugation. Valuable objects, perhaps symbolic faces of different allies or frontier communities, were buried at the world's axis. There is one significant temporal aspect of this collection because the most remarkable mask is a small, mint-condition, Olmec jade mask that was probably carved a full 2,000 years before the first of the temple's eleven facades were constructed (see pl. 39). In this precious Olmec treasure and in a number of Teotihuacan-style masks, we see the Aztec concern with integration of the symbols of the ancient civilization in its shrine.

Twin Temples

When the Chichimec tribes, from whom the Aztecs emerged as conquerors, came into the central plateau during the thirteenth century, they encountered a world that had long been dominated by complex state societies.[58] It is important to understand that while the Aztecs did evolve from an insignificant political group into an imperial people in less than 200 years, the institutions that they developed had been in existence for over 1,500 years. Complex state societies with great capital cities dominating lesser cities and communities had been the order of life in central Mesoamerica since the beginning of the first millennium A.D.

The magnificent cities of Teotihuacan, Tollan, and Chollolan, with their great pyramids, imposing stone sculpture, complex social structures, long-distance trade systems, religious iconography, and sacred genealogies for kings, intimidated and inspired the Aztecs to measure up to and integrate the Classic heritage.[59] As noted, the truly monumental four-section city of Teotihuacan (Abode of the Gods) was revered as the place where the present cosmogonic era was created.[60] Aztec kings periodically visited the ancient shrines to perform sacrifices and reestablish ties to the divine ancestors and sanctity that dwelt there. The prestige of Teotihuacan was reflected in the two "red temples" found at Templo Mayor containing Teotihuacan-style architecture and symbolism. The Toltec civilization of the Great Tollan and the cult of Quetzalcoatl were viewed as the "golden day" of artistic excellence, agricultural abundance, ritual renewal, and place where giants had perceived the divine plan for human society.[61] One of the last discoveries at the Templo Mayor was the splendid "Eagle Temple," which contained not only the life-size eagle warriors (see pl. 53), statues of Mictlantecuhtli, and images of Tlaloc but also a long, winding, sculptured frieze of warriors replicating, in general terms, a similar frieze at Tula. As Esther Pasztory has shown, these cities "cast a giant shadow over the Aztecs who could not help feeling small and inferior by contrast."[62] Plagued by a sense of illegitimacy and cultural inferiority, the Aztecs made shrewd and strenuous efforts to encapsulate the sanctified traditions of the past into their shrine. This is reflected in the fact that the Templo Mayor was a "twin temple," a form invented by the Aztecs and their contemporaries. The Templo Mayor supported great shrines to Tlaloc, as well as Huitzilopochtli. On the obvious level, Tlaloc's presence (see pls. 48–51) represents the great forces of water and moisture, which were absolutely critical for agricultural conditions of the lake and surrounding lands. Elaborate ceremonies were held, involving the sacrifice of children to Tlaloc, in order to bring the seasonal rains to the land.[63] Tlaloc's prominence at the shrine displays another Aztec concern as well. Tlaloc was the old god of the land who had sustained the great capitals of pre-Aztec Mexico. He represented a prior structure of reality in a cultural and supernatural sense. He had granted permission to the Aztecs to settle in the lake; therefore, he was the indigenous deity who adopted the newcomers. As a means of legitimating their shrine and city, the Aztecs were forced to integrate the great supernatural and cultural authority of the past into the Templo Mayor.

The practice of integrating the images of the great cultural past is also reflected in the discovery of an elaborately painted Chac Mool in front of one of the earliest Templo Mayor constructions (see pl. 52). This backward reclining figure, who was a messenger to the fertility gods, holds a bowl on his lap which was used to hold the heart of a sacrificial victim. Chac Mools were originally Toltec figures that had appeared in prominent ceremonial centers of the Toltec cities. The statue's surprising appearance at the Templo Mayor suggests again the Aztec insecurity and concern to bring the superior cultural past into their mighty present.

Human Sacrifice and the Historical Periphery

As is well documented in the ethnohistorical and archaeological sources, the Templo Mayor was the scene of elaborate human sacrifices, which increased to incredible numbers during the last eighty years of Aztec rule (see pl. 1).[64] The usual justification for this increment has been the belief that the Aztecs were feeding their gods in order to keep the cosmos in motion. Before looking more closely at this scandalous development, let us consider a short survey of the practice and paraphernalia of human sacrifice, to demonstrate the basic pattern of ritual violence.

It must be understood that human sacrifice was carried out within a larger, more complex ceremonial system in which a tremendous amount of energy, wealth, and time was spent in a variety of ritual festivals dedicated to a crowded and hungry pantheon.[65] This dedication is reflected in the many metaphors and symbols related to war and sacrifice. Blood was called *chalchiuh-atl* (precious water). Human hearts were likened to fine burnished turquoise, and war was *teoatl tlachinolli* (divine liquid and burned things). War was the place "where the jaguars roar," where "feathered war bonnets heave about like foam in the waves." Death on the battlefield was called *xochimiquiztli* (the flowery death).

The many ritual festivals were organized by two calendars, a divinatory calendar of 260 days and a solar calendar of 360 days with 5 "dangerous days" at the end. The divinatory calendar appears to have organized the birthday festivals of the patron deities of the neighborhoods and local communities. The solar calendar marked the major festivals for the prominant deities of war, sun, rain, and fertility. Some festivals included rituals dedicated to both local and major gods and dramatized the relationships between them.

This crowded ceremonial schedule was acted out in the many ceremonial centers of the city and empire. The greatest ceremonial precinct formed the axis of Tenochtitlan and measured 440 meters on each of its four sides. It contained, according to some accounts, over eighty ritual temples, skull racks (see pl. 10), schools, and other ceremonial structures. Book II of Sahagún's *Florentine Codex* contains a valuable list with descriptions of most of these buildings, including "the Temple of Uitzilopochli . . . of Tlaloc . . . in the middle of the square, . . . it was higher, it was taller . . . faced toward the setting of the sun." Also we read of the "Teccizcalli: there Moctezuma did penances; . . . there was dying there; captives died there" and "Mexico Calmecac: there dwelt the penitents who offered incense at the summit of the Temple of Tlaloc, quite daily," and "Teccalco: there was casting (of men) into the fire there," and "The Great Skull Rack: there also there used to be slaying," followed by "The Temple of Cinteotl: there the impersonator of Chicome coatl died, at night only. And when she died, then they flayed her . . . the fire priest put on her skin" and "Coaapan; there the fire priest of Coatlan bathed himself" and for cooking "Tilocan; there cooked the (amaranth seed dough for) the image of Uitzilopochtli" and finally for cannibalistic preparation, "Actl Yiacapan Uey Calpulli; . . . there they gathered together the sacrificial victims called Tlalocs . . . when they had slain them, they cut them to pieces there and cooked them. They put squash blossoms with their flesh . . . then the noblemen ate them, all the high judges: but not the common fold—only the rulers."

Important variations of ritual activity were carried out at these temples, schools, skull racks, and bathhouses; however, the general pattern of human sacrifice was as follows. Most Aztec rituals began with a four-day (or multiples of four) preparatory period of priestly fasting (*nezahualiztli*). An important exception was the year-long fast by a group of priests and priestesses known as the *teocuaque* (god eaters) or the greatly feared *in iachhuan Huitzilopochtli in mocexiuhzauhque* (the elder brothers of Huitzilopochtli who fasted for a year). This preparatory period also involved nocturnal vigil (*tozohualiztli*) and offerings of flowers, food, cloths, rubber, paper, poles with streamers, as well as incensing (*copaltemaliztli*); the pouring of libations; and the embowering of temples, statues, and ritual participants. Dramatic processions of elaborately costumed participants moving to music ensembles playing sacred songs passed through the ceremonial precinct before arriving at the specific temple of sacrifice. The major ritual participants were called *in ixiptla in teteo* (deity impersonators). All important rituals involved a death sacrifice of either animals or human beings.

The most common sacrifice was the decapitation of animals such as quail, but the most dramatic and valued sacrifices were the human sacrifices of captured warriors and slaves. These victims were ritually bathed, carefully costumed, taught to dance special dances, and either fattened or slimmed down during the preparation period. They were elaborately dressed to impersonate specific deities to whom they were sacrificed.

The different primary sources reveal a wide range of sacrificial techniques, including decapitation (usually for women) (see pl. 1), shooting with darts or arrows, drowning, burning, hurling from heights, strangulation, entombment and starvation, and gladiatorial combat. Usually, the ceremony peaked when splendidly attired captors and captives sang and danced in procession to the temple, where they were escorted (sometimes unwillingly) up the stairways to the sacrificial stone. The victim was quickly thrust on the sacrificial stone (techcatl) and the temple priest cut through the chest wall with the ritual flint knife (see pl. 32) (tecpatl). The priest grasped the still beating heart, called "precious eagle cactus fruit," tore it from the chest, offered it to the sun for vitality and nourishment, and placed it in a carved circular vessel called the *cuauhxicalli* (eagle vessel). In many cases, the body, now called "eagle man," was rolled, flailing, down the temple steps to the bottom where it was dismembered. The skull was decapitated, the brains taken out (see pl. 22), and after skinning, it was placed on the tzompantli (skull rack) consisting of long poles horizontally laid and loaded with skulls. In many cases, the captor was decorated, for instance, with chalk and bird down, and given gifts. Then, together with his relatives, he celebrated a ritual meal consisting of "a bowl of stew of dried maize called tlacatlaolli . . . on each went a piece of the flesh of the captive."

While this pattern of ritual preparation, ascent and descent of the temple, heart sacrifice of enemy warriors, dismemberment and flaying of the victim, and cannibalism was usually followed, it is important to emphasize the diversity of sacrificial festivals that involved variations and combinations of these elements. For instance, during the feast of Tlacaxipehualiztli, "the feast of the flaying of men," a prisoner of war "who came here from lands about us" was taken by a priest called the "Bear Man" and tied up to a huge round sacrificial stone (temalacatl) placed horizontally on the ground. The captive was provided with a pine club and a feathered staff to protect himself against the attacks of four warriors armed with clubs of wood and obsidian blades. When he was defeated he was removed from the stone and short temple base, his heart was taken out, and he was flayed.

Another distinctive festival was called Toxcatl, dedicated to the ferocious god *Tezcatlipoca* (Smoking Mirror). Elaborate efforts were made to find the perfect deity impersonator for this festival. The captive warrior had to have a flawless body, musical talents, and rhetorical skills. For a year prior to his sacrifice he lived a privileged existence in the capital. He had eight servants, who ensured that he was splendidly arrayed and bejeweled. He had four wives given to him during the last twenty days of his life. Just before the end of the sacrificial festival we are told that he arrived at a "small temple called Tlacochalco . . . he ascended by himself, he went up of his own free will, to where he was to die. As he was taken up a step, as he passed one step, there he broke, he shattered his flute, his whistle" and was then swiftly sacrificed.

A very remarkable festival, celebrated on the first day of the month of *Atlcahualo*, involved the paying of debts to Tlaloc, the rain god. On this day, children (called "human paper streamers") with two cowlicks in their hair and favorable day signs were dressed in such colors as dark green, black striped with chili red, light blue, some set with pearls, and were sacrificed in seven different locations (see pl. 15). The flowing and falling of tears of the children ensured rain.

Besides these theatrical ritual killings, everyone in the Aztec world participated in some form of self-sacrifice or bloodletting. Bloodletting was either an offering or penitential rite involving the pricking of earlobes with maguey thorns or, in more severe circumstances, the drawing of strings through holes cut in the tongues, ears, genitals, and other fleshy parts of the body. Often blood was placed on slips of paper and offered to the gods.[66]

The claim that this ceremonial system was developed to feed the gods may be partly true; however, my interpretation of the two cosmogonic episodes reveals that human sacrifice and incremental human sacrifice was an act of cosmic repetition that functioned not only as a feeding ritual but also as a ritual re-creating Aztec dominance and power established in their sacred history. The Aztecs were reestablishing a mythic structure that revealed that military aggression against the forces from the periphery created a new world—the world of Huitzilopochtli or the cult of the Fifth Sun. A conference held at the University of Colorado in 1979, "Center and Periphery: the Aztec, the Templo Mayor, and the Aztec Empire," showed it was a combination of myth and history that led to the increments of ritual killing at the Templo Mayor. Papers and discussions at this conference focused on the powers of peripheral city-states and the abundant number of objects that originated from the distant tributary towns in the empire. As Johanna Broda in particular pointed out, this near obsession with the periphery had a peculiar social significance. We know that within the Valley of Mexico the Aztec warrior and priestly nobility managed a high degree of centralization of agricultural schedules, technological developments, labor management, and ritual processes. In all directions beyond the valley, however, there was little continued success in peacefully controlling the internal organization of conquered or enemy city-states.[67] The Aztec capital, while expanding its territory and tribute controls, was repeatedly shocked by rebellions that demanded complex and organized military and economic reprisals. My own survey of the opening chapters of Bernal Díaz del Castillo's eyewitness account of the Aztec empire shows the tenuous and emotionally charged relationship between the capital city and the coastal settlements. From the earliest stages of the military campaigns in Mexico, Cortés discovered that a combination of allegiance, fear, and resentment on one hand and outright defiance on the other hand motivated caciques and populations located in the peripheral areas of the Aztec empire. In fact, it was partly Cortés's ability to perceive the weaknesses in the extension of Aztec authority to the eastern flanks of the empire that led to the eventual conquest of Tenochtitlan. This antagonism between the core area and the surrounding city-states created immense stresses within all the institutions of Tenochtitlan, contributing to the astonishing increases in human sacrifice carried out at the Templo Mayor between 1440 and 1521. Not only did the political order appear unstable but the divine right to conquer and subdue all peoples and enemies also seemed unfulfilled. The anxiety that the Aztecs already experienced in regard to their universal order, after all cosmic life as an unending war, was intensified to the point of cosmic paranoia. In this situation, the ritual strategy to rejuvenate the cosmos became the major political instrument to subdue the enemy and control the periphery.

Broda has shown that the role of the Templo Mayor in this explosive process can be seen in at least three important events. During the reign of Moctezuma Ilhuicamina (1440 to 1455), the shrine of Huitzilopochtli received its first large reconstruction (see pls. 2, 4).[68] As a means of ensuring quality of workmanship and allegiance to the new temple, workers from a number of city-states under Aztec control were ordered to do the job. One independent community, Chalco, refused to participate and was declared in rebellion against the Aztecs, however. A ferocious war was launched, and eventually the Chalcans were defeated. Their captured warriors were brought to the Templo Mayor and, along with other prisoners of war, sacrificed at its rededication. This pattern of celebration—the expansion of the Great Temple with warfare and the sacrifice of enemy warriors—was followed by subsequent Aztec kings who increased the sacrificial festivals as a means of controlling resistance and peripheral territories. In 1487 Ahuitzotl celebrated the renovation of the Templo Mayor by ordering great quantities of tribute brought into Tenochtitlan. Newly conquered city-states were ordered to send their tribute in the form of sacrificial victims who were slain at the inauguration.

Curiously, at these ceremonies of massive human sacrifice, the kings and lords from allied and enemy city-states were invited to the ceremonial center to witness the spectacular festival. The ritual extravaganza was carried out with maximum theatrical tension, paraphernalia, and terror in order to amaze and intimidate the visiting dignitaries, who returned to their kingdoms trembling with fear and convinced that cooperation, and not rebellion, was the best response to Aztec imperialism.

On another occasion, the Aztec king, this time Moctezuma Xocoyotzin (1503 to 1520), ordered the construction of a temple within the main ceremonial precinct to house the images of all the gods worshipped in the imperial domain. Before the dedication of the shrine, he ordered a war against a rebellious coastal city-state, Teuctepec. From this campaign, 2,300 warriors were brought to Tenochtitlan and sacrificed while the king initiated the sacrifices.

All this suggests that the tension between the capital and peripheral towns and the political threats and cosmic insecurities that Aztec elites experienced as a result contributed in a major way to the increase of human sacrifice at the Templo Mayor.

The significant changes in Aztec religion between 1440 and 1521, manifested primarily in the increment of human sacrifice at the Templo Mayor, require further discussion here. One fact the excavation and ethnohistorical analysis proves is that pervasive changes were taking place throughout Aztec society during the period of the rapid expansion and rebuilding of the Templo Mayor. Friedrich Katz, in his excellent general history of the Aztec state, reveals how the royal counselor Tlacaelel set in motion a number of innovations to ensure Aztec dominance in the face of the intense rebellions and threatening agricultural crises that periodically plagued the capital. This flexibility and increment in the religious rituals of the Aztecs can be partly understood with reference to Roy Rappaport's work on the capacity of the sacred to assist a society in adapting to new social circumstances without weakening the cherished cultural conceptions of a people. We have long known, says Rappaport, that sanctity supports and conserves the social order. Traditionally, scholars have viewed adaptations and innovations as signs of secular advances and the break with conventional theologies and ideologies. Rappaport, however, uses Hockett and Ascher's formulation of "Romer's rule" to argue a different approach. This formulation "proposes that the initial effect of an evolutionary change is conservative in that it makes it possible for a previously existing way of life to persist in the face of changed conditions." Rappaport argues that the sacred can actually enhance the flexibility in social structure and symbolic organization to persist in the face of innovation and change. In other words, the threatening aspects of changed conditions can be somewhat neutralized by incorporation into sacred tradition. This ability to combine flexibility and rigidity derives from the fact that some elements of the sacred are not restricted in their meaning to specific social goals or institutions. Rappaport states:

> They can, therefore, not only sanctify any institution while being bound by none but can also sanctify changes in institutions. Continuity can be maintained while allowing change to take place, for the association of particular institutions or conventions with ultimate sacred postulates is a matter of

interpretation, and that which must be interpreted can also be reinterpreted without being challenged. So, gods may remain unchanged while the conventions they sanctify are transformed through reinterpretation in response to changing conditions.[69]

Rappaport shows that sacred concepts communicate much more than information about temple activity. They convey information about the political arrangements and the regulation of society, and they imbue these arrangements with an aura of the sacred. Sanctity is infused in all systems and subsystems of society in order to maintain the fundamental order of social life. Sanctity allows the persistence of traditional forms in the face of "structural threats and environmental fluctuations."

From this perspective, the time-honored tradition (human sacrifice) underwent a significant innovation (large-scale human sacrifice in relation to conquered warriors) in order to maintain Aztec dominance in the face of threats (rebellions) and fluctuations (droughts). The increment in human sacrifice is an example of Romer's rule, and not the expression of protein deficiency or merely a response to environmental pressures. It was a religious strategy carried out to conserve the entire cosmogonic structure of the Aztec city-state.

There is a remarkable parallelism between these events and the mythic structure of Huitzilopochtli's myth, where enemy warriors from distant and rebellious communities were slain with unceasing aggression at the sacred mountain. One important difference is that, within the myth, these killings intensified the power of the temple on the mountain and served as the origin of Huitzilopochtli's cult. In history, the increment of ritual killing served to both strengthen *and* weaken the authority of Tenochtitlan. Many city-states were securely integrated by terror into the Aztec sphere; however, some were alienated into the direction of other kingdoms and the capacity of rebellion increased. Nowhere is this pattern of social fission more clear than in the alliance-building process that Cortés directed as he traveled through the outskirts of the empire and met both vicious resistance and vital support from communities both loyal and disloyal to Moctezuma's capital. All the more reason, then, for the Aztecs to sacrifice those Spanish warriors at the Templo Mayor during their "rebellion" against the capital. In the eyes of the eagle and jaguar knights, the Spaniards were the threatening personification of the 400 children who had come to destroy the temple.

Myth and the Conquest

One final example of the alignment of mythic thought, sacred space, kingship, and ritual action in Aztec religion appears in several indigenous accounts of the conquest of Tenochtitlan. In these accounts we see the vivid expression of what I have called the "apocalyptic view" of the world in which the sacred order dissolves when cosmic things lose their place.

The opening section of the last volume of Bernardino de Sahagún's *Florentine Codex*, a volume entitled *The Conquest*, tells that omens of great portent appeared in the valley of Mexico a full decade before Cortés and his soldiers arrived. Like so many historical events in the Aztec world, these strange happenings were viewed as cosmological messages about the destiny of the fifth sun. The first chapter of Book XII begins with the sentence, "Here are told the signs which appeared and were seen when the Spaniards had not yet come here to this land, when they were not yet known to the natives here." It is important that the text is emphatic about the fact that omens appear in relation to, but before the invasion of, the Spaniards in Mexico. In fact, in the three different accounts of these omens this priority of the celestial signs over the actions of the Spaniards in relation to the conquest is emphasized. The Indians' informants appear to be demonstrating that from their perspective, supernatural forces communicated that the connection between the cosmos and the state was disintegrating long before the Spaniards appeared to complete the process. In Sahagún, the omens appear as a message of destruction, reversal, and the end of the capital. The first omen, in a sense, tells it all. "A fiery signal . . . it seemed to bleed fire, drop by drop like a wound in the sky." The Aztecs witness a "rip" in their universe, a rip that bleeds fire, threatening the death of their cosmos that is centered by the Templo Mayor. Then a catastrophe at the Great Temple takes place. The text reads, "The Temple of Huitzilopochtli burst into flames. It is thought that no one set it afire, that it burned down of its own accord. . . . The flames swiftly destroyed all the temple . . . and the temple burned to the ground." The center of the Aztec world is mysteriously ignited and destroyed. The identification of temple and city is strong in Mesoamerican thought, as demonstrated in illustrated books such as the *Codex Mendoza*, where the image of a temple tipped, and burning or smoking is a sign that the city has been conquered. In this frightening event, the shrine of the sun and war was burned and toppled, reflecting the image just discussed—a burning, falling temple signifies that a city has been conquered. A series of shocking omens follow in which the "Temple of Xiuhtecuhtli (the Old God, the Fire God) was struck by a lightning bolt," a comet raced across the sky from west to east—the reverse direction of the solar motion, the lake flooded the city, a weeping woman haunted the city at night, a bird with a mirror on its head reflected marching soldiers coming to the capital, and a two-headed man appeared on the streets of the city. The interplay of omens and political events continues to be displayed in the accounts of the subsequent battles and fall of the city. The informants have also described Moctezuma's suffering, the battles between the two armies, and are telling of the siege of Tenochtitlan. Then comes a passage full of piercing fate. We read that, just before the surrender of the city:

> at nightfall it began to rain, but it was more like a heavy dew than a rain. Suddenly the omen appeared, blazing like a great bonfire in the sky. It wheeled in enormous spirals like a whirlwind and gave off a shower of sparks and red-hot coals, some great and some little. It also made loud noises, rumbling and hissing like a metal tube placed over a fire. It circled the wall nearest the lakeshore and then hovered for a while above Coyoncazco. From there it moved out in the middle of the lake where it suddenly

157

disappeared. No one cried out when the omen came into view; the people knew what it meant and they watched in silence.[70]

What they knew was that their mythic structure, their cosmological connection was dissolving into disorder, chaos, and the destruction of the temple. The precise ordering of costume, sculpture, cardinal axiality, and central place was breaking up and going haywire in one way or another.

These omens and their strategic location in the narrative about the conquest shows the tenacity of the interplay of cosmology, nature, sacred space, and cosmic collapse. It is very remarkable that thirty years after the conquest, in a society ruled by Spaniards, Aztec survivors poignantly reaffirm the mythic conviction lodged in their minds that the life and death of their city was animated not solely by Aztecs or Spaniards but also by the patterns of their own heavens.

Notes

1. Bernal Díaz del Castillo, *The Discovery and Conquest of Mexico* (New York: Farrar, Straus, and Giroux, 1956), p. 191.

2. The vital human need for "orientatio" has been elaborately described in a number of works by Mircea Eliade, including *The Myth of the Eternal Return* (New York: Pantheon Books, 1965), *Patterns in Comparative Religions* (New York: Meridian Books, 1967), and recently in his three-volume *The History of Religious Ideas* (Chicago: University of Chicago Press, 1983), especially vol. I, p. 3.

3. Besides Johanna Broda's article, "Templo Mayor as Ritual Space," see Bernardino de Sahagún's *General History of the Things of New Spain: Florentine Codex*, A. J. O. Anderson and C. E. Dibble (Salt Lake City: University of Utah, 1951–1959), especially Book III, pp. 47–48, 52–53, and Book IX, pp. 66–67. See also numerous passages in Diego Durán's *Book of the Gods and Rites and the Ancient Calendar*, Fernando Horcasitas and Doris Heyden, eds. (Norman: University of Okalahoma Press, 1971). For a general view of ritual killing in Mesoamerica, see Elizabeth H. Boone, ed., *Ritual Human Sacrifice in Mesoamerica* (Washington, D.C.: Dumbarton Oaks Research Library and Collection, Trustees for Harvard University, 1984).

4. See Miguel León-Portilla's study of Nahuatl philosophy, *Aztec Thought and Culture* (Norman: University of Oklahoma Press, 1963); George Kubler, *The Art and Architecture of Ancient Americas: The Mexican, Maya and Andean Peoples* (Baltimore: Pelican History of Art, 3d ed., 1984); and most recently, Esther Pasztory's truly remarkable *Aztec Art* (New York: Harry N. Abrams, 1983). Pasztory's work is the first comprehensive attempt at defining and integrating the awesome and puzzling art of the Aztecs. Also, Richard Fraser Townsend's *State and Cosmos in the Art of Tenochtitlán* (Washington, D.C.: Dumbarton Oaks, Trustees for Harvard University, 1979) describes the "living structural affinity between natural and the social orders" of the Aztec world in a fresh and penetrating way. Also note Davíd Carrasco, "Axtec Religion," *The Encyclopedia of Religion*, Mircea Eliade, Editor-in-Chief, vol. 2, 23–29 (New York: Macmillan Publishing Co., 1987).

5. See Alfonso Caso's authoritative introduction to the Mesoamerican Calendar in "Calendrical Systems in Central Mexico" in G. F. Eckholm and Ignacio Bernal, eds., *Handbook of*

Middle American Indians (Austin: University of Texas Press, 1971), vol. 10, pp. 332–348 (hereafter referred to as *Handbook*).

6. H. B. Nicholson, "Major Sculpture in Pre-Hispanic Central Mexico," *Handbook* (1971): 10:92–134.

7. Pedro Armillas, *Program of the History of the American Indian* (Washington, D.C.: Pan American Union, 1958); Philip Phillips and Gordon Willey, *Method and Theory in American Archaeology* (Chicago: University of Chicago Press, 1958); Paul Kirchhoff, "Mesoamerica: Its Geographic Limits, Ethnic Composition and Cultural Characteristics," in *The Heritage of Conquest*, Sol Tax, ed. (Chicago: University of Chicago Press, 1977), pp. 17–30; and Pedro Carrasco, "The Peoples of Central Mexico and Their Historical Traditions," in *Handbook* (1971): 11:459–474.

8. Edward Calnek, "Tenochtitlán in the Early Colonial Period," *Actes du XLII Congres International des Americanistes*, Congres du Centenaire, Paris, 2–9 September 1976, vol. VIII, pp. 35–40, 1979.

9. Paul Wheatley, "City as Symbol," Inaugural lecture delivered at the University College, London, 20 November 1967, p. 7.

10. This phrase, "mythic structure," has been used convincingly by Jacob Neusner in his introductory study of Judaism, *The Way of Torah* (Belmont, Calif.: Wadsworth Publishing, 1976). Specific applications of this idea appear usefully in Cornelious Loew's *Myth, Sacred History and Philosophy* (New York: Harcourt, Brace and World, 1967), Henri Frankfort's *Kingship and the Gods* (Chicago: University of Chicago Press, 1948), and Charles H. Long's *Alpha: Myths of Creation* (Chico, California: Scholars Press, 1963), as well as Davíd Carrasco's *Quetzalcoatl and the Irony of Empire: Myths and Prophecies in the Aztec Tradition* (Chicago: University of Chicago Press, 1983). For a discussion of the ways in which a mythic structure gains power in novel situations see Davíd Carrasco, "Quetzalcoatl's Revenge: Primordium and Application in Aztec Religion," *History of Religions* 19 (May 1980): 296–319.

11. Among Jonathan Z. Smith's exciting works, see *Map Is Not Territory: Studies in the History of Religions* (Leiden: E. J. Brill, 1978) and the article from which this quote was taken, "The Influence of Symbols upon Social Change: A Place upon Which to Stand," *Worship* (October 1970): 14:457–474.

12. See Mircea Eliade's *The Sacred and the Profane* (New York: Harcourt Brace Jovanovich, 1959) and *Myth and Reality* (New York: Harper & Row, 1963).

13. This chapter, "Cosmogonic Myth and Sacred History," in *The Quest* (Chicago: University of Chicago Press, 1969), pp. 72–88, constitutes the most succinct statement of Eliade's view of the range of mythic influences in ritual life and human consciousness.

14. Loew, *Myth, Sacred History and Philosophy*: 5.

15. See Paul Wheatley's "The Suspended Pelt: Reflections on a Discarded Model of Spatial Structure" in *Geographic Humanism, Analysis and Social Action*, Donald R. Deskin, Jr., George Kish, John D. Nystuen, and Gunnar Olsson, eds. (Ann Arbor, Mich., 1976), Geographic Publications, no. 17, pp. 47–108.

16. See Smith, *Map Is Not Territory*: 100–103 for a discussion of the significance of this term in relation to Eliade's terminology.

17. Benjamin Keen, *The Aztec Image in Western Thought* (New Brunswick, N.J.: Rutgers University Press, 1971).

18. Peter Brown, *Society and the Holy in Late Antiquity* (Berkeley, Los Angeles, and London: University of California Press, 1982), p. 8.

19. Paul Wheatley, *The Pivot of the Four Quarters* (Chicago: Aldine Publishers, 1971). Besides this swollen seed of urban studies, Wheatley's expansive vision of the history and meaning of the city can be explored in his most recent work, *Nagara and Commandery: Origins of*

the Southeast Asian Urban Tradition (Chicago: University of Chicago, Department of Geography Research Papers nos. 207–208, 1983).

20. Wheatley, *Pivot*: 414.

21. Townsend, *State and Cosmos*: 17–22.

22. Alfonso Caso, *El Pueblo del Sol* (Mexico: Fondo de Cultura Economia, 1975).

23. See Henry B. Nicholson's remarkable summary article, "Religion in Pre-Hispanic Central Mexico," in *Handbook* (1971): 10:395–445 for a concise description of Mesoamerican cosmology.

24. Miguel León-Portilla, *Pre-Columbian Literatures of Mexico* (Norman: University of Oklahoma Press, 1969), p. 87.

25. See León-Portilla's *Aztec Thought and Culture* for an elaborate discussion of this Aztec High God, especially chapters 2 and 3.

26. Diego Durán, *Historia de Las Indias de Nueva España y Islas de Tierra Firma* (Mexico: Imprenta de J. M. Andrade y F. Escalante, 1867–1880), vol. 2, p. 343.

27. Alvarado Tezozómoc, *Crónica Mexicana* (Mexico: Editorial Leyenda, S.A., 1944).

28. See Davíd Carrasco, "City as Symbol in Aztec Thought: The Clues from the Codex Mendoza," *History of Religion* (20 February 1981): 199–220, for discussion in the footnotes regarding the symbolism. See also Carrasco's "Templo Mayor: The Aztec Vision of Place," *Religion* (London) 11 (1981): 275–297.

29. A recent publication, *Native Mesoamerican Spirituality*, Miguel León-Portilla (Paulist Press, 1980), contains a large number of *teocuicatls* (divine songs) and *huehuetlatollis* (ancient words), making the volume the best collection of indigenous fragments available in English. The following quotes regarding Huitzilopochtli are taken from pp. 220–225.

30. For an interpretation of Tula's religious significance see Davíd Carrasco's *Quetzalcoatl and the Irony of Empire*, especially pp. 72–92 and 104–128, plus the bibliography.

31. Alfredo López-Austin's *Hombre-Dios: Religión y Política en el Mundo Nahuatl* (Mexico: Universidad Nacional Autonoma de Mexico, 1973) is a complex and brilliant interpretation of Mesoamerican religion.

32. See Mircea Eliade's discussion of "magical heat" and "berserker" experiences in the history of religions for useful connections to not only the myth of Huitzilopochtli but also the warrior mentality, which animated segments of Aztec religion, in *Rites and Symbols of Initiation* (New York: Harper and Row, 1958), pp. 81–107.

33. See Henry B. Nicholson's detailed description of the Coyolxauhqui stone in "The New Tenochtitlán Templo Mayor Coyolxauhqui-Chantico Monument" (in press), in Festschrift honoring Professor Gerdt Kutscher, Ibero-Amerikanisches Institut, Berlin, Germany.

34. Diego Durán, *Book of the Gods and Rites*: 458.

35. See Anthony Aveni's wealth of publications on the patterns of archaeoastronomy in Mesoamerican and native American traditions, including his *Skywatchers of Ancient Mexico* (Austin: University of Texas Press, 1980).

36. Bernardino de Sahagún, *The Florentine Codex*, II: 25–30.

37. See Carlos Ginzberg, "Morelli, Freud and Sherlock Holmes: Clues and the Scientific Method," in *The Sign of Three, Dupin, Holmes, Pierce* (Bloomington: Indiana University Press, 1983).

38. See Johanna Broda's exhaustive account in "La Fiesta Azteca del Fuego Nuevo y el culto de la Pléyades," In *Space and Time in the Cosmovision of Mesoamerica*. Franz Tichy ed. *Lateinamerika-Studien*, vol. 10 (Munich: Wilhelm Fink-Verlag, 1982*b*), pp. 129–158.

39. This quote is actually Clifford Geertz's gloss on Shils's work in "Centers, Kings and Charisma: Symbolics of Power," in *Local Knowledge*: 122. For a more extensive discussion of

astronomy and symbolism in Aztec Mexico, see Davíd Carrasco, "Star Gatherers and Wobbling Sons: Astral Symbolism in The Aztec Tradition," *History of Religions* 26 (Feb. 1987): 279–294.

40. See H. B. Nicholson's "Religion in Pre-Hispanic Central Mexico" for a precise description of Aztec cosmology, in *Handbook* (1971): 10:395–446.

41. One of the most vivid examples of this replication and miniaturization can be found in the *Codex Borgia*'s representations of the rain gods.

42. See Miguel León-Portilla, *Aztec Thought and Culture*, especially chapters 2 and 3.

43. Edward Calnek, "The Internal Structure of Tenochtitlan," in *The Valley of Mexico*, Eric Wolf, ed. (Albuquerque: University of New Mexico Press, 1976).

44. Ibid.

45. Durán, *Historia de los Indias*: 2:343.

46. Johanna Broda, "El Tributo en Trajes Guerreros y la Estructura del Sistema Tributario Mexica," in *Economía Política*, Carrasco and Broda, eds.: 122–140.

47. Rudolph Van Zantwijk, "The Great Temple of Tenochtitlán: Model of Aztec Cosmovision," in *Mesoamerican Sites and World Views*, Elizabeth P. Benson, ed. (Washington, D.C.: Dumbarton Oaks, 1981), pp. 71–84.

48. Numa Denis Fustel de Coulanges, *The Ancient City* (New York: Doubleday Anchor Books, n.d.).

49. Sahagún, *Florentine Codex*, III:1.

50. Ibid.

51. Sahagún, *Florentine Codex*, VII:6.

52. Ibid.

53. Ibid., 7.

54. Ibid., 8. My work with myths of creation is deeply indebted to the superior work of Charles H. Long, especially his *Alpha: Myths of Creation* (Chico, California: Scholars Press, 1963).

55. Edward Shils, *"Center and Periphery" Selected Essays* (Chicago: University of Chicago Press, 1970), pp. 7–8.

56. Stanley Tambiah, "The Galactic Polity: The Structure of Traditional Kingdoms in Southeast Asia," *Annals of the New York Academy of Sciences* (1977): 293:69–97.

57. Pedro Carrasco, "Social Organization of Ancient Mexico," *Handbook* (1971): 10:347–375.

58. Ibid.

59. Esther Pasztory, *Aztec Stone Sculpture* (The Center for Inter-American Religions, January 1977).

60. Ibid.

61. Ibid.

62. Ibid.

63. Durán, *Book of the Gods and Rites*: 160.

64. Broda, "Ideology of the Aztec State and Human Sacrifice" (manuscript delivered at 1979 Conference in Boulder, Colorado, pp. 24–35), to be published in *Societies in Transition: Essays in honor of Pedro Carrasco*, Roger Joseph, Frances F. Berdan and Hugo G. Nutini, eds. (in press).

65. Broda, "Ideology of the Aztec State," pp. 24–38. See also Davíd Carrasco, "Human Sacrifice: Aztec Rites," *The Encyclopedia of Religion* vol. 6: 518–523 (New York: Macmillan Publishing Co., 1987).

66. This general discussion of ritual human sacrifice is derived from H. B. Nicholson's

"Religion in Pre-Hispanic Central Mexico" in *Handbook* (1971), 10: and the *Florentine Codex*, Book II, *The Ceremonies*. See especially the appendix.

67. Broda, "Ideology of the Aztec State," pp. 30–31.

68. Ibid.

69. Roy Rappaport, *Ecology, Meaning and Religion* (Richmond, Calif.: North Atlantic Books, 1979), p. 148.

70. This entire sequence of references comes from Sahagún, *Florentine Codex*, XII:3–10. Book XII contains the closest thing we have to an Aztec and Tlatelolca account of the conquest. For a collection of omen accounts associated with the Aztecs, see Miguel León-Portilla, *The Broken Spears* (Boston: Beacon Press, 1962), pp. 3–15.

Glossary

GUIDE TO PRONUNCIATION

Nahuatl was transcribed by Spaniards and normally stresses the penultimate syllable.
Vowels follow Spanish pronunciation:

a	as in b*a*r	Amatl
e	as in r*e*d	Mexica
i	as in k*ee*p	Tizoc
o	as in p*o*se	Toltec
u	as in *u*se	Tula, Motecuhzoma
y	as in *y*et	Yucatan

Consonants correspond to English equivalents, except for the following:

h	is like *w*	Huitzilopochtli
que, qui	is like *k*	quetzal
qua, quo	is like *kw*	Atamalqualiztli
x	is like *sh*	Xipe
z	is like *s*	Zapotec

LIST OF INDIAN LANGUAGE TERMS (CLASSIC NAHUATL (CN), MODERN NAHUATL, AND MODERN MAYAN DIALECTS

Acamapichtli—first Aztec tlatoani (king) who ruled from 1375 to 1395

ah-ilix—"guardian," "protector" (modern Quiché Maya), name referring to small stone idols

Ahuitzotl—eighth Aztec tlatoani who ruled from 1486 to 1502

aj choch—"protector of the house" (modern Quiché Maya, Chichicastenango), name referring to small stone idols

aj ixim—"protector of the corn kernels" (modern Quiché Maya, Chichicastenango), name referring to small stone idols

aj su'ts—"beings or lords of the clouds" (modern Quiché Maya, Chichicastenango), name referring to small stone idols

alaxic—"lineage" (modern Quiché Maya, Chichicastenango)

163

altepetl—"mountain filled with water" (CN), term for "village," "community"

alxic—"little gods of destiny" (modern Quiché Maya, Chichicastenango), small stone idols

amatetehuitl—"paper strips" (CN), high paper banners used in rites of the rain gods

anecuyotl—(CN) emblem mentioned in Aztec myths and in certain rites where it symbolizes the destiny of the deity

asihuaw—"water woman" (modern Nahuatl, Sierra de Puebla)

atagat—"man or lord of water" (modern Nahuatl, Sierra de Puebla)

Atemoztli—the "Falling of the Water" (CN), sixteenth month of the Aztec solar calendar

atl—"water" (CN)

atl tlachinolli—"water-fire" (CN), Aztec metaphoric concept for warfare

atlatlayan—"water of conflagration" (CN)

Atlcahualo—"Detention of Water," possibly "Shortage of Water" (CN), first month of the Aztec solar calendar

Axayacatl—sixth Aztec tlatoani who ruled from 1468 to 1481

Aztlan—controversial term that, according to the majority of authors, is to be translated as "place of the white heron," derived from *aztatl*, "heron" (CN)

calmecac—"file of houses" (CN), Aztec temple schools for the nobility

calpixque—"stewards" (CN), tribute collectors of the Aztec empire

camahuil—"deity," "idol" (also *kabavil*) (modern Quiché Maya, Totonicapan), type of small stone or clay idol

Cemanahuac—"land surrounded by water," "the world" (CN)

centzon huitznahua—the "four-hundred Southerners" (CN), Coyolxauhqui's 400 brothers in the myth of the birth of Huitzilopochtli

Chac—Maya rain god, equivalent to the Aztec Tlaloc

Chac Mool—"red jaguar," term derived from Mayan language referring to the Toltec style reclining seated sculptures found at Chichén Itzá and Tula and in Aztec art

chalchihuitl—"precious stone or jade" (CN), symbol for preciousness; *chalchihuites* is a Mexican-Spanish term derived from Nahuatl (plural)

chalchiuh-atl—"precious water" (CN)

Chalchiuhtlicue—"She of the Jade Skirt" (CN), Aztec goddess of the surface water, streams, and lakes

Chantico—"At the Hearth" (CN), goddess of fire and the hearth, patron deity of Xochimilco

Chicomecoatl—"Seven Serpent" (CN), Aztec goddess of maize and sustenance

Chicomoztoc—the "Seven Caves" (CN), mythic place of origin of the Aztecs

Cihuacoatl—"Woman Serpent" (CN), important Aztec earth and mother goddess; Cihuacoatl was also the title of the Aztec political dignitary next in importance after the tlatoani

cihuateotl—"divine woman" (CN), singular of *cihuateteo*, the spirits of women who died in childbirth and became converted into female monsters

164

Cihuatlampa—"region of women" (CN), referring to the west

Cinteotl—"Maize-Ear Lord" (CN), Aztec male corn deity

cipactli—"alligator" (CN); the cipactli was the earth monster on whose back the world rested

Coaapan—"place of serpent water" (CN)

coatepantli—"serpent wall" (CN)

Coatepec—"on the serpent hill" (CN)

Coatepetl—"serpent mountain" (CN)

Coatlicue—"She with the Serpent Skirt" (CN), Aztec mother and earth goddess

Cocij—Zapotec rain god, equivalent to the Aztec Tlaloc

copal—pre-Hispanic Indian incense (CN)

copaltemaliztli—"incensing" (CN)

copalteteo—"gods made of copal" (CN)

Copil—according to Aztec mythology, the leader of a conspiracy against the Mexica while they occupied Chapultepec; he was defeated and sacrificed and his heart was thrown into the lake (this site later marked the foundation of Tenochtitlan)

Coyolxauhqui—"She Who Is Adorned (or Painted) With Copper Bells" (CN), Huitzilopochtli's rebellious sister in the myth of the birth of the Aztec patron deity

cu—temple, pyramid, term from the Antilles incorporated into sixteenth-century Spanish

cuauhxicalli—"eagle vessel" (CN), sculptured recipient for human hearts

Ehecatl—"Wind God" (CN), another name for the Aztec god Quetzalcoatl.

Etzalcualiztli—a "Food Made of Beans and Maize" (CN), sixth month of the Aztec solar calendar

huauhtli and *michihuauhtli*—(CN), varieties of amaranth

Huehueteotl—the "Old God" (CN), Aztec fire god

huehuetlatolli—ancient words, wisdom of the ancients (CN)

huey atl—the "great water" (CN), referring to water in its absolute form, or the sea

Huey miccailhuitl—"Great Festival of the Dead" (CN), tenth month of the Aztec solar calendar

Huey tecuilhuitl—"Great Festival of the Lords" (CN), seventh month of the Aztec solar calendar

Huey tozoztli—the "Great Vigil" (CN), fourth month of the Aztec solar calendar

Huitzilopochtli—"Hummingbird to the Left" (CN), patron deity of the Aztec ethnic group

Huitztlampa—"region of thorns" (CN)

Huixtocihuatl—Aztec goddess of salt; sister of the rain gods; the name derives from *Huixtotin*, an ethnic group (CN)

Ilamatecuhtli—"Old Lady" (CN), Aztec earth and fertility goddess

ilhuica atl—"heavenly water," "water of the sky" (CN), referring to the sea

inan atl—"mother of the water" (modern Nahuatl, Ameyaltepec, Guerrereo), referring to the sea

165

in iachhuan Huitzilopochtli in mocexiuhzauhque—"elder brothers of Huitzilopochtli (priests) who fasted for a year" (CN)

in ixiptla in teteo—"deity impersonators" (CN)

Ipaina—"haste, velocity, swiftness" (CN), a footrace forming part of certain Aztec calendar rites

Itzcoatl—fourth Aztec tlatoani who ruled from 1426 to 1440

ixiptla tepetl—"mountain images" (CN), small idols formed of maize dough

Izcalli—"growth" (CN), eighteenth month of the Aztec solar calendar

Iztac Cihuatl—"White Woman" (CN), Aztec goddess, the second-highest volcano of the Valley of Mexico

Juyubtak'aj—"Mountain-Plains" (modern Quiché Maya, Chichicastenango), name of the earth deity or "world"

kabavil—"deity, idol" (modern Maya Quiché); see *camahuil*

Malinalxochitl—"Malinalli-grass flower" (CN); according to the Aztec migration myth, Malinalxochitl was the sorceress sister of Huitzilopochtli, who became the founder of the province of Malinalco, where an important Aztec religious shrine was built

matlalatl—"blue water" (CN)

Matlalcueye—"She with the Blue (Green) Skirt" (CN), water and mountain goddess, name of the volcano La Malinche, Tlaxcala

maxtlatl—loincloth (CN)

Miccailhuitontli—"Small Festival of the Dead" (CN), ninth month of the Aztec solar calendar

Mictlampa—the "region of the underworld" (CN)

Mictlan—the "land of the dead, underworld" (CN)

Mictlantecuhtli—the "Lord of the Underworld" (CN), Aztec god of the abode of the dead

Mixcoatl—"Cloud Serpent" (CN), name of an important Aztec god, patron of hunters, and of the fourteenth Aztec month *Quecholli*

Motecuhzoma Ilhuicamina or *Motecuhzoma I*—fifth Aztec tlatoani who ruled from 1440 to 1469

Motecuhzoma Xocoyotzin or *Motecuhzoma II*—ninth Aztec tlatoani who ruled from 1502 to 1520

Nahuatl—an Uto-Aztecan language spoken by the autochthonous inhabitants of central Mexico on the eve of the Spanish Conquest; the Mexica or Aztecs were one of these groups

Nanahuatl, Nanahuatzin—the "Pimply One" (CN), Aztec god figuring in the myth of the creation of the fifth sun

nauhcampa—"four parts, quarters" (CN)

nezahualiztli—"priestly fasting" (CN)

Ochpaniztli—"Sweeping of the Way" (CN), twelfth month of the Aztec solar calendar and an important festival with fertility connotations *ollas*—(earthenware) pots (Spanish)

Ometeotl—"God Two" (CN), lord of duality, Aztec deity

Omeyocan—"place of duality" (CN)

Panquetzaliztli—"Raising of Banners" (CN), fifteenth month of the Aztec solar year; main annual festival of the Aztec patron deity Huitzilopochtli

pillis, pipiltin—nobility, ruling class within Aztec society (CN)

Popocatepetl—"Smoking Mountain" (CN), the highest volcano in the Valley of Mexico

Quetzalcoatl—"Feathered Serpent," "Precious Serpent," or "Precious Twin" (*coatl*) (CN), one of the major Aztec deities with a complex symbolism

sihuawchan—"house of the women" (modern Nahuatl, Sierra de Puebla)

Tajin—Totonac rain god, equivalent of the Aztec Tlaloc

techcatl—(CN) sacrificial stone for human sacrifice

tecpatl—"flint" (CN), term for sacrificial knife in Aztec ritual

tecuacuiltin—"statue, image, idol" (CN), small idols used in Aztec cult

Tecucciztecatl—"Lord of Snails" (CN), the Aztec moon god

temalacatl—"circular stone" (CN), sacrificial stone on which the gladiatorial sacrifice was performed

teoatl tlachinolli—"divine liquid and burned things" (CN), an Aztec metaphor referring to warfare

teocalli—"house of the god" (i.e., temple) (CN)

teocuaque—"god eaters" (CN), a form of penitence in Aztec ritual

teocuicatl—"divine song" (CN)

Teotihuacan—"Abode of the Gods" (CN), important archaeological site in central Mexico dating from the Classic period

Teotleco—"the Gods Arrive" (CN), twelfth month of the Aztec solar calendar

tepehua—"rain boys; owners of the mountains" (modern Nahuatl, Pipil, El Salvador)

Tepeilhuitl—"Mountain Festival" (CN), thirteenth month of the Aztec solar year; festival in honor of all the mountains of the Valley of Mexico

tepetl—"mountain" (CN)

Tepeyollotl—"Heart of the Mountain" (CN), Aztec deity related to the night, to caves, the earth, and the jaguar

tepictoton—"small sculptured figurines" (CN), small idols formed of maize dough used in Aztec ritual

Teteo innan—"the Mother of the Gods" (CN), Aztec mother and earth goddess

Tezcaapan—"place of water of the mirror" (CN)

Tezcatlipoca—"Smoking Mirror" (CN), one of the major Aztec deities related to rulership, magic, and the night

tezontle—volcanic rock, Mexican-Spanish term derived from Nahuatl

tianquiztli—"marketplace" (CN), Aztec concept for the constellation of the Pleiades

tipeyolohtle—"heart of the mountain" (modern Nahuatl, Zongolica, Veracruz), with the same meaning as tepeyollotl (CN)

Tititl—"Stretching" (CN), seventeenth month of the Aztec solar calendar

Tizoc—seventh Aztec tlatoani who ruled from 1481 to 1486; he was unsuccessful in military campaigns

Tlacaelel—long-lived and politically brilliant counselor or cihuacoatl to five Aztec emperors (Itzcoatl, Motecuhzoma I, Axayacatl, Tizoc, and Ahuitzotl); great innovator in politics and religious matters

tlacatlaolli—"human maize" (CN), a dish prepared from human flesh and maize, consumed in the ritual context

Tlacaxipehualiztli—"The Flaying of Men" (CN), second month of the Aztec solar calendar and important religious festival during which the gladiatorial combat and the rite of flaying of men was performed

tlachinolli—"burned object" (CN), term forming part of the metaphor *tlachinolli teoatl*, "warfare, battle"

tlallo—"full of earth, or covered with earth" (CN)

Tlaloc—"He Who Has the Quality of Earth" (CN), name of the Aztec rain god

Tlalocan—"place of Tlaloc" (CN), the paradise of the rain god

tlaloque—plural form of Tlaloc (CN), the small servants of the Aztec rain god

Tlaltecuhtli—"Earth Lord" (CN), conceived in the form of an earth-monster

tlalxicco—"center, or navel of the earth" (CN)

tlaquaian—"place where one eats" (CN), referring to a stone altar at the Templo Mayor

tlaquechpanyotl—(CN), large paper fan (worn at the nape of the neck); insignia of Aztec rain and water deities

Tlatelolco—twin city of Tenochtitlan

tlatoani—the "speaker" (CN), name of the Aztec ruler or king

tlatocayotl—the "domain of a tlatoani" (CN), small local states, or city-states of which the Aztec empire was composed

tlatoque—rulers, plural of tlatoani (CN)

tlatsinihkeh—"those who produce thunder and lightning" (modern Nahuatl, Zongolica, Veracruz)

tleatl—"water of fire" (CN)

tlenamacaque—Aztec fire priests (plural) (CN)

Tlilapan—"place of black water" (CN)

Tlillan—"the dark place" (CN), the temple of the goddess Cihuacoatl situated next to the Great Double Pyramid at the Templo Mayor

tochtli—"rabbit" (CN), one of the twenty signs of the Aztec ritual calendar

Tonacatecuhtli—"Lord of Sustenance" (CN), Aztec creator deity

Tonacatepetl—"mountain of sustenance" (CN)

tonacayotl—"human sustenance" (CN), referring primarily to maize

tonalco—"time of heat and the sun" (CN), referring to the dry season

Toxcatl—controversial translation of the name, probably meaning "Dryness, Drought" (CN), fifth month of the Aztec solar calendar *toxpalatl* or *tozpalatl*—"yellow water" (CN)

tozohualiztli—nocturnal vigil (CN)

Tozoztontli—the "Little Vigil" (CN), third month of the Aztec solar calendar

Tutek'aj or *Turuk' aj*—name of a large stone idol situated on the most prominent mountain near Chichicastenango (modern Quiché Maya, Chichicastenango)

tzitzimime—"astral bodies that shine in the night" (CN), Aztec female demons with skeletal features

tzoalli—dough consisting of maize mixed with other seeds and honey, used to form the mountain images in Aztec ritual (CN)

tzompantli—skull rack at the Templo Mayor (CN)

ulteteo—"gods made of liquid rubber" (CN), small idols used in Aztec rites to the rain deities

Xilonen—"She Who Is Like Tender Maize" (CN), the young maize goddess

xiuhcoatl—"fire serpent" (CN)

xiuhpohualli—the "counting of the years" (CN), referring to the solar count or 365-day calendar

Xiuhtecuhtli—"Turquoise Lord, or the Lord of the Year" (CN), name of the Aztec fire god, the eldest of the gods

xihuitl—"year, turquoise, grass, or comet" (CN)

xochimiquiztli—"flowery death" (CN), referring to ritual warfare

Xochipilli—"Flower Prince" (CN), Aztec solar deity with fertility aspects

Xolotl—the monstrous twin brother of the god Quetzalcoatl (CN)

xopan—"when it is green" (CN), referring to the rainy season

Yollotlicue—"She With the Skirt of Hearts" (CN), referring to a monumental sculpture of the Aztec mother-and-earth goddess

Selected Bibliography

Acosta Saignes, Miguel. "Los Teopixque: Organización Sacerdotal entre los Mexica." *Revista Mexicana de Estudios Antropológicos* 8 (1946): 147–205.

Adams, Robert Mc. C. *The Evolution of Urban Society.* Chicago: Aldine, 1967.

Aguilera, Carmen, *Coyolxauhqui: Ensayo Iconográfico.* Cuadernos de la Biblioteca, Serie Investigación, no. 2. Biblioteca Nacional de Antropología e Historia. Mexico: INAH, 1978.

———. "Xolpan y Tonalco. Una Hipotesis Acerca de la Correlación Astronómica del Calendario Mexica." *Estudios de Cultura Nahuatl* (Mexico: UNAM) 15 (1982): 185–208.

———. "Iztac Mixcoatl en la Vasija del *Templo Mayor.*" In *Memoria del Primer Coloquio de Historia de la Religión en Mesoamerica y Areas Afines.* Edited by Barbro Dahlgren. Instituto de Investigaciones Antropológicas. Mexico: UNAM (in press).

Ahuja, Guillermo. "Excavación de la Cámara II." In *El Templo Mayor: Excavaciones y Estudios.* Edited by Eduardo Matos Moctezuma. Mexico: INAH, 1982. Pages 191–212.

Alcina Franch, José. "Pequeñas Esculturas Antropomorfas de Guerrero, México." *Revista de Indias* (Madrid) XXI (1961): 295–350.

Alcocer, Ignacio. *Apuntes sobre la Antigua México-Tenochtitlan.* Mexico: Instituto Panamericano de Geografía e Historia, 1927.

Armillas, Pedro. *Program of the History of American Indians.* Washington, D.C.: Pan American Union, 1958.

Aveni, Anthony F., and Gary Urton, eds. *Ethnoastronomy and Archaeoastronomy in the American Tropics. Annals of the New York Academy of Sciences*, vol. 385. New York: The New York Academy of Sciences, 1982.

Batres, Leopoldo. *Teotihuacan, Ciudad Sagrada de los Dioses.* Mexico: Imprenta de Hull, 1906.

———. "Exploraciones en las Calles de las Escalerillas" (1902). In *Trabajos Arqueológicos en el Centro de la Ciudad de México.* Edited by Eduardo Matos Moctezuma. Mexico: INAH, 1979. Pages 61–90.

Beyer, Hermann. "La Procesion de los Señores" (1955). In *Trabajos Arqueológicos en el Centro de la Ciudad de Mexico.* Edited by Eduardo Matos Moctezuma. Mexico: INAH, 1979. Pages 149–166.

Bonfil Batalla, Guillermo. "Los que Trabajan con el Tiempo." *Anales de Antropología* (Mexico: Instituto de Investigaciones Históricas, UNAM) V (1968): 99–128.

Broda, Johanna. "Tlacaxipehualiztli: A Reconstruction of an Aztec Calendar Festival from 16th Century Sources." *Revista Española de Antropología Americana* (Madrid) 5 (1970): 197–274.

———. "Las Fiestas Aztecas de los Dioses de la Lluvia." *Revista Española de Antropología Americana* (Madrid) (1971): 245–327.

———. "Los Estamentos en el Ceremonial Mexica." In *Estratificacíon Social en la Mesoamérica Prehispánica*. Edited by Pedro Carrasco, Johanna Broda, et al. Mexico: SEP-INAH, 1976. Pages 37–66.

———. "Relaciones Políticas Ritualizadas: El Ritual Como Expresión de Una Ideología." In *Economía Política e Ideología en el México Prehispánico*. Edited by Pedro Carrasco and Johanna Broda. Mexico: Nueva Imagen—CIS-INAH, 1978. Pages 219–255.

———. "Estratificacíon Social y Ritual Mexica: Un Ensayo de Antropología Social de los Mexica." *Indiana* (Berlin) 5 (1979): 45–82.

———. "Aspectos Socio-económicos e Ideológicos de la Expansión del Estado Mexica." In *Economía y Sociedad en los Andes y Mesoamérica*. Edited by José Alcina Franch. *Revista de la Universidad Complutense* XXVIII (117): 73–94. Madrid: Universidad Complutense de Madrid, 1980a.

———. "Astronomy, Cosmovision and Ideology of Prehispanic Mesoamerica." In *Ethnoastronomy and Archaeoastronomy in the American Tropics*. Edited by Anthony F. Aveni and Gary Urton. *Annals of the New York Academy of Sciences*, vol. 385. New York: The New York Academy of Sciences, 1982a. Pages 81–110.

———. "La Fiesta Azteca del Fuego Nuevo y el Culto de las Pléyades." In *Space and Time in the Cosmovision of Mesoamerica*. Edited by Franz Tichy. *Latinamerika-Studien,* vol. 10. Munich: Wilhelm Fink-Verlag, 1982b. Pages 129–158.

———. "El Culto Mexica de los Cerros y del Agua." *Multidisciplina* (Mexico: Escuela Nacional de Estudios Profesionales, Acatlan—UNAM) 3, no. 7 (1982c): 45–56.

———. "Cíclos Agrícolas en el Culto: Un Problema de la Correlación del Calendario Mexica." In *Calendars in Mesoamerica and Peru: Native American Computations of Time*. Edited by Anthony F. Aveni and Gordon Brotherston. Oxford: BAR International Series 174, 1983. Pages 145–165.

———. "The Provenience of the Offerings: Tribute and '*Cosmovision.*'" In *The Aztec Templo Mayor*. Edited by Elizabeth H. Boone. Washington, D.C.: Dumbarton Oaks 1987. Pages 211–256.

———. "Ideology of the Aztec State and Human Sacrifice." Paper presented at the Symposium on "Center and Periphery: The Templo Mayor and the Aztec Empire," University of Colorado at Boulder, 5–9 November 1979. To be published in *Societies in Transition: Essays in Honor of Pedro Carrasco*. Edited by Roger Joseph, Frances F. Berdan, and Hugo G. Nutini (in press).

Brown, Peter. *Society and the Holy in Late Antiquity*. Berkeley, Los Angeles, and London: University of California Press, 1982.

Brundage, Burr. *A Rain of Darts*. Austin: University of Texas Press, 1972.

Burgoa, Francisco de. *Geográfica Descripción de la Parte Septentrional del Polo Ártico de América*, 2 vols. Publicaciones del Archivo General de la Nación, XXV–XXVI. Mexico: Talleres Gráficos de la Nación, 1934.

Calnek, Edward. "The Internal Structure of Tenochtitlan." In *The Valley of Mexico*. Edited by Eric Wolf. Albuquerque: University of New Mexico Press, 1976.

———. "Myth and History in the Founding of Tenochtitlán." Unpublished manuscript, 1977.

———. "Tenochtitlan in the Early Colonial Period." *Actes du XLII Congres International des Americanistes*, Congres du Centenaire, Paris, 2–9 September 1976, vol. VIII, 1979. Pages 35–40.

Carmack, Robert M. *Evolución del Reino Quiché*. Guatemala City: Piedra Santa, 1979.

Carrasco, Davíd, "Quetzalcoatl's Revenge: Primordium and Application in Aztec Religion," *History of Religions* 19 (May 1980): 296–319.

———— "City as Symbol in Aztec Thought: Clues from the Codex Mendoza," *History of Religions* 20 (1981*a*): 199–220.

————. "Templo Mayor: The Aztec Vision of Place." *Religion* (London) 11 (1981): 275–297.

————. *Quetzalcoatl and the Irony of Empire. Myths and Prophecies in the Aztec Tradition.* Chicago: University of Chicago Press, 1983.

———— "Aztec Religion," *The Encyclopedia of Religion*, Mircea Eliade, Editor-in-Chief. Vol. 2, pp. 23–29. New York: MacMillan Publishing Co., 1987.

———— "Human Sacrifice: Aztec Rites," *The Encyclopedia of Religion*, Mircea Eliade, Editor-in-Chief, vol. 6: 518–523. New York: Macmillan Publishing Co., 1987.

———— "Star Gatherers and Wobbling Sun: Astral Symbolism in The Aztec Tradition," *History of Religions* 26 (February 1987): 279–294.

Carrasco, Pedro. "Un Mito y Una Ceremonia entre los Chatinos de Oaxaca." In *A William C. Townsend en el XXV Aniversario del Instituto Lingüístico del Verano*. Mexico, 1960. Pages 43–48.

————. "The Peoples of Central Mexico and Their Historical Traditions." In *Handbook of Middle American Indians, Guide to Ethnohistorical Sources*, vol. 11. Austin: University of Texas Press, 1971. Pages 459–474.

————. "La Economía del México Prehispánico." In *Economía Política e Ideología en el México Prehispánico*. Edited by Pedro Carrasco and Johanna Broda. Mexico: Nueva Imagen— CIS-INAH, 1978. Pages 13–74.

————. "Las Fiestas de los Meses Mexicanos." In *Mesoamérica: Homenaje al Dr. Paul Kirchhoff*. Edited by Barbro Dahlgren. Mexico: SEP-INAH, 1979. Pages 52–60.

Carrasco, Pedro and Johanna Broda, eds. *Economía Política e Ideología en el México Prehispánico*. Mexico: Nueva Imagen—CIS-INAH, 1978.

Carrasco, Pedro, Johanna Broda, et al. *Estratificación Social en la Mesoamérica Prehispánica*. Mexico: SEP-INAH, 1979. Pages 52–60.

Ciudad Ruíz, Andrés. "Comentarios a la Religiosidad Popular en el Altiplano Guatemalteco Durante la Época Prehispánica: Los Camahuiles de Cerámica." *Mayab*, no. 2. Madrid: Sociedad Española de Estudios Mayas, 1986.

Codex Borbonicus. Facsimile edition. Commentary by Karl Anton Nowotny. Akademische Druck-und Verlagsanstalt, Graz-Austria, 1974.

Codex Borgia. Facsimile edition. Commentary by Karl Anton Nowotny. Akademische Druck-und Verlagsanstalt, Graz-Austria, 1976.

Cohodas, Marvin. "The Iconography of the Panels of the Sun, Cross, and Foliated Cross at Palenque: Part II." In *Primera Mesa Redonda de Palenque, Part I*. Edited by Merle Greene Robertson. Pebble Beach, Calif.: The Robert Louis Stevenson School, 1974. Pages 95–107.

————. "The Iconography of the Panels of the Sun, Cross, and Foliated Cross at Palenque: Part III." In *Segunda Mesa Redonda de Palenque, Part III*. Edited by Merle Greene Robertson. Pebble Beach, Calif.: The Robert Louis Stevenson School, 1976. Pages 155–176.

Cordan, Wolfgang. *Das Buch des Rates*. Düsseldorf-Köln: 1962.

Coulanges, Numa Denis Fustel de. *The Ancient City*. New York: Doubleday Anchor Books, n.d.

Dahlgren, Barbara, Emma Pérez-Rocha, Lourdes Suáres Díez, and Perla Valle de Revueltas, eds. *Corazón de Copil*. Mexico: INAH, 1982.

Díaz del Castillo, Bernal. *The Discovery and Conquest of Mexico*. New York: Farrar, Straus & Giroux, 1956.

Durán, Fray Diego. *Historia de las Indias de Nueva España*, 2 vols. Edited by Angel María Garibay. Mexico: Editorial Porrúa, 1967.

————. *Book of the Gods and Rites and the Ancient Calendar.* Edited and translated by Fernando Horcasitas and Doris Heyden. Norman: University of Oklahoma Press, 1971.

Edmonson, Munroe. *Quiché-English Dictionary.* Middle American Research Institute, publication no. 30. New Orleans: Tulane University, 1965.

————. *The Book of Counsel: The Popol Vuh of the Quiché Maya of Guatemala.* Middle American Research Institute, publication no. 35. New Orleans: Tulane University, 1971.

Eliade, Mircea. "Methodological Remarks on the Study of Religious Symbolism." In *The History of Religions.* Edited by Joseph Kitagawa. Chicago: University of Chicago Press, 1959.

————. *The Myth of the Eternal Return.* New York: Pantheon Books, 1965.

————. *Patterns in Comparative Religions.* New York: Meridian Books, 1967.

————. *Tratado de Historia de las Religiones.* Mexico: Biblioteca Era, 1975.

Elzey, Wayne. "Mythology of the Ages of the World." Ph.D. dissertation, University of Chicago, 1975.

Fernández, Justino. *Coatlicue: Estética del Arte Indígena Antiguo.* Instituto de Investigaciones Históricas. Mexico: UNAM, 1959.

Frankfort, Henri. *Kingship and the Gods.* Chicago: University of Chicago Press, 1948.

Fuente, Julio de la. "Las Ceremonias de la Lluvia entre los Zapotecos de Hoy." In XXVII Congreso Internacional de Americanistas, *Actas de la Primera Sesion,* vol. III. Mexico, 1939. Pages 479–481.

————. *Yalalag. Una Villa Zapoteca Serrana.* Museo Nacional de Antropología, Serie Cientifica, no. 1. Mexico: INAH, 1949.

Garibay, Angel María, ed. "Histoyre du Mechique (Historia de México)." In *Teogonia e Historia de los Mexicanos.* Angel María Garibay, ed., Colección Sepan Cuántos no. 37. Mexico: Editorial Porrúa, 1965.

Gibson, Charles. "Structure of the Aztec Empire." In *Handbook of Middle American Indians,* vol. 10, part I. Austin: University of Texas Press, 1971. Pages 376–394.

Ginzberg, Carlos. "Morelli, Freud and Sherlock Holmes: Clues and Scientific Method." In *The Sign of Three, Dupin, Holmes, Pierce.* Bloomington: Indiana University Press, 1983. Pages 48–74.

Girard, Rafael. *Los Mayas Eternos.* Mexico: Libro Mexicano, 1962.

González González, Carlos Javier. "Materiales de Estilo Mezcala en el *Templo Mayor.*" In *The Aztec Templo Mayor.* Edited by Elizabeth H. Boone. Washington: Dumbarton Oaks, 1987. Pages 145–160.

Good, Catherine. *Hacienda la Lucha: Arte y Comercio Nahua.* Mexico: Fondo de Cultura Económica, in press.

Gossen, Gary. "Temporal and Spatial Equivalents in Chamula Ritual Symbolism." In *Reader in Comparative Religion: An Anthropological Approach.* Edited by William Lessa and Evon Z. Vogt. New York and London: Harper and Row, 1972. Pages 135–149.

Graulich, Michel. *Mythes et Rites des Vingtaines du Mexique Central Préhispanique,* 3 vols. Ph.D. thesis, Université Libre de Bruxelles, 1979–1980.

————. "Templo Mayor, Coyolxauhqui und Cacaxtla." *Mexicon* (Berlin) V, no. 5 (1983): 91–94.

————. "Quelques Observations sur les Sculptures Mesoamericaines Dites 'Chac Mool.'" Unpublished manuscript, n.d.

Guiteras-Holmes, Calixta. *Perils of the Soul: The World View of a Tzotzil Indian.* New York: The Free Press of Glencoe, 1961.

Hardoy, Jorge. *Pre-Columbian Cities.* New York: Walker, 1973.

Heyden, Doris. "An Interpretation of the Cave Underneath the Pyramid of the Sun in Teotihuacan, Mexico." *American Antiquity,* 40(2) (1975): 131–147.

173

————. "Caves, Gods and Myths: World-View and Planning in Teotihuacan." In *Mesoamerican Sites and World Views*. Edited by Elizabeth Benson. Washington, D.C.: Dumbarton Oaks, 1981. Pages 1–40.

Holland, William R. *Medicina Maya en los Altos de Chiapas*. Serie de Antropología Social, no. 2. Mexico: Instituto Nacional Indigenista, 1978.

Ichón, Alain. *La Religión de los Totonacas de la Sierra*. Colección SEP-INI, no. 16. Mexico: Instituto Nacional Indigenista, 1973.

Katz, Friedrich. *The Ancient American Civilizations*. New York: Praeger, 1972.

Keen, Benjamin. *The Aztec Image in Western Thought*. New Brunswick, N.J.: Rutgers University Press, 1971.

Kirchhoff, Paul. "Mesoamerica: Its Geographic Limits, Ethnic Composition and Cultural Characteristics." In *The Heritage of Conquest*. Edited by Sol Tax. Chicago: University of Chicago Press, 1977.

Kirchhoff, Paul, Lina Odena Güemes, and Luís Reyes García (introductory study; translation and notes). *Historia Tolteca-Chichimeca*. Mexico: INAH, 1976.

Klein, Cecelia. *The Face of the Earth: Frontality in Two-Dimensional Mesoamerican Art*. Outstanding Dissertations in the Fine Arts (series). New York and London: Garland, 1976.

————. "Rethinking Cihuacoatl: Aztec Political Imagery of the Conquered Woman." Paper presented at the XLIII International Congress of Americanists. Vancouver, 1979, unpublished.

————. "Who was Tlaloc?" *Journal of Latin American Lore* 6(2) (1980): 155–204.

————. "The Ideology of Autosacrifice at the *Templo Mayor*." In *The Aztec Templo Mayor*. Edited by Elizabeth H. Boone. Washington, D.C.: Dumbarton Oaks, 1987. Pages 293–370.

Knab, Tim. *Words Great and Small: Sierra Nahuat Narrative Discourse in Everyday Life*. Unpublished manuscript, copyright 1983.

Köhler, Ulrich. *Čonbilal Č'ulelal. Grundformen Mesoamerikanischer Kosmologie und Religion in einem Gebetstext auf Maya-Tzotzil*. Acta Humboldtiana. Series Geographica et Ethnographica, no. 5. Wiesbaden: Franz Steiner-Verlag, 1977.

LaFarge, Oliver, and Douglas Byers. *The Year Bearer's People*. Middle American Research Series, publication no. 3. New Orleans, 1931.

Lehmann, Walter, ed. *Die Geschichte der Königreiche von Colhuacan und Mexiko*. Quellenwerke zur Alten Geschichte Amerikas, vol. I. Stuttgart and Berlin: Verlag Kohlhammer, 1938.

León-Portilla, Miguel, ed. *The Broken Spears*. Boston: Beacon Press, 1962.

————. *Aztec Thought and Culture*. Norman: University of Oklahoma Press, 1963.

————. *Pre-Columbian Literature of Mexico*. Norman: University of Oklahoma Press, 1969.

————. *México-Tenochtitlan: Su Espacio y Tiempo Sagrados*. Mexico: INAH, 1978.

————, ed. *Native Mesoamerican Spirituality*. New York: Paulist Press, 1980.

————. "Los Testimonios de la Historia." In Miguel León Portilla and Eduardo Matos Moctezuma, *El Templo Mayor*. Mexico: Bancomer, S.A., 1981. Pages 33–102.

León-Portilla, Miguel, and Eduardo Matos Moctezuma. *El Templo Mayor*. Mexico: Bancomer, S.A., 1981.

Loew, Cornelious. *Myth, Sacred History and Philosophy*. New York: Harcourt, Brace and World, 1967.

Long, Charles H. *Alpha: Myths of Creation*. (Chico, California: Scholars Press, 1963).

López-Austin, Alfredo. *Hombre-Dios: Religión y Política en el Mundo Náhuatl*. Instituto de Investigaciones Históricas. Mexico: UNAM, 1973.

174

———. "Iconografía Mexica. El Monolito Verde del Templo Mayor." *Anales de Antropología* (Mexico: UNAM) XVI (1979): 135–153.

———. *Cuerpo Humano e Ideología: Las Concepciones de los Antiguos Nahaus*, 2 vols. Instituto de Investigaciones Antropológicas. Mexico: UNAM, 1980.

Lorenzo, José Luís. "Las Zonas Arqueológicas de los Volcanes Iztaccihuatl y Popocatepetl." In *Dirección de Prehistoria*, publication no. 3. Mexico: INAH, 1957.

Madsen, William. *Christo-Paganism: A Study of Mexican Religious Syncretism.* Middle American Research Institute, publication no. 19. New Orleans: Tulane University, 1957.

Martínez, Hildeberto, and Luís Reyes García. "Culto en las Cuevas de Cuautlapa en el Siglo XVIII." *Comunidad* (Mexico: Universidad Iberoamericana) V (1970): 541–551.

Matos Moctezuma, Eduardo, ed. *Trabajos Arqueológicos en el Centro de la Ciudad de México (Antología).* Mexico: SEP-INAH, 1979.

———. "Los Hallazgos de la Arqueología." In Miguel León-Portilla and Eduardo Matos Moctezuma, *El Templo Mayor.* Mexico: Bancomer, S.A., 1981*a.* Pages 103–284.

———. "El Templo Mayor: Economía e Ideología." In *El Templo Mayor: Excavaciones y Estudios.* Edited by Eduardo Matos Moctezuma. Mexico: INAH, 1982*a.* Pages 109–118.

———, ed. *El Templo Mayor: Excavaciones y Estudios.* Mexico: INAH, 1982*b.*

———. *El Templo Mayor: Planos, Cortes y Perspectivas.* Dibujos Victor Rangel. Mexico: INAH, 1982*c.*

———. "El Simbolismo del *Templo Mayor.*" In *The Aztec Templo Mayor.* Edited by Elizabeth H. Boone. Washington, D.C.: Dumbarton Oaks, 1987. Pages 185–210.

Mendelson, E. Michael. "A Guatemalan Sacred Bundle." *Man* (London) 170 (1958): 1–7.

Molina, Fray Alonso de. *Vocabulario en Lengua Castellana y Mexicana.* Facsimile edition. Mexico: Editorial Porrúa, 1970.

Monjarás-Ruíz, Jesús. *La Nobleza Mexica: Surgimiento y Consolidación.* Mexico: Edicol, 1980.

Mönnich, Anneliese. *Die Gestalt der Erdgöttin in den Religionen Mesoamerikas.* Ph.D. thesis, West Berlin: Freie Universität, Berlin, 1969.

Moreno de los Arcos, Roberto. "Los Territorios Parroquiales de la Ciudad Arzobispal, 1325–1981." *Gaceta Oficial del Arzobispado de Mexico*, XXII, nos. 9–10 (1982): 152–173.

Nagao, Debra. *Mexica Buried Offerings: A Historical and Contextual Approach.* BAR International Series 235. Oxford, 1985*a.*

———. "The Planting of Sustenance: The Symbolism of the Two-Horned God in Mexica Offerings from the Templo Mayor." In *Res-Anthropology and Aesthetics*, no. 10. Cambridge, Mass.: Peabody Museum, Harvard University, 1985*b.* Pages 5–27.

Navarrete, Carlos, and Doris Heyden. "La Cara Central de la Piedra del Sol: Una Hipótesis." *Estudios de Cultura Nahuatl* (Mexico) 11 (1974): 355–376.

Navas, Fray Francisco de las. *Calendario de Fray Francisco de las Navas, de don Antonio de Guevara y Anónimo Tlaxcalteca.* Colección Ramírez, Opúsculos Históricos, vol. 21. Colección Antigua, vol. 210. Archivo Histórico del INAH, Museo Nacional de Antropología e Historia, Mexico, unpublished manuscript. Pages 93–203.

Neusner, Jacob. *The Way of Torah.* Belmont, Calif.: Wadsworth Publishing, 1976.

Nicholson, Henry B. "Religion in Pre-Hispanic Central Mexico." In *Handbook of Middle American Indians, Guide to Ethnohistorical Sources*, vol. 10. Austin: University of Texas Press, 1971. Pages 395–445.

Nicholson, Henry B., and Eloise Quiñones Keber. *Art of Aztec Mexico: Treasures of Tenochtitlan.* Catalog of an Exhibition at the National Gallery of Art. Washington, D.C., 1983.

Nisbet, Robert, *The Sociological Tradition.* New York: Basic Books, 1966.

Nowotny, Karl Anton. *Tlacuillolli*. In *Monumenta Americana* (series), vol. III. Berlin: Verlag Gebrüder Mann, 1961.

———. "Die Aztekischen Festkreise." *Zeitschrift für Ethnologie*, 93(1, 2) (Braunschweig) (1968): 84–106.

———. *Rituale in Mexiko und im Nordamerikanischen Südwesten*. Jahrbuch für Geschichte von Staat, Wirtschaft und Gesellschaft Lateinamerikas, vol. 8. Cologne: Böhlau Verlag, 1970. Pages 4–38.

———. "Herkunft und Inhalt des Kodex Borbonicus." In *Codex Borbonicus: Bibliotheque Nationale de l'Assemblee Nationale, Paris (4120)*. Facsimile edition. Graz-Austria: Akademische Druck-und Verlagsanstalt, 1974a. Pages 11–25.

———. *Codex Borbonicus*, Commentary, Facsimile Edition. Graz-Austria: Akademische Druck-und Verlagsanstalt, 1974b.

———. *Codex Borgia*, Commentary, Facsimile Edition. Graz-Austria: Akademische Druck-und Verlagsanstalt, 1976.

Olivera, Mercedes. "Huémitl de Mayo en Citlala: Ofrendas para Chicomecoatl o Para la Santa Cruz?" In *Mesoamérica: Homenaje al Doctor Paul Kirchhoff*. Edited by Barbro Dahlgren. Mexico: INAH, 1979. Pages 143–158.

Parsons, Elsie Clews. *Mitla, Town of the Souls and Other Zapotec-Speaking Pueblos of Oaxaca, Mexico*. Chicago: University of Chicago Press, 1936.

Pasztory, Esther. "The Xochicalco Stelae and a Middle Classic Deity Triad in Mesoamerica." In *Actas del XXIII Congreso Internacional de Historia del Arte*, vol. I. Granada, 1973. Pages 185–215.

———. *The Iconography of the Teotihuacan Tlaloc*. Studies in Pre-Columbian Art and Archaeology, no. 15. Washington, D.C.: Dumbarton Oaks. 1974.

———. "Artistic Traditions of the Middle Classic Period." In *Middle Classic Mesoamerica*, A.D. 400–700. Edited by Esther Pasztory. New York: Columbia University, 1978. Pages 108–142.

———. *Aztec Art*. New York: Harry N. Abrams, 1983.

———. "The Aztec Tlaloc: God of Antiquity." In *Thelma Sullivan*, in press.

Paz, Octavio. *The Other Mexico*. New York: Grove Press, 1972.

Phillips, Philip, and Gordon Willey. *Method and Theory in American Archaeology*. Chicago: University of Chicago Press, 1958.

Pomar, Juan Bautista. "Relación de Tezcoco." In Pomar-Zurita: *Relaciones de Texcoco y de los Señores de la Nueva España*. Colección de Documentos para la Historia de México, vol. 2. Mexico: S. Chavez Hayhoe, 1941. Pages 1–64.

Rappaport, Roy. *Ecology, Meaning and Religion*. Richmond, Calif.: North Atlantic Books, 1979.

Reyes García, Luís, ed. *Der Ring aus Tlalocan. Mythen und Gebete, Lieder und Erzählungen der heutigen Nahua in Veracruz und Puebla*. Quellenwerke zur Alten Geschichte Amerikas, vol. 12. West Berlin, 1976.

———. "La Visión Cosmológica y la Organización del Imperio Mexica." In *Mesoamérica: Homenaje al Doctor Paul Kirchhoff*. Edited by Barbro Dahlgren. Mexico: SEP-INAH, 1979. Pages 34–40.

Rickards, Constantine G. "The Ruins of Tlaloc, State of Mexico." *Journal de la Societé des Américanistes* (Paris) 21 (1929): 197–199.

Román Berrelleza, Juan Alberto. "La Ofrenda No. 48 del Templo Mayor: Un Caso de Sacrificios Infantiles." In *The Aztec Templo Mayor*. Edited by Elizabeth H. Boone. Washington, D.C.: Dumbarton Oaks, 1987. Pages 131–143.

Sahagún, Fray Bernardino de. *(FC): Florentine Codex: General History of the Things of New Spain*, 13 parts. Edited and translated by Arthur J. O. Anderson and Charles E. Dibble. Monographs of the School of American Research, no. 14. Santa Fe, N.M.: The School of American Research and the University of Utah, 1951–1982.

———. *(HG): Historia General de las Cosas de Nueva España*, 4 vols. Edited by Angel María Garibay. Mexico: Editorial Porrúa, 1956.

Schultze-Jena, Leonhard. *Leben, Glaube und Sprache der Quiché von Guatemala.* In *Indiana* (series), vol. I. (Jena: G. Fischer-Verlag), I (1933).

———. *Mythen in der Muttersprache der Pipil von Izalco in El Salvador.* In *Indiana* (series), vol. II Jena: G. Fischer-Verlag, II (1935).

———. *Bei den Azteken, Mixteken und Tlapaneken der Sierra Madre del Sur von Mexiko.* In *Indiana* (series), vol. III. Jena: G. Fischer-Verlag, (1938).

———. *La Vida y las Creencias de Los Indígenas Quichés de Guatemala.* In *Biblioteca de Cultura Popular*, vol. 40. Translated by Antonio Goubaud Carrera and Herbert D. Sapper. Guatemala: Ministerio de Educación Pública, 1947.

Seler, Eduard. *Gesammelte Abhandlungen (GA)*, 5 vols. Facsimile edition. Graz-Austria: Akademische Druck-und Verlagsanstalt, 1960*a*.

———. "Die Ausgrabungen am Orte des Haupttempels in Mexiko" (1901). *Gesammelte Abhandlungen* vol. II Graz-Austria: Akademische Druck-und Verlagsanstalt, 1960*b*, Pages 767–904.

Sepúlveda, Ma. Teresa. "Petición de Lluvias en Ostotempa." *Boletín INAH* (Mexico: INAH) II(4) (1973): 9–20.

Shils, Edward. *"Center and Periphery" Selected Essays.* Chicago: University of Chicago Press, 1970*a*.

———. *Selected Essays.* Chicago: Center for Social Organization Studies, 1970*b*.

Smith, Jonathan Z. "The Influence of Symbols upon Social Change: A Place on Which to Stand." *Worship* 44 (8) (October 1970): 457–474.

———. *Map is Not Territory: Studies in the History of Religions.* Leiden: E. J. Brill, 1978.

Suárez Jácome, Cruz. "Petición de Lluvia en Zitlala, Guerrero." *Boletín INAH* (Mexico: INAH) III (22) (1978): 3–13.

Sullivan, Thelma D. "Tlaloc: A New Etymological Interpretation of the God's Name and What it Reveals of His Essence and Nature." In *Atti del XL Congreso Internationale Degli Americanisti*, Roma and Genova, 1972, vol. II. Genova: Casa Editrice Tilgher, 1974. Pages 213–219.

Tambiah, Stanley. "The Galactic Policy: The Structure of Traditional Kingdoms in Southeast Asia." *Annals, New York Academy of Sciences* (1974): 293: 69–97.

Tarn, Nathaniel, and Martin Prechtel. "Eating the Fruit: Sexual Metaphor and Initiation in Santiago Atitlan." Paper presented at the *XVIII Mesa Redonda de la Sociedad Mexicana de Antropología*. Chiapas: San Cristobal, 1981.

Tedlock, Barbara. *Time and the Highland Maya.* Albuquerque: University of New Mexico Press, 1982.

———. "Earth Rites and Moon Cycles: Mayan Synodic and Sidereal Lunar Reckoning." In *Ethnoastronomy: Indigenous Astronomical and Cosmological Traditions of the World.* Edited by John B. Carlson and Von Del Chamberlain. Washington, D.C.: Smithsonian Institution Press, in press.

Tezozómoc, Hernando Alvarado. *Crónica Mexicana.* Mexico: Editorial Leyenda, 1944.

———. *Crónica Mexicayotl.* Translated by Adrián León. Instituto de Investigaciones Históricas. Mexico: UNAM, 1949.

BIBLIOGRAPHY

Thompson, Eric. "The Role of Caves in Maya Culture." In *Amerikanische Miszellen: Festband Franz Termer*. Edited by W. Bierhenke. *Mitteilungen aus dem Museum für Völkerkunde*, vol. 25. Hamburg, 1959. Pages 122–129.

Tichy, Franz, ed. *Space and Time in the Cosmovision of Mesoamerica*. In *Lateinamerika-Studien*, vol. 10. Universität Erlangen-Nürnberg. Munich: Wilhelm Fink-Verlag, 1982.

Townsend, Richard F. *State and Cosmos in the Art of Tenochtitlan*. Studies in Pre-Columbian Art and Archaeology, no. 20. Washington, D.C.: Dumbarton Oaks, Trustees for Harvard University, 1979.

———. "Pyramid and Sacred Mountain." In *Ethnoastronomy and Archaeoastronomy in the American Tropics*. Edited by Anthony F. Aveni and Gary Urton. *Annals of the New York Academy of Sciences*, vol. 385. New York: The New York Academy of Sciences, 1982. Pages 37–62.

Turner, Victor. *Dramas, Fields and Metaphors*. Ithaca, N.Y.: Cornell University Press, 1974.

Van Zantwijk, Rudolph. "La Paz Azteca. La Ordenación del Mundo por Los Mexica." *Estudios de Cultura Nahuatl* (Mexico: UNAM) 3 (1962): 101–135.

———. "Los Seis Barrios Sirvientes de Huitzilopochtli." *Estudios de Cultura Nahuatl* (Mexico: UNAM) 6 (1966): 177–185.

———. "The Great Temple of Tenochtitlan: Model of Aztec Cosmovision." In *Mesoamerican Sites and World Views*. Edited by Elizabeth P. Benson. Washington, D.C.: Dumbarton Oaks, 1981. Pages 71–86.

Vogt, Evon. "Some Aspects of the Sacred Geography of Highland Chiapas." In *Mesoamerican Sites and World-Views*. Edited by Elizabeth Benson. Washington, D.C.: Dumbarton Oaks, 1981. Pages 119–143.

Wach, Joaquin. *The Sociology of Religion*. Chicago: University of Chicago Press, 1967.

Weitlaner, Roberto J., and Carlo Antonio Castro. *Usila (Morada de Colibries)*. In *Papeles de la Chinantla* VII, Serie Científica, no. 11. Mexico: Museo Nacional de Antropología. 1973.

Wheatley, Paul. "The Suspended Pelt: Reflections on a Discarded Model of Spatial Structure." In *Geographic Humanism, Analysis and Social Action*. Edited by Donald R. Deskin Jr., George Kisch, John D. Nystuen, and Gunnar Olsson. Geographic Publications, no. 17. Ann Arbor, Mich., 1966. Pages 47–108.

———. "City as Symbol." Inaugural lecture delivered at the University College, London, 20 November 1967.

———. *The Pivot of the Four Quarters: A Chinese City*. Chicago: Aldine Publishing, 1971.

Wicke, Charles, and Fernando Horcasitas. "Archaeological Investigations on Monte Tlaloc, Mexico." *Mesoamerican Notes* 5 (1957): 83–96.

Wolf, Eric. *Sons of the Shaking Earth*. Chicago: University of Chicago Press, 1959.

Index

Designer: U.C. Press Staff
Compositor: Freedmen's Organization
Text: 10/13 Sabon
Display: Sabon
Printer: Malloy Lithographing, Inc.
Binder: John H. Dekker and Sons